An Essay

ON THE CAUSES OF THE

REVOLUTION AND CIVIL WARS

OF

HAYTI,

BEING

A SEQUEL TO THE POLITICAL REMARKS

UPON CERTAIN

FRENCH PUBLICATIONS AND JOURNALS

CONCERNING

HAYTI,

BY

THE BARON DE VASTEY

Chancellor of the King, Member of the Privy Council, Field Marshal of the Army of Hayti, Knight of the Royal and Military Order of St. Henry, &c. &c. &c. &c.

TRANSLATED FROM THE FRENCH, BY

W. H. M. B.

NEGRO UNIVERSITIES PRESS
NEW YORK

972.94
V341e
1969

Originally published in 1823

Reprinted 1969 by
Negro Universities Press
A DIVISION OF GREENWOOD PRESS, INC.
NEW YORK

SBN 8371-2709-2

PRINTED IN UNITED STATES OF AMERICA

CONTENTS.

Introduction... 1
Chapter I. *Of the principal causes of the Revolutions in St. Domingo*... 15
    II. *Of Hayti under the Governor General Jean Jaques Dessalines*............................. 43
    III. *Of the Empire, with an account of the assassination of the Emperor*.......................... 46
    IV. *Of the Civil Wars*................................ 56
    V. *The subject continued. Presidency of the two sides* 67
    VI. *Of the Monarchy and Republic of Hayti, with the attempts of the French*........................104

APPENDIX.

A. Reply to H. Henry's Pamphlet............................. 1
B. Documents relative to Lavaysse's mission, Published by Pétion's authority................................. xiii
    No. 1, to 8 inclusive, correspondence between Pétion and Dauxion Lavaysse xiii
    No. 9, The President's address to the People...... xxx
C. Farther documents relative to Lavaysse's mission... x xiii
    No. 1, Instructions for M M. Lavaysse, Medina, and Dravermann................................ xxxii
    No. 2, Process Verbal of the examination of Medina xli
    No. 3, Extract from the Columbian.................. xlvi
D Correspondence of Catineau Laroche................. xlviii
E. Correspondence of the French Commissioners...... lvi
    No 4, Ordinance of the King of France.......... lxi
    No. 8, Copy of a letter to General Christophe...... lxv

CONTENTS.

No. 16, *Proclamation of the President of Hayti*	lxxxiv
F. No. 1, *Declaration of the King of Hayti*	lxxxv
No. 2, *Copy of a Letter from Dauxion Lavaysse to General Christophe*	xcvi
No. 3, *Extract from the Moniteur*	ci
No. 4, *Address of the General Council*	ci
G. No. 1, *Proclamation of the King of Hayti*	cvi
No. 2, *Letter from the King of Hayti to the Magistrates &c. at Port-au-Prince*	cviii
No. 3, *Reply to the King's Letter and Proclamation*	cx
H. *Address of the King on the Anniversary of the Expulsion of the French*	cxi
I. *State of Education and Commerce, in Hayti*	cxv
No. 1 *Report of the National Schools*	cxv
No. 2, *Commercial Report for the year 1817*	cxvi
No. 3, *Order in Council, for a Free Trade with Hayti*	cxvii

Advertisement
BY
THE TRANSLATOR.

A History of St. Domingo, from the commencement of its revolution to the present day, freed from the distortions of prejudice, and the colouring of party, is yet a desideratum in the annals of literature. Such a work, executed by a competent and impartial writer, would furnish a most impressive and valuable illustration of the *impolicy*, no less than the *injustice* of slavery, and the evils which unavoidably flow from the *colonial system*. It would enable us to trace the slow, but certain progress of the causes of that fearful convulsion, which, after deluging the fertile plains of Hayti with human blood, and exhibiting a display of horrors to which the page of history furnishes no parallel, tore from the royal diadem of France one of its brightest and most valuable jewels, and laid the foundation of those civil dissensions which yet distract that lovely country, and oppose a formidable obstacle to the improvement of its inhabitants. It would likewise *practically* demonstrate, that superiority both of *intellectual* and *moral* power, is *not* confined to any one complexion, and that *generous* and *virtuous feelings* are *not* the exclusive privilege of Europeans.

In the instructive records of such a history, we should see a people, sunk but a few short years ago in the lowest depths of ignorance, and brutalized by the most barbarous despotism, calling into action, after their emancipation from bondage, those dormant energies of the soul, and those latent virtues of the heart, which we had been taught to believe them incapable of possessing, and, not only forming themselves into an organised and well regulated community, but starting, almost *per saltum*, into notice, as statesmen, legislators and historians.

ADVERTISEMENT.

As a statesman and a legislator, no less than as a warrior, the illustrious hero who sways the sceptre of the North, stands pre-eminently conspicuous, and the code of laws which bears his name, the wholesome regulations he has established in the administration of the state, the order and punctuality which he has introduced nto all the details of office, and, above all, the institutions he has founded for diffusing the light of moral and intellectual improvement throughout his dominions, are so many splendid monuments of the extent of his genius, and the liberality of his heart. While the writings of Boisrond Tonnere, de Limonade, de Dupuy, de Vastey, the Chevalier Prezeau and others, prove the Haytians to be no less capable of excelling with the *pen*, than with the sword.

But, that we may the better appreciate the rapidity of the progress made by this calumniated race in the arts of civilization, let us dispassionately peruse the account given of himself and his countrymen, by the author of the present volume, in a note upon a former work, to which this is in fact but a sequel.

"To form a just idea of our progress in civilization, arts and sciences, we ought never to lose sight of what we were, and what we now are.

"We were sunk, twenty-five years ago, in slavery and the most profound ignorance.—"We had no idea of human societies, no thought of happiness, no kind of energy.—"Our physical and moral faculties were so completely depressed under the weight of despotism, that I, who am writing this, imagined that the world terminated with the horizon. So contracted in my notions that I could not conceive the most simple idea. All my countrymen were as ignorant as myself, and, if it were possible, even more so.

"The civil, executive and military offices of the kingdom, are now filled by Haytians only, since foreigners are rendered incapable of holding situations in the kingdom. Necessity overcame all obstacles; almost every one acquired learning by the help of books. I was intimately acquainted with many of them who learned to read and write of themselves,

ADVERTISEMENT. [v

'without an instructor. They walked about "with books in their hands, inquired of persons "whom they met, whether they could read; if "they could, they were then desired to explain "the meaning of such a particular sign, or such "a word. In this way many of the natives "succeeded, without the help of education, "though already advanced in years. They be-"came notaries, barristers, judges, statesmen, "and astonished every one by the solidity of "their judgment. One may readily conceive "what such men would have been, had they "been trained with the care and method of a "classical education."*

And yet such are the men whom the colonial faction, both in France and elsewhere, has hitherto been in the habit of representing, not only as inferior to the whites in intellect, but even as forming, contrary to scriptural evidence, a distinct species, "*possessing indeed,*" as Mazeres (one of those to whom the baron has

---

* See note, at page 46, of the translation of Baron de Vastey's "*Reflexions Politiques,*" inserted in the Pamphleteer, No. xxv. page 210.

replied) admits in his letter to M. Sismonde de Sismondi, "*a certain degree of affinity, but yet destitute of all identity with them.*"

How triumphantly have all these puerile assertions---assertions as contradictory to the express records of the Bible, as they are repugnant to the plainest dictates of reason---been disproved by the exertions of the Haytians, since their emancipation from slavery, and from its concomitant, ignorance. Under the benignant auspices of a wise and virtuous prince, schools are now to be found in almost every village,* and the cultivation of the mind has succeeded to the degrading influence of the cart-whip. The calumnies of the ex-colonists have been practically refuted by the literary exertions of men, to whom they denied the possession of the commonest intellect---and by none more convincingly, than by those of our

* Besides the schools founded by the king, and of which an account will be found in Appendix I, page cxv. there are multitudes of elementary schools dispersed throughout the kingdom, in which the Haytian youth are instructed in the first rudiments of knowledge: and all parents are required to send their children to these schools as soon as they have attained a sufficient age.

present author, who is indebted to the innate powers of his own unassisted genius for all the literary attainments he has made, and now comes fearlessly forward on the great arena of politics, to encounter, in vindication of his brethren and country, men who, to no inconsiderable talents, unite all the advantages of a regular and finished education.

The objects of the present volume are to shew the causes which led to the emancipation of the Blacks from the bondage of the colonial system---to trace the events which produced the memorable declaration of independence--- and to demonstrate the firmness of their determination never again to submit to the yoke of France, *even though their extermination should be the fearful alternative.*

The author has also renewed his former efforts to expose to his countrymen at large the true character of the designs of France and the agency of French intrigue, in fomenting and perpetuating those civil feuds, which have hitherto opposed so lamentable an obstacle to the security and improvement of the country.

ADVERTISEMENT.

In the prosecution of this plan, his duty to his king, and his zeal for his country, have occasionally betrayed him into an asperity of language, which, when the provocation is fairly and impartially considered, is not without considerable claims to indulgence.

With respect to the justice of his animadversions upon the conduct and motives of the late president of the republic, the evidence adduced by the baron, corroborated as it is by the language uniformly held by the French writers when speaking of Pétion, and also by his questionable behaviour in the negociation with Dauxion Lavaysse, goes far to establish it, and affords a strong presumption that want of power, rather than want of inclination, prevented him from attempting to betray Hayti into the hands of the French.

The wretched remains of SIXTY THOUSAND* men who accompanied or followed the unprin-

---

* Of this number not quite FOUR THOUSAND lived to evacuate the island with the detestable Rochambeau.——By an oversight in the correction of the press, the number of troops sent from France in Leclerc's time, is stated in the note at the bottom of page 41, to have been 6,000, in place of 60,000.

ADVERTISEMENT. [ix

cipled Leclerc in his memorable expedition, loudly proclaim the madness, as well as the wickedness, of any similar attempt, against men who are no longer open to the seductions of flattery, or the intimidations of power—against men who have already had sufficient experience of the promises and professions of French generals—against men who are now amply prepared and unanimously resolved to resist invasion, and fully instructed in the most effectual methods of harassing and overcoming an European foe. May France then be wise enough to profit by the experience of the past—resign pretensions which she has no longer the power to maintain—and by the prudent forbearance of her future conduct with respect to Hayti, entitle herself to the gratitude of a people who only require to be known to be admired.

Postscript to the Translator's Advertisement.

The following work was within a few pages of being ready for publication, when the melancholy intelligence of the death of the patriotic Henry, and the unfortunate overthrow of his wise system of administration, arrested the progress of the press, and put a stop to the completion of the translation. Anxious however to give the work in a perfect form, to a few of the more zealous friends of the African Cause, the Translator has ventured to complete a limited impression of only One hundred copies, for private distribution—not for sale, hoping that the interest which its perusal can hardly fail to excite, at the present period more especially, may eventually lead to its more extensive circulation, through the medium of a larger impression.

Stonehouse, July 1st. 1823.

INTRODUCTION.

POLITICAL discussions have always been repugnant to our feelings and our principles. We have always studiously avoided them through the fear of becoming the aggressors; and, if we have been tempted at times to enter the lists of controversy, it has always been from the impulse of necessity and sorely against our inclination. But, when summoned by the call of duty to the defence of our country, our cause and our rights, we have never hesitated a moment to mount the breach and combat with our utmost ability the enemies of our Government, under whatever colour or disguise they presented themselves.

The colonial hydra is again in motion. Again have its roarings, traversing the wide expanse of ocean which divides us, echoed in our ears. Another Antæus, it multiplies itself, assails us under every possible variety of form, and seeks, by sowing dissensions amongst ourselves, to render us the unsuspecting instruments of its own perfidious views, and to employ our own hands to plunge the suicidal dagger into our bosoms. In aid of this favourite design it employs against us its accustomed weapons of fraud, of calumny, and of falsehood: those never-failing resources of the weak, the cowardly and the wicked: to which we oppose those of truth, of justice, and of reason; weapons which it is the peculiar privilege of the brave and upright to wield, and which, inspiring us with the courage and skill of an Hercules, will enable us to strangle in their birth the hideous projects of this artful and perfidious monster.

In my last work entitled "*Reflexions Politiques, &c.*"* which has reached France, I have, from facts within my own knowledge, refuted Mr. *Borgne de Boigne's* "*New Plan of Colonization for St. Domingo, with the formation of a Commercial Company for the restoration of the intercourse between France and that Island.*" After combatting all the objections and even the cavils urged by this writer against the recognition of our independence, I have established in the most incontestible manner, the justice of our rights and the validity of our claims.

The refutation of the falsehoods and mistatements advanced by *Mr. le Borgne de Boigne* with respect to our political situation, has led to a developement of the nature and principles of the Haytian Government, and an exposition, in conformity with the Royal Declaration of the 20th of November, 1816,† of the fixed

* See a translation of this in the 25th No. of the Pamphleteer, page 165. † See Appendix, F. No. 1.

and unalterable line of policy determined upon with respect to France, by his Haytian Majesty. Satisfied that I had explained myself sufficiently in that work, I little expected to see not only the objections which I had already confuted, but others even still less tenable, marshalled anew against me.

But it is not information which our enemies desire, since their knowledge already exceeds their wishes. It is not a fuller acquaintance with our internal situation and resources, for this they abundantly possess. Their real object is to catch us in the new toils which they have spread for us: to lure us from an adherence to our maxims of sound policy, and thus either to reconduct us insensibly and step by step into the bonds of slavery, or to overwhelm us with inevitable destruction.

This point gained, nothing more would be left for them to desire. Our life then must be passed in ceaseless conflict with the planters, for we shall ever be inaccessible alike to their artifices, their blandishments or their threats: and *never—no, never!* shall they tempt us to swerve from the immoveable determination proclaimed in our motto " INDEPENDENCE OR DEATH," a determination consecrated by our laws, and cemented by our blood. Behold! Tyrants, this is the ceaseless object of our vows—the unalterable resolution of our hearts!

From the course of events in Europe, however, and

from the triumph of liberal sentiments so loudly proclaimed, we were led to hope that the Government of France, no longer ignorant of our real situation, would have renounced with candour and sincerity pretensions equally unjust and chimerical, and have adopted in their room sentiments more in unison with the general interests of France. We had flattered ourselves that, convinced of their folly and extravagance, the French Government would no longer have permitted the intrigues and clamours of the Ex-Colonists to sway its councils.

Nor was the aspect of affairs less promising in the south-west of Hayti, than in France. Pétion, the ambitious chieftain, who had kindled the flames of civil discord in the bosom of his afflicted country, died of inanition, of remorse, and grief: during his short illness he refused to take those remedies and that sustenance which his recovery demanded: he was mortified at beholding the odious plots he had concerted with the *Dauxion Lavaysses,* the *Colombels,* and the *Milcents,* against his country, wholly detected: ashamed to see himself compelled to retract the disgraceful offers he had made of paying tribute to France and to the Ex-Colonists; convicted of high treason, and of being the accomplice of a spy; proved by fifteen heads of accusation, grounded upon legal and authentic documents bearing his own signature, to have conspired against the liberty and independence of the Haytian people; disgraced in the eyes both of his countrymen and strangers; sick in a word of a loathsome existence, and torn by remorse, Pétion went down into the tomb, without having either the boldness or the ability to clear himself from so horrible a charge.

Thus fell the hero, the legislator, and the benefactor of the Republic, stigmatized with the charge of treason against his country, and against humanity: his accomplices decreed him no less than the honours of an apotheosis. Thus also *Marat*, surnamed *The Friend of the People!* received the honours of the Pantheon: but when the day of reason and of truth returned, his impure remains were thrown into the slaughter-house. Let us hope that the day of reason and of truth will arise for this traitor, and that justice will be done to him also. I am sorry, in the mean time, to disturb his ashes: but it is necessary to give every one his due, and treat him according to his actions. In discharging this imperative duty, I still feel that I pay but a feeble tribute to his memory.

After the death of this traitor, who appeared to have carried with him, in his last moments, the spirit of evil, of discord, and of civil war, our Government imagined the moment was favorable for bringing back and directing the national spirit to the same end, to an unity of interests and wishes. Yet, though our offers of *peace,* of *union,* and of *reconciliation* were not received, according to our reasonable expectations, our august and well beloved Sovereign was not the less satisfied with having followed the impulse of his own heart, and again used his utmost efforts to promote the general welfare and true interests of the nation. His Majesty waits till time and reflection enable the more respectable and intelligent inhabitants of this part of Hayti, to appreciate the magnanimity of his overtures, and the generosity of his sentiments.

The voice of reason being unable as yet to prevail over that of the passions, his Majesty directed his care and attention to the internal situation of his dominions, and employed himself in devising means for ameliorating and improving the state of society. With this view, Public Instruction,* the foundation of schools and academies, with their discipline and police; the improvement of agriculture and the increase of landed proprietors, with the restoration of good morals by the respect paid to marriage, and the encouragement given to it, have been the ceaseless objects of his Majesty's solicitude.

During the kind of truce which has existed between all parties, the paper war, the only one we have waged for a length of time, had ceased : our foes internal, as well as external, appeared sunk in the most profound

* See Appendix, I. No. 1.

repose, and we no longer assailed by our writings men who seemed, by their silence, to acknowledge themselves vanquished. We employed our inexperienced pens on objects which were more agreeable and better suited to our tastes and our inclinations, in the cultivation of the literature and science which adorn life and form its solace.

But at that time the Congress of *Aix la Chapelle* had not taken place; the army of occupation had not yet evacuated France. The period for the Ex-Colonists to renew their intrigues had not yet arrived. No intelligence which could awaken the smallest suspicion of the continued existence of the most deadly hatred against us had been received from *Port-au-Prince*. We felicitated ourselves on the prevalence of an amicable disposition. We imagined that the private interests of the adherents of Pétion, and respect for themselves, had suggested the wisdom of silence, and prevented their exposing themselves in the eyes of the world, as they had hitherto done. We conceived they would have been satisfied of the impossibility of realizing the guilty projects of their leader *by reducing the Blacks to slavery under the dominion of France*; and that, foiled in their diabolical attempts they would have returned to better principles. We thought that men like these, branded with the crime of *treason not only against their country, but against humanity itself*, would, for their own sakes, have feared to re-exhibit themselves upon the great theatre of the world, and that they never would have the assurance to stir up the sink of crime into which their perfidy had plunged them; certain that in so doing they could not fail to awaken the most hateful recollections, and expose the deformity of their proceedings in the strongest light.

Strange mistake under which we laboured! Was there then no human consideration capable of checking these senseless—these obstinate and wicked men. Not even their own selfish interests? But what do I say? Honour! Glory! Patriotism! Nothing—nothing was capable of influencing them!!!

Whilst we felt secure, these men were silently plotting fresh treasons against Hayti—against their brethren and fellow citizens. They resumed the broken thread of the former confederacy, for the purpose of pursuing it to its accomplishment. *Colombel* and *Milcent* formed a conspiracy at *Port-au-Prince*, in concert with the Ex-Colonists in *France*. They there fabricated and disseminated, by means of the press, the grossest libels and the lowest and most atrocious calumnies against the Haytian character, and exerted their utmost ingenuity to injure the generous hero who had just been speaking to them of *peace, union, harmony, and the common good*; he, in short, who had shewn, in all circumstances in which the safety of his country was menaced, that he possessed the *skill*, the *power* and the *inclination*, to maintain her rights and defend her cause.

O! you who have suffered yourselves to be prejudiced by reading these disgusting pamphlets, and have perhaps lent an attentive ear to them, consider for a moment with me what cause could have provoked such falsehoods and abuse, what motives could have given birth to them, to rekindle the wrath, the fury and the malice, of these traitors against the great man who is their object. *A generous and conciliatory overture*—the language of *peace, union, and common interests!*—such are the objects, the motives and the causes, of these vituperations. In fact, it is in the union of the Haytians, in the paternal harmony which ought to prevail among men who have the same interests, and the same cause to maintain, that real danger threatens traitors sold to the Ex-Colonists; and never can we give them higher offence, or injure them more deeply, that by speaking to them of the re-union and reconciliation of the great Haytian family. We can never touch them in a tenderer or more formidable spot. But let them do what they may, let them exert themselves never so much to procrastinate this happy moment, sooner or later this reconciliation will take place, and their countrymen and brethren will, in spite of them, clasp each other in a fraternal embrace, never again to be disunited.

Whilst we were holding out the olive-branch of peace to our brethren and fellow citizens of the south-west, *Colombel, Milcent* and the Ex-Colonists, were actively engaged in counteracting our efforts, and endeavouring, by their publications, to goad the Haytians anew to conflict and to carnage: and the French Journals, their *faithful echoes*, responded to their shouts of war. According to them, Haytian blood was streaming afresh, in the plains of *Cibert* and of *Santo*, where *four thousand men* had fallen on either side; (being so much gain to the Ex-Colonists). Unfortunately however for them, this dreadful expenditure of human life had no existence but in their disordered fancy and in their publications. As for us *Savages of the North!* we were in the most perfect tranquility, celebrating marriages, and giving fêtes and entertainments in our good town of SANS SOUCI at the very time that our enemies were circulating with the most malignant activity the grossest falsehoods and libels against us, throughout France and other parts of Europe; spreading wide their baleful poison, injuring us in public opinion, filling the hearts of the philanthropic with grief and dismay, and elating our implacable foes with imaginary triumphs, and fallacious hopes.

INTRODUCTION.   [11

We were far from entertaining the most remote suspicion of such vile plots, of so base a conspiracy against us.

Meanwhile, besides the descriptions of the bloody contests in which we were *represented as engaged*, the French Journals were filled from time to time with the most outrageous articles against the personal character of our revered Monarch. These were copied word for word from pamphlets manufactured at *Port-au-Prince*, the French Editors artfully and malignantly taking the precaution to insert them in their journals without signature, or any intimation of their origin: fearing lest by betraying the cloven-hoof they should provoke us to a reply: insomuch that we paid them no manner of regard. Such indeed was the atrocious character of their impostures and the extravagance of their facts that the King himself, as they were read to him, laughed at the madness and folly of the French news writers: and so fully were we satisfied that these productions, which had not even a shadow of common sense or probability, and whose veracity was hardly on a par with the Arabian Nights Entertainments, were the hallucinations of French novelists in the pay of the Ex-Colonists, that instead of replying, we held them in the most sovereign contempt.

However agreeable this conduct on our part was to the suggestions of reason, it proved nevertheless injurious to us for the moment in other countries, where our silence was misconstrued; our enemies profiting by the temporary credit which it gave to their calumnies. These vile fabrications were hailed with joy by the Ex-Colonists, who hastened, by dispersing them, to swell the ranks of their partizans, and add to the number of our foes. Those who were already biassed against us had their prejudices strengthened, while others of good intentions, but who were unacquainted with the true posture of our affairs, allowed themselves to be prejudiced against us. Even our very friends received an unfavourable impression.

Hence it became of importance to us to break silence with a view to rectify public opinion (which had been misled by these falsehoods) and to refute and confound our calumniators. This is no longer a difficult task for us to accomplish, especially now that we are apprised by whom the blow has been struck. For who could have imagined that these pamphlets, *composed and printed at Port-au-Prince, should first reach us by way of Paris!!!* Colombel and Milcent, those traitors in the pay of the Ex-Colonists, have employed a circuit of *two thousand leagues* to transmit to us their infamous productions; and to fill up the measure of their enormities, they would summon us before a tribunal of their accomplices; but, while we accept their challenge, we protest against this hostile tribunal, which we will not consent to make the umpire between us. We make our appeal to the tribunal of the world at large, and to the judgment of the virtuous and enlightened of every country—

Such are the powerful motives which have led me to undertake my present task.

The perfidious machinations of the enemies of Hayti have led in the first place to—

Fresh remarks upon the political structure of our Government, of which they have attacked the nature and the monarchical principle, in order to compare it with its opposite, the Republican form of Government:

From an attack upon the *Form* of our Government, they have proceeded in the second place to the most libellous invectives against the person and character of the Sovereign who holds the reins: these attacks having a close and natural connection, the one arising out of the other:

They have in the third place strengthened the system of duplicity and falsehood adopted by the Ex-Colonists, who mislead and pervert anew the opinion of the public in France; and they have given birth to fresh objections, and fresh pretentions still more erroneous and ridiculous than those which have preceded them.

From a careful examination of these various opinions, as they appear in the different documents now lying before me, I am convinced that the great majority of persons in France labour under the greatest delusion with respect to the true situation of affairs in Hayti, owing to the want of other grounds for forming their judgment than the false reports, the calumnious and sophistical reasonings, of the Ex-Colonists and their adherents.

Satisfied that a continuance of such errors must be highly prejudicial to the best interests of both countries, I felt that I should perform an eminent service not only to France and Hayti, but also to humanity at large, by rectifying public opinion and reinstating truth in her just rights.

Moreover, men, estimable in every point of view notwithstanding their differing from us in political feelings and interests, might have been themselves deceived and have led others into error, and thus unintentionally do us the greatest injury. Hence then it becomes imperative upon us to undeceive both the one and the other.

My only regret is, that the shortness of my time, and the weakness resulting from an afflicting indisposition, have prevented me from executing my task as I could have desired, and compelled me to sue to my readers for the utmost latitude of their indulgence.

ESSAY
ON THE CAUSES OF THE REVOLUTION AND THE CIVIL WARS IN HAYTI.

CHAPTER I.

OF THE PRINCIPAL CAUSES WHICH LED THE HAYTIANS TO THEIR EMANCIPATION FROM SLAVERY, AND THENCE TO THE ESTABLISHMENT OF THEIR INDEPENDENCE.

HAYTI has no general history written by a native of the country. The few detached fragments which we possess are chiefly from the pens of European writers, who have principally confined themselves to those parts more immediately connected with themselves, and who, when led by the subject to speak of the native inhabitants, have done so with that spirit of prejudice and partiality which never fails to appear whenever there arises a question involving the competition of Blacks with Whites.

It should further be borne in mind, that those historians had nothing to guide them except statements furnished by Whites, in which facts and events were most strangely garbled, truth was exhibited in a false light, and the scale made to preponderate to one side, without at any time inclining to the other. And as to give a correct history of any country, a thorough acquaintance with its inhabitants and transactions is an indispensible requisite, it cannot be a matter of surprise that these writers, notwithstanding their great talents, should have fallen into the most egregious errors in even the meagre fragments they have given of Haytian history.

From this want of a general history upon whose fidelity reliance can be placed, inconceivable difficulties arise to the political writer, who finds himself every moment stopped and embarrassed in his progress: and to enable himself the better to confute his opponents and render his meaning clear and intelligible to his readers, he is obliged to trace events to their source, in order to free the truth from those mists of falsehood in which his adversaries have involved it.

It is on this account that I have been led to give a succinct exposition of the leading events of the Haytian Revolution, together with the causes that gave it birth. These I have set as land-marks to guide my readers and myself through this labyrinth, without however wandering from the narrow limits I have prescribed to myself, lest I should become prolix, and thus lose sight of the essential object of my labours. Without further preamble then, I will now enter upon my subject.

Prior to the Revolution of 1789, the population of Hayti consisted of three distinct classes, each of which was further sub-divided, according to the established prejudices of the Colonial system; namely—

40,000 Whites, sub-divided into *Great Planters*, and *Inferior Whites, (Petits blancs.)*

30,000 Persons of Colour and Blacks, *nominally free,* likewise sub-divided into *as many sections as there were gradations of complexion more or less approaching to white.**

---

* See the secret instructions of the Minister Malonet, the Works of *Moreau de Saint Méry*, and of Ex-Colonists.

500,000 Black Slaves, Natives and Africans, who likewise participated in the colonial prejudices, the *Creoles* separating themselves from the *Africans*; and in these two sub-divisions the domestics, coachmen, and drivers,* in a word all who were about the persons of the Whites and were known by the appellation of good subjects, were again distinguished from the great majority of wretched slaves that were fixed to the hoe.

In all these classes, the same spirit of pride, of arrogance and of vanity, prevailed. The *Great Planters* held the *Inferior Whites* in contempt. These again despised the *People of Colour and Free Blacks*, who in their turn looked down upon their unfortunate brethren in bondage.

Such are the foundations of the Colonial System. They rest upon *slavery* and the *prejudice of colour*, as the means of preserving to the Whites that superiority of which the Ex-colonists are so jealous.

I shall be silent on the subject of *exclusive commerce*, that being a branch of the system which concerned only the Ex-colonists and the mother country: *at that period we* had nothing to do with trade; *we* only furnished the means of carrying it on.

A population so considerable, and consisting of such incongruous and heterogeneous elements, could not by any possibility avoid sensibly feeling the effects of a Revolution. It wanted but the smallest spark to

---

* For the information of persons unversed in the manners and phraseology of the Planters, it may be proper to observe, that this word is *exclusively* applied to those who *drive the negroes in the field, and are distinguished from their brethren of the hoe by the characteristic badge of the* CART WHIP, that *justly terrific* emblem of authority. *Translator.*

ignite the highly inflammable materials which lay hid within its bosom.

The French Revolution hallowed in that country the eternal and indestructible rights of social man. The cry of *Liberty and Equality*, re-echoed in the ears of men *groaning beneath the barbarous and most oppressive yoke of colonial bondage*, could not fail to produce tremendous effects calculated by their explosion to overturn and crumble into atoms the colonial system of St. Domingo.

There were but two methods of subverting a system so long and deeply rooted by time and prejudice as the colonial: the one gradual, and emanating from our oppressors themselves; the other sudden and violent, originating with the oppressed, contrary to the wishes of our tyrants and productive of a bloody and protracted contest, pregnant with crimes, with carnage and with horrors. It was accomplished by this last method.

The unconceding character, the injustice, and the cruelty of the Ex-colonists, produced the sanguinary conflict which has been prolonged even to the present day; and the colonial hydra in its agony bellowed in vain.

While the Royalists and Republicans were at issue in France, the Revolution in St. Domingo followed with giant strides the impulse given by the mother country. The *Great Planters* and *Inferior Whites* quarrelled and fought among themselves, the one wishing to display the *white*, the other the *tricolor cockade*. In all their meetings, whether public or private, the *rights of man* and the doctrines of *liberty and equality* formed the only topics of discussion.

The domestics and other confidential slaves employed about the Whites, lent an attentive year to discussions which had for them a deep interest, in addition to their novelty; they were the subject of their conversations among themselves, and were reported by them to their companions. The Whites used no reserve with respect to what passed in their presence, conceiving possibly that they were too dull of comprehension to attend to or understand political disquisitions: so blinded were they by the prejudices which they entertained against the Blacks; prejudices of which they are even at this moment unable to divest themselves.

I have already remarked the spirit of pride and jealousy inherent in the Colonial System, and pervading every class. The *Great Planters* refused to make any cession of rights to the *Inferior Whites,* who, on their side wanted to have the same rights with the former, but refused them to the *Men of Color:* and those who desired to become equal to the *Inferior Whites,* refused to yield any of their own rights to the *blacks.*

It was thus that the unfortunate Ogé, claiming a participation of civil and political rights for his *coloured brethren alone,* refused to follow the advice of the brave and generous Chavanne, who undertook to extend these advantages to the Blacks: and thus Ogé voluntarily deprived himself of the aid of an immense force: he became the unhappy victim of his error: the Whites held him in no esteem; and he expired on the wheel with his adherents.

It was thus also that in the several accommodations which took place between the Whites and the Men of Colour, the Blacks were uniformly sacrificed by both parties.

Nevertheless the blood of those martyrs, Ogé and Chavanne, ignominiously shed upon the scaffold, cried aloud for vengeance and served to accelerate the Revolution.

The white population split into two distinct parties. The *Great Planters*, whom we now distinguish by the appellation of *Ultra-Colonists*, for they have made no change in their system, constituted the *Royalist faction*, which, in conjunction with the emigrants, the English and the Spaniards, made head against France.

The *Whites* who espoused the principles of the Revolution, whom we now call the *Liberals* or *Constitutionals*, formed the *Republican Faction*.

The Black and Coloured population became the tools of both factions. The *Great Planters* armed the *Blacks* in the name of the Kings of France and Spain to oppose the *Republicans*; and the *Republicans* saw themselves compelled to proclaim universal liberty in order to oppose the Spaniards, the Planters, and the English.*

Generals Jean François, Biassou, Candi, Bouquemand, and others, fought in the name of the the Kings of France and Spain, against the forces of the Republic: and Generals Toussaint Louverture, Villate, Leveille, with a multitude of other Haytian warriors, fought in the name of the French Republic against the Emigrants, the Spaniards, and the English.

Each of these parties became equally the victims of their credulity and attachment to the Whites.

Jean François, Biassou, Candi, and all ye other heroes, who shed your blood for the Kings of France and Spain! what has become of you? Jean François terminated his existence in exile. Biassou and Candi were basely and inhumanly replunged into slavery, and buried alive in the mines of Mexico. And you,

---

* See the Proclamation of the Commissioner Santhonax, declaring *Universal Freedom*; occasioned by the Insurrection of Galbaud and the Planters.

Touissant Louverture, Villate, and the other Haytian warriors, what has been the recompense of your services, and the blood you shed in the cause of these ungrateful Republicans? Toussaint expired amid the horrors of a dungeon, from cold, from torture, from famine, and from misery. Villate perished in the most horrible agonies from poison. Thousands of our brethren became in like manner the victims of their blind fidelity. Base ingratitude! detestable perfidy! O, my fellow countrymen, when will you cease to be the tools and victims of these monsters? Of the men of colour and the free blacks, part joined with the Royalists, and part with the Republicans; the mass of the black population followed the impulse which was given, and divided itself between the contending factions. On one side the *white*, on the other the *tri-colour* cockade was displayed, and under the specious names of *King*, *Liberty*, or the *Republic*, we fought and shed our blood without knowing wherefore, without even suspecting that we were mere tools employed for our own destruction by the *Whites*, both *Royalists* and *Republicans:* for we were far from imagining that the *Whites*, divided among themselves on political subjects, were perfectly unanimous in their views with respect to us, and that, however, the *method* by which they sought its attainment might differ, their *object* was the same, *namely, to make one party the means of crushing the other, and in the end reducing the victorious side to slavery.*

Thus they employed Gen. Rigaud to crush Gen. Toussaint, and afterwards endeavoured to plunge the victorious Toussaint and his companions into slavery.

But lest their object should be mistaken, they welcomed General Rigaud under all the circumstances of his defeat, while they marked the successful General Touissaint for their destined victim, as he eventually became. Had victory, on the contrary, crowned the arms of Gen. Rigaud with success, Toussaint would in his turn have been welcomed by them, and both would have been their victims in the end. Whichever was victorious, the French Expedition would have equally taken place: the civil war was but the prelude, and the conqueror would have found himself compelled either to fight, or tamely to submit to slavery.

Surely the proceedings in France, and the fate which overtook the unfortunate *Pélage, the valiant Delgresse and the wretched *indigenes* who after *having enjoyed the sweets of liberty* now groan in bondage in the Island of Guadeloupe, might convince us that had we the misfortune to be weaker, we should have been treated in an equally cruel, unjust, and barbarous manner.

The General in Chief, Toussaint Louverture, had reduced the whole of the island under the banners of France, and expelled the strangers and great planters who opposed it.

The Republic was triumphant.

Toussaint exerted himself without intermission to efface the evils of war, to restore order, and promote agriculture. He extended his special protection to the Ex-colonists, who enjoyed their former properties as under the ancient regime, with the exception of being no longer allowed to flog and put the Blacks to death at pleasure.

But *slavery was at an end!* and *Toussaint was supreme.* This order of affairs suited neither France

---

* Pelage, with the armed mulattoes of Guadeloupe fell, like Petion and his party, into the snare prepared for them. They assisted Richepanse to subdue and destroy the armed negroes, or rather performed that service wholly for him, and were rewarded by deportation and death.—Ext. from a note on the *Fœdera Africana,* No. ix. *Translator.*

nor the Ex-colonists: and to accomplish the restoration of slavery, it was necessary to begin by weakening the forces, and sapping the power of Gen. Toussaint.

Such were the views with which Gen. Hédouville was sent to St. Domingo by the French Government, with secret instructions to kindle a civil war between the Blacks and Men of Colour.

At this period Gen. Rigaud commanded the province of the South under General Toussaint. He was one of the oldest and most confidential of the generals of colour, and the only one who could rival Gen. Toussaint.

Hédouville, who burned to throw the apple of discord between these two chieftains, summoned them both to the Cape, where, in one of his conferences with Gen. Toussaint, he proposed to him to arrest General Rigaud. " *Arrest Rigaud!*" exclaimed the virtuous Toussaint, " *much rather would I arrest myself.*"

Hédouville, unable to seduce General Toussaint, turned his attention to General Rigaud, whom he found more complying; he flattered his ambitious views, conferred on him the brevet of general in chief, and embarked for France after kindling the flames of civil war.

The tri-colour standard was seen to wave in both armies; each fought for and in the name of the French Republic. What then was the source of this civil war? What its necessity? Who its author? Answer me, ye traitors and fomentors of civil discord! Colombel, Milcent and your colleagues, answer me and say, who were the authors and promoters of this disastrous feud? To whom can the innumerable misfortunes it occasioned be justly ascribed? Doubtless to Hédouville and Rigaud: to Hédouville for having the treachery to set up a *Commander in Chief*, while *another who had never been legally superseded held the office*: and to Rigaud who had the baseness, the injustice, and the ambition to accept the brevet of General in Chief, contrary to every principle of honour and military discipline. Did not General Rigaud know that the rank of General in Chief could not devolve upon him? Did he not know that by accepting it he would plunge his country, his brethren and fellow-citizens, into all the horrors of a cruel and disastrous civil war? Had not General Rigaud been a traitor, and an ambitious tool in the hands of the French, would he have driven General Toussaint against his wish into the field of battle, and compelled him in his turn to become an instrument for furthering the vengeance and the deadly projects of the Whites and of the French Government. Would he not have shrunk with horror and affright from the incalculable evils he was bringing on his country? Alas, the history of our past civil wars, is but the mirror which reflects the present. Heaven grant their termination be not the same!

The first civil war was produced by the ambition of Rigaud: and the second, which was only the reaction of the former, by that of Pétion. Both of these Generals were merely the instruments employed by the French to divide and destroy us.

In this war, destructive to the Haytians, and profitable only to the Whites, these last sided, *some* with General Toussaint, and *others* with General Rigaud. On both sides they were the warmest advocates for civil war, and the most zealous promoters of massacre and carnage. Incalculable were the mischiefs resulting from their perfidious councils.* O! ye tools of the Ex-colonists Colombel and Milcent, who, by your clamours and pitiful abuse, endeavour to spirit up the Haytians

---

* The *Abbé Bosquet* drew up the Proclamations of General Rigaud: and a person of the name of Salenave, those of General Toussaint.

anew to civil commotions! you who have the assurance to reproach us with the calamities of the war kindled by Gen. Pétion, why do you not equally charge General Toussaint with the misfortunes produced by Rigaud? What! it is you who incessantly goad us to civil war; it is you who summon us to murder, to carnage, and to fight: and it is you who are the persons that now calumniate us, and upbraid us with the death of those unhappy victims who have been cut off by your perfidious machinations. Ye murderers! it is ye who have assassinated them; it is ye who led them into error to serve your passions, and who have dug their graves: and had we been weak enough to have been led astray by your deceitful provocations; had we not penetrated your black designs, Haytian blood would have again flowed in the plains of Cibert and of Santo, while you would have remained during the action secure behind the curtain to publish fresh pamphlets, relate the numbers who fell, and make a pompous display of the public calamities, in order to figure to your accomplices the scattered limbs of your compatriots, the earth bathed with their blood, and to congratulate each other on the result of your perfidies and crimes; and after having been the authors and instigators of these misfortunes, would you again endeavour to impute them to us, and load our shoulders with the weight of your own guilt?

After Rigaud's departure the WHITES, both *Royalists and Republicans, Great Planters,* and *Inferior Whites,* all rallied around General Toussaint. Rigaud failed in overthrowing Toussaint, as Hédouville had proposed; the Ex-colonists took other means to accomplish this end: aided by the non-conformist *(non-concordatistes)* priests who swayed the mind of General Toussaint, they surrounded this unfortunate chieftain, lavishing upon him the most sumptuous entertainments, and the basest flattery. He was a second Spartacus, the illustrious hero predicted by the Abbé Raynal, and at the same moment they were both in France and in the country plotting fresh contrivances for his destruction.

To accomplish their perfidious projects, they recommended to General Toussaint the establishment of a system of police nearly as rigorous as that of the ancient regime, in order thus to alienate from him the affections of the Blacks. They led him to sacrifice his own nephew, Gen. Moyse, upon the pretext of a conspiracy against the Whites. They suggested to him the formation of a Constitution which should render Hayti *nearly* independent of France; which he should have done completely or not at all; for such a measure admitted of no medium: it was necessary to be either *dependent* or *independent*, the one or the other; and Gen. Toussaint, by rendering himself partially independent of France, exposed himself to her vengeance, without giving himself the means of resisting her. The Ex-colonists likewise suggested to him the idea of granting furloughs to a large part of the troops in order to send them back to agricultural pursuits. Nay, they went still further, and carried their assurance to the extent of persuading him to repair and improve the roads, so as to facilitate the transportation of artillery and the march of the French troops. Thus, while really adopting the most erroneous measures, the unfortunate Toussaint believed he was only promoting the welfare of his brethren and country: a mistake of which he was but too clearly convinced.

Whilst the Ex-colonists were thus paving the way within the country for Gen. Toussaint's downfal, those who were in France, were busied in exerting their influence with Bonaparte; whom they supplied with pecuniary aid, and gave him those perfidious counsels, which speedily brought upon us the expedition under the command of Leclerc.

Then all joined against the unfortunate Toussaint. *White Royalists, White Republicans, Great Planters* and *Inferior Whites, Lawyers, Conformist* and *Nonconformists Priests (Prêtres concordatistes, non-concordatistes)* all were now *for once* unanimous: the cause was common; *the Restoration of Slavery or the extermination of the Blacks*, was the question at issue: and upon such a subject no diversity of opinion could prevail.

And *we* too—infatuated that we were! how did *we* act? We rushed in crowds with frantic impatience to meet the iron yoke prepared for our necks.

We are French, said they:—France had bestowed freedom upon us:—France could not now bring us new fetters, after having burst the old: the mere suspicion was criminal:—the mention of it unpardonable.

The whole of the Department of the South submitted without firing a shot. This was one of the consequences of the war of Rigaud. Men of Colour and Blacks, both those who had been originally free, and those whom the Revolution had enfranchised, were to be seen hastening in crowds to throw themselves into the arms of the French, of *their brethren before God and before* the *Republic*.* Never was conquest more easy: hardly did a twentieth part of the population oppose a feeble resistance.

* As the memorable Proclamation of the First Consul referred to in this passage, may not be in the recollection of all who read these pages, and as it furnishes a curious illustration of the perfidious duplicity which enabled the Consular, and afterwards the Imperial Government of France, to obtain at one time the sovereignty of nearly the whole of Europe, the Translator here subjoins an English version of that memorable document.

Toussaint's own brother, Gen. Paul Louverture, at St. Domingo, and Clerveaux at St. Jago, surrendered to the French, without a blow, the Spanish division of the Island, and the troops under their command. These two Generals had been gained over by their confessor Bishop Mauviel, and General Kerverseau.

Paris, 17th Brumaire, 10th year of the Republic of France one and indivisible.

PROCLAMATION

Of the First Consul to the Inhabitants of St. Domingo.

Whatever be your origin or complexion, you are all Frenchmen, *you are all free and equal before God and before the Republic.*

France, as well as St. Domingo, has been the prey of factions, torn both by foreign and domestic wars; but all is changed. All nations have embraced the French, and sworn to them peace and friendship. All the French have likewise embraced each other and sworn eternal amity: come ye likewise to embrace the French, and enjoy the satisfaction of again beholding your friends and brethren from Europe.

Government sends you the Captain General Leclerc; he takes with him a large force to protect you against your enemies and those of the Republic. Should any one say to you, *These forces are designed to rob you of your freedom,* reply, *the Republic has given us freedom—the Republic will never suffer us to be deprived of it.*

Rally around your Captain General; he brings you back peace and plenty. Rally ye all around him He who dares to separate himself from the Captain General is a traitor to his country, and the wrath of the Republic will devour him as the fire devours your dried canes.

Given at Paris, at the Palace of the Government, the 17th Brumaire, in the 10th year of the French Republic.

(Signed)   BONAPARTE.

By the First Consul.

(Signed)   HUGHUES B. MARET, Secretary of State.

A true copy.

(Signed)   LECLERC, Captain General.

A true copy.

(Signed)   DUGUA, General, Chief of the Etat Major of the Army.

Governor Toussaint was unprepared for war. He had issued no orders to his Generals, for he had no hostile design against France, which he had, on the contrary, served with the warmest zeal, and the most approved fidelity.

Generals Jean Jacques Dessalines and Henry Christóphe alone opposed the French. Maurepas indeed made a stout resistance at first but, deceived by the advice of the Whites, he soon surrendered.

I will not trace the march of the armies in this campaign, nor enter into details of the engagements, the ambuscades, and traits of heroism which ennobled our valiant warriors. One day perhaps I shall be able to do this ; but at present these details would lead me too far from my subject. Time presses, and I must hasten to my purpose.

In France Bonaparte had rallied all parties ; *Jacobins* and *Republicans, Emigrants and Royalists, both of the old and new school,* all fell into the train of his powerful genius. It was the same with the Whites in St. Domingo; they all flocked around Leclerc, and the most inveterate of the Ex-colonists* formed his privy council.

But if the most perfect unanimity prevailed among the Whites, it was the reverse among the Indigénes, who split into two distinct factions, the one adhering to Governor Toussaint, the other joining with the French. This last was thrice as numerous as the former: I will divide it into two classes; composed, the

---

* At the Cape, Belin de Villeneuve, Colet, Dumas, Domergue, O'Gorman, and Camfranq ; at Port-au-Prince, Desrivieres, a kind of chevalier, Guieu, and Bion, Ange, Baudomant, St. Cyr, Lecune, and Cottel; at Cayes, Mongin, formerly a Judge, and distinguished for his ferocity, Labiche, Lothon, Desongards, the curate Grisset, Gravet, &c. formed Leclerc's council.

first of *voluntary instruments,* the second of those who were *involuntary.*

The first class, and it was fortunately the least numerous, was composed of men bought over by the French, and initiated in their plans; these were indigénes, *Blacks and Mulattoes in their outward complexion alone,* but *Ex-colonists in heart and principle,* and they were and yet are, the most inveterate enemies of their brethren and their country. Such as Pétion, Laplume, Bardet, Lariviere, Louis Labelinais, Noël Mathieu, Jolicœur, Colombel, Milcent, &c. these therefore I shall regard as Ex-colonists, or even worse, for they were traitors, they deserve to be slaves, and one can wish them nothing better. These then I shall rank under the class of *voluntary instruments.*

The second class embraced a large number of the most enlightened and virtuous Haytians, who sincerely believed that the French were come to maintain liberty. Such were Maurepas, Médard, Thomany, Lamahotiere, &c. in a word, all those Haytians who fought under the French, and afterwards became their victims, may be regarded as *blind and involuntary instruments.*

What—it will be asked—were the most enlightened of the Haytians the *blindest* tools of the French?—Assuredly so. Men of the greatest information and strictest probity, found it difficult to persuade themselves that a great nation like France would stoop to disgrace herself by an act of such unparralleled ingratitude and perfidy! while the mistrust natural to our highland fellow-citizens benefitted us much more than the feeble glimmerings of our own knowledge: *they* saw the Whites armed, this was sufficient for *them*:— trembling for their *liberty,* they secretly provided themselves with arms, entrenched themselves in the deep recesses of the woods, and prepared for war.

It is from these brave inhabitants of the forests, these true founders of our liberty and independence, that we received this great and salutary lesson, which we should preserve for ever as a preventative against surprise; *that we ought to be perfectly on our guard before we suffer a crafty and perfidious foe to approach us; but that the shortest and safest method is to keep as far as possible out of their reach, and never to go near them without arms in our hands.*

The war proceeded with vigour: the *indigénes* on the French side rancorously assailed their brethren and fellow-citizens, who, in the fastnesses of the mountains, maintained the cause of Governor Toussaint, under the command of Generals Jean Jacques Dessalines, Henry Christóphe, and Andrew Vernet, who alone preserved unshaken fidelity.

The Indigénes who fought in the ranks of the French, were invariably made their advanced guards, served as guides, detected ambuscades, and were employed in assaults. The most perilous posts and destructive fires were reserved for them, under the pretence of their perfect acquaintance with the localties of the country.

Governor Toussaint, however, in compliance with the repeated solicitations of Gen. Leclerc, resolved to treat for peace: he selected for his negociator General Henry Christóphe, and General Leclerc took General Hardy for his.

Toussaint had already received long and signal services from Henry. He knew his honour, his integrity, and his incorruptible character. Leclerc doubtless was also acquainted with Hardy, and had *substantial* reasons for his choice.

These two Generals opened the negotiations: the correspondence between them has been printed and published,* and reflects no less credit upon Gen. Christóphe, than disgrace upon Leclerc who had the baseness to propose to him to arrest Governor Toussaint.†

* See the Documents subjoined to the *Manifeste du Roi* of the 18th of Sept. 1814.

† It is curious to observe the coincidence of this attempt of Leclerc's with a similar proceeding of Hedouville's already related at page 23.

The following correspondence, extracted from the documents subjoined to the *Manifeste du Roi* of the 18th of September 1814, is so highly creditable to the feelings and integrity of the great man who now governs the Northern division of Hayti with so much reputation to himself and benefit to his subjects, that the Translator feels no occasion to apologize for its introduction here.

"Head Quarters at the Cape, 29th Germinal, year 10 of the French Republic.
"*The General in Chief to General Christophe.*

"You may give credit, Citizen General, to all that Citizen Vilton has written to you on behalf of General Hardy. I will keep the promises which have been made to you. But, if you design to submit to the Republic, consider what a service you could render her by furnishing the means of securing the person of Gen. Toussaint.   (Signed) LECLERC."

"Head Quarters, Robillard, Grand Boucan, 2d Floreal, year 10.
"*Henry Christóphe, General of Brigade, to General Leclerc.*

"I have received yours of the 29th of last month. Wishing to give credit to what Citizen Vilton has written to me, I only wait for a proof which must convince me of the maintainance of liberty and equality in favour of the population of this colony. The laws which consecrate these principles, and which the mother country has doubtless enacted, will carry this conviction to my heart; and I protest to you that on obtaining this desired proof, by a knowledge of these laws, I will instantly submit.

"You propose to me, Citizen General, to furnish you with the means of securing the person of General Toussaint Louverture. To do so would on my part be an act of perfidy and treason; and

On the termination of this negotiation Governor Toussaint concluded a war of three months by signing a treaty of peace, and, with his Generals, submitting to the authority of Leclerc.

Then began the disarming of the cultivators, who were all compelled to return to the plantations, and apply themselves to the labours of agriculture.

Universal peace prevailed! Yet a few years—what do I say? *a few short months of dissimulation*, and our liberty was at an end. Before they shackled us anew with the bonds of slavery, it was necessary that we should be disarmed, and rendered incapable of resistance: it was necessary to make us resume our bonds

this proposition, disgraceful to me, is in my eyes a convincing proof of your invincible repugnance to believe me susceptible of the smallest sentiment of delicacy and honour. He is my chieftain and my friend. Is friendship, Citizen General, compatible with such monstrous baseness?

The laws of which I have spoken, have been promised to us by the mother country, by the Proclamation which her Consuls addressed to us when they transmitted the Constitution of the year 8. Fulfil, Citizen General, fulfil this maternal promise by unfolding to our view the code which contains it, and you will see all her children rushing into the arms of this beneficent mother, and amongst them Gen. Toussaint Louverture, who then undeceived like the rest, will correct his mistake. It is only when this error shall be thus rectified, that, if he persevere in spite of evidence, he can be regarded as criminal, and justly incur the sentence you have launched against him, the execution of which you propose to me.

Consider, General, the happy effects which will result from the simple publication of these laws to a people formerly crushed beneath the weight of irons, lacerated by the lash of a barbarous slavery; pardonable doubtless for apprehending a similar fate: of a people in fine who, after having tasted the sweets of liberty and equality, covet only to enjoy happiness among themselves, with an assurance of having nothing more to apprehend from the bonds and return to that state of annihilation from which we had emerged: it was necessary that we ould enter anew the horrible circle of tears, of suffering and of disgrace; it was necessary we should again live and bow the head beneath the yoke of these despots, to submit to their pride, their disdain and our own degradation.—No--no—no—sooner let a thousand poignards bury themselves in our hearts!!!

The unbridled passions and unbending character of the Ex-colonists, ought yet to save us. Just and omnipotent God! thou God the rewarder and avenger of crimes and perfidy! thou inspiredst their hearts with that spirit of madness, that thirst of gain, of hatred and of vengeance, which blinded them; and thou madest their very vices subservient to our deliverance.

No slavery, no colonies, vociferated these maniacs, *the blacks must either be all slaves, or they must be drowned, hanged, or burned. We must make a new plantation* (bois neuf*) added they.

they have burst. The exhibition of these laws will stop the effusion of French blood by French hands, will restore to the Republic children who may yet serve her, and cause peace, tranquility and prosperity, to return after the horrors of civil war to the bosom of this unhappy colony. The object is doubtless, Citizen General, worthy of the greatness of the mother country, and to accomplish it, General would cover you with glory and the blessings of a people which will take pleasure in forgetting the evils they have alreado experienced from the delay of their promulgation. Consider that to refuse a participation in these laws so necessary to the welfare of these countries, would be to perpetuate these evils even to the utter destruction of the inhabitants. In the name of my country, in that of the mother country I call for these salutary laws; produce them and St. Domingo is saved.

I have the honour to salute you

(Signed) H. Christophe.

* *Bois neuf*, signifies to *eradicate wholly from the soil*, (dessoucher un terrein) so as not to leave the smallest vestige.

The season of intrigue was past: they drove Gen. Leclerc into the adoption of the most violent measures against the unfortunate Haytians.

Governor Toussaint was arrested, gagged and pinioned, like a felon, while at table with General Brunet, and embarked with his family and officers for France. *You dare to arrest me! you insult an honorable officer!* exclaimed the unfortunate Toussaint to General Brunet and his aides-de-camp, who acted in the honorable capacity of police-officers and catch-poles upon the occasion. *Is it thus that you observe the faith of treaties? You are traitors and perjurers; heaven is just! I shall be avenged.* These were the last words uttered by this great man upon the land of his nativity, upon that land which he had conquered for France, and filled with the renown of his exploits. He has *indeed* been avenged, but he was not permitted to behold the day of retribution.

From this moment, the signal for proscriptions was given from one end of the island to the other.

The detail of horrors and cruelties which make nature shudder with affright, would lead me too far from my purpose: it is sufficient for me to say that *women and infants,* the *aged and infirm, friends and foes alike,* who had hitherto been spared in our wars, were all indiscriminately butchered with every possible aggravation. To *arrest* and *hang* became synonymous. The wretches even created a new vocabulary. *To drown two hundred individuals,* was to *make a national haul*; to *hang,* was to *promote a step*; to be *torn in pieces by blood hounds,* was to *descend into the arena*; to *shoot,* was to *wash the figure with lead*; and to *burn alive,* was to *operate warmly.** The antient regime was re-organized.

* See details of some of these enormities in the Baron's " *Systeme colonial devoilée,*" and his " *Reflexions sur les noirs et*

Every negro or mulatto who had been a slave before the Revolution, returned to the authority of his master, who hired, sold or disposed of them at pleasure.

Our misfortunes had reached their height, and partial insurrections had every where commenced.

Leclerc then saw Dessalines for the first time, (says Boisrond Tonnere, from whom I borrow the account, in the 45th page of his " *Memoirs pour servir à l'Histoire d'Hayti.*") " He had begun to conform himself
" to colonial cruelty, and was consequently apprised
" of the opinion of the Ex-colonists, that to overthrow
" the two classes of men combined in St. Domingo in
" the support of liberty, it was necessary to sow dis-
" sension between them. He applied himself there-
" fore to the completion of what Hédouville had
" begun. Leclerc flattered Dessalines and loaded him
" with praises, to which he pretended his conduct was
" entitled: he assured him he might count on the
" special favour of the Government, and that the First
" Consul, after the advantageous reports he had made
" in his behalf, would not be slow in bestowing on
" him a reward worthy of him. In a word he em-
" ployed all those political common places by which
" the Whites, and above all the French, hoped to gull
" the Blacks and Mulattoes. Dessalines saw with
" what sort of a man he had to deal, and was conse-
" quently upon his guard. After thanking the Captain
" General, he begged him to believe that his most
" anxious wish was to retire with the whole of his
" family to France, and that as for the rest, he placed
" every reliance on the good intentions of the Govern-
" ment to which he was entirely devoted. You are
" too necessary here, replied Leclerc, you must not

---

les blancs;" of which last a translation has been published by Hatchard.   *Transl.*

" embark for France till I accompany you, which will
" not be at the soonest in less than six months. Allow
" me the pleasure of presenting you to the First
" Consul. You know he is my brother in law. It is
" a long time to wait, answered Dessalines; neverthe-
" less I submit to your wishes."

Whether Leclerc was really the dupe of Dessalines, or whether he thought him too dull to perceive the traps laid for him, he began by insinuating that up to that period he had been unable to discover who were really hostile to the French Government: but he hoped by his assistance to learn who they were whom he ought to combat in order to restore peace and harmony. " As to the Planters," said he, " they are so unfortu-
" nate and possess so little influence, that it cannot be
" supposed that they have any interest in continuing
" the troubles: they have their families and properties
" in France. Is it not rather to the Men of Colour
" that we owe all our misfortunes?" Dessalines felt all the consequence of his reply, and framed it according to the views of the Captain General. " Since we
" are of the same opinion," said the latter, " I think
" our only plan will be to *exterminate the whole of*
" *them:* but I am embarrassed in the choice of means.
" The French troops are so reduced by disease that
" hardly enough remain to garrison the towns. I
" think you ought to levy an army of five thousand
" men for this expedition, which need not continue
" longer than you find expedient." "Wait," he added,
" I will give you an order to receive whatever arms
" and ammunition you require." In fact, he wrote the order with his own hand, and sent it to Gen. Dessalines along with 500 double louis, for the expences of the expedition, acquainting him that he might set off as soon as he thought fit. Before quitting the Cape, Dessalines took care to see all the French Generals,

and to sound their dispositions. He saw Dugua, chief of the *Etat major* of the army, who, discontented, no doubt, with the Captain General, informed him that the 13th Demibrigade,* was going to be incorporated as sappers in the Guard of Honour, and that he saw with regret, that the unfortunate soldiers of that corps were about to be sacrificed. Nothing more was wanting to awaken the vigilance of Dessalines, who immediately after his visit to Dugua, became acquainted with the transactions at Gonaïves.†

Fully enlightened with respect to the perfidious projects of Gen. Leclerc, Gen. Dessalines hastened to communicate them to the other Generals his companions in arms, who unanimously resolved on hostilities against the French. Dessalines, as the oldest and most elevated in rank, was acknowledged as *General in Chief of the army of Indigénes.*

It is remarkable that the *Black* Generals *always* resisted the seductions of the Whites, and defeated their perfidious plots.

The Commissioner Santhonax, proposed to General Toussaint the destruction of the Men of Colour by the Blacks: indignant at this base proposition, he had him arrested and sent on board ship. Hédouville made him a similar proposition with respect to Rigaud;‡ it was rejected with similar indignation, and he compelled Hédouville also to embark for France.

Leclerc, as I have just mentioned, made the same proposition to Dessalines, who not only spurned such infamy, but hastened to communicate it to the Men of Colour.

Equally noble was the conduct of King Henry. When he was General of Brigade, quartered with his

* Black troops.
† It was here General Toussaint was arrested.
‡ See page 22.

troops at Petite Anse, he lost no time in acquainting Pétion, then a Colonel under his command, and Gen. Clerveaux, who was stationed at Haut-du-Cap, with the deadly fate that menaced them; and they resolved to take arms in concert, and defend themselves from the vengeance and treachery of the French. Since that time, similar propositions have been suggested to the King, who rejected them with horror. But let me not anticipate. Meanwhile, I do not hesitate to say, that it is to the patriotism, the firmness, and the deep discernment of this great man, that the Haytians owe their security, their freedom and their independence.

If the Black Generals have principally resisted the seduction of the Whites, the same has not been the case with the Generals of Colour, who have always been so weak as to suffer themselves to be made the tools of the Whites against the Blacks.

Yet Colombel and Milcent accuse the Blacks of a desire to exterminate the Men of Colour, though the history of the country and the truth of facts demonstrate on the contrary, that the Men of Colour owe their preservation to the Black Generals, who never would become the tools of the Whites for their destruction.

What then, exclaim Colombel and Milcent, is it not true that the Blacks have destroyed thousands of Coloured Men in our civil wars? How then can you say that the Men of Colour owe their preservation to the Black Generals? To this I reply, that if the Men of Colour have been destroyed, it is Pétion and Rigaud who have been to blame; for had they resisted the seductions of the Whites, like the Black Generals, there would not have been any civil war: and it is so true that the Coloured people owe their safety to the Black Generals Toussaint Louverture, Dessalines and Henry Christóphe, that had these been so weak as to lend an ear to the perfidious suggestions of the Whites, and yielded to their persuasions, not a person of Colour would be in existence at this moment; and the Whites would have gained their utmost wishes. But these wise and considerate patriots felt that the interests of both classes were indissolubly connected: and had the Coloured Generals been equally patriotic, sage, and prudent, and had they yielded less to their insatiable ambition, we should have enjoyed unbroken harmony, and never had to deplore the evils of civil war.

It was at the period of this general arming, of which I have just spoken, that death freed us from Leclerc. Of his personal character I shall be silent, yet he was an angel of light compared with the monster* who succeeded him.

The Commander-in-Chief of the Indigéne army soon rallied all parties. Both the voluntary and involuntary instruments were obliged either to accompany the French in their flight, or to throw themselves into the arms of their brethren, against whom they had hitherto so blindly fought: too happy again to find a secure refuge amongst them.

Pétion was one of the *voluntary* instruments who joined General Dessalines, in order to escape the fate which threatened him: this General welcomed him kindly, admitted him into his friendship, and vowed to him a tender and eternal friendship from which he never swerved. He was far from thinking that he welcomed to his bosom one that was one day to assassinate him, and who reserved a similar fate for his successor.

In short, after having experienced every vicissitude of fortune, and been bowed down beneath the pressure of affliction; after having been for twelve years the sport and victims of all the factions which succeeded each other in St. Domingo; after having shed our

* Rochambeau.

blood in a thousand battles without conferring any real benefit on our country; we now, *for the first time* fought for our true interests, and were no longer the mere instruments of our own destruction for a cause which was foreign to us. For the first time we maintained a *national war*; we fought for liberty—for independence—for our country—for ourselves—to rescue ourselves from death and the tyranny of our executioners. On one side were the French—the Indigénes on the other: hatred and vengeance inflamed our courage—patriotism and liberty guided our steps—we had both our own individual injuries, and the death of our martyred brethren to avenge. We rushed to the combat with shouts of frantic joy; we fought man for man, each panting to slay his opponent—each burning to shed his blood in defence of his country, his freedom and his independence. Happy to be able to shed it, to the last drop, in so good a cause. After a dreadful and sanguinary struggle, the victims of oppression were left the sole and undisputed masters of the field.

The veil of error and of falsehood was at length torn away. Before the radiant sun of independence, faction fled as the clouds before the impetuosity of the wind: our political atmosphere became purified by victory, and we began to inhale the healthful breezes of liberty and independence. Victorious, surrounded by the ruins of the vanquished, we boldly looked around us. The *forty thousand* Ex-colonists, Great Planters and Inferior Whites—the numerous and well appointed army of the expedition—had all vanished from our soil.* The frightful Colonial System, slavery with the prejudice of colour, and a restrictive commerce, were all overturned

* Of 6000 [60,000] troops who had been sent from France during Leclerc's administration, little more than 4000 quitted it alive along with Rochambeau; this loss occurred in less than two years.——*Transl.*

from the foundation. The phantom of France, that chimera which had so long deluded us, had disappeared from before our eyes, and in the warmth of our enthusiasm we reared upon the yet smoking embers of their ruins, the lovely and immortal pillar of our independence.

Emancipated children of Hayti! prostrate yourselves in grateful humility at the feet of the Eternal, and return to him unnumbered thanks: let us admire the wisdom of his designs and the impenetrable methods which he has employed to deliver the oppressed and chastise their oppressors.

We had been the victims and blind tools used by the Ex-colonists to accomplish our own ruin, and we were ourselves in the hands of God the instruments of our own deliverance. They made us the panders to their vile passions; and contrary to their intention they conducted us to FREEDOM. Blind and infatuated, they attempted to rob us of this inestimable blessing, and fill up the measure of their injustice and their guilt, and again, in despite of themselves, they led us to INDEPENDENCE.

It is then to the unbridled passions, and unnumbered crimes of the Ex-colonists, that France should ascribe the loss of the richest and most lovely of her transatlantic possessions.

Such then, in brief, were the leading causes which conducted us to LIBERTY—and from LIBERTY to INDEPENDENCE.

CHAP. II.

OF THE GOVERNMENT OF THE HAYTIANS UNDER THE GOVERNOR GEN. JEAN JACQUES DESSALINES.

AFTER the expulsion of the French, the victors set themselves about framing a form of Government, and rendering themselves a free and independent nation.

Great knowledge, and a profound acquaintance with the fundamental principles of legislation, were not to be expected among men so recently emerged from the night of slavery and ignorance, among men whose hearts yet rankled, and whose feelings were yet irritated by misfortune: who had but just terminated an obstinate and savage warfare; and had always lived amid the danger and din of arms, in the solitude of forests or the dust of camps. Nevertheless, we find in the acts of that period an energy and enthusiasm strongly characteristic of the spirit which animated their authors.

On the 1st of January, 1804, nearly two months after the expulsion of the French, the Commander-in-Chief of the Indigéne forces convoked a general assembly of the Generals and Chiefs of the army and nation at Gonaïves, to take into consideration such measures as would be most conducive to the happiness, the liberty and the independence, of the people.

On our first step in the career of legislation ought to depend the prosperity or misfortunes of our country: but we then committed a capital error, from which perhaps flow all the calamities of our civil wars. This arose from our ignorance of the best form of Government for our adoption.

But we had not then acquired the knowledge and experience which we now possess: we did not understand the mechanism of representative and monarchical Governments, and our Legislators were more expert at the sword than the pen. It was natural then, that an assembly of soldiers, should adopt a form of Government purely military.

The Act of Independence was proclaimed. The Generals, Officers, People and Troops, unanimously swore in the face of the universe *to renounce France for ever, and to die rather than live under her dominion.*

There was as yet no Constitution.

Jean Jacques Dessalines, Commander-in-Chief of the army of Indigénes, was appointed and proclaimed head of the Government, under the title of GOVERNOR GENERAL FOR LIFE, with the power of making peace and war.

This title was by no means suited to an independent Government: but having been that of General Toussaint, it was from a spirit of habit conferred upon General Dessalines, without reflecting upon the true acceptation of the word, which no longer corresponded with the change in our situation. The name of the island was altered, and the Saint Domingue of the French was superseded by the original name of Hayti, whence the Black and Coloured Indigénes adopted the generic appellation of Haytians. And here it is worth remarking, that while *we* uniformly adopt these new names, the *French* pertinaciously adhere to the term Saint Domingue, both in their Acts and writings.

The Governor General made an highly patriotic address to the people of Hayti, in which he energetically retraced the calamities and sufferings, the horrors and injustice, we had experienced from the French, together with the necessity which there was for living free and independent, or submitting to death.

On the dissolution of the meeting, the Generals returned each to his respective command. The Generals of Division were stationed as follows: Henry Christóphe at the Cape; Clerveaux at Marmelade; Vernet at Gonaïves; Gabart at St. Marc; Pétion at Port-au-Prince, and Geffrard at Cayes.

Next to the Governor General, Henry Christóphe was the oldest General in the army, and the only Black of this high rank. The five remaining Generals of Division were *Men of Colour*. This single fact proves more than words how favourably General Dessalines was disposed towards persons of this description.

The Governor General first fixed the seat of Government at the ci-devant plantation Laville, whence he removed it to the plantation Marchand, situated in the plain of Artibonite, at the foot of the great chain of mountains of Cahos. Here he founded a town called after his own name, and secured it by the establishment of fortresses at the base, on the sides, and on the summit of the mountain.

Never was a position worse chosen in every point of view. Had he established the seat of Government at Port-au-Prince or in its vicinity, he would have been better able to watch over the West and South, and have possibly prevented the civil war. But Artibonite had been the theatre of his military exploits: he had defeated the French at la Crête-à-Pierrot, at Verrettes, at St. Marc, and Camp Marchand: an acquaintance with the place and people, his taste, and the force of habit, led him to this preference of the centre of the country to every other situation for establishing the seat of Government.

Meanwhile, in proportion as he proceeded in the career of Government, Dessalines became himself more and more convinced of the defects of its Constitution. The title of GOVERNOR GENERAL was found unsuitable to our situation. There was no Constitutional compact, and at the end of six months he resolved without further deliberation to change the form

CHAP. III.

OF THE EMPIRE.

WANT of reflection, or rather the influence of habit had given the title of GOVERNOR GENERAL to the *Commander-in-Chief of the army of Indigénes* ; a spirit of imitation conferred upon him that of EMPEROR.

Bonaparte, the First Consul, had assumed this title. The Governor General was therefore equally at liberty to take it. This however was going from one extreme to another; for if the title of GOVERNOR GENERAL, as implying a dependence upon some higher authority, was ill suited for the Chief of an independent people, the imposing one of EMPEROR, which implies in the person who bears it real power in territory, population, &c. was equally inapplicable to our situation.

In the enactments respecting the nomination of the Emperor, it is stated, that *the supreme authority does not admit of partition : the Emperor was named for life, with power to nominate his successor : he formally relinquished the custom of limiting the succession to his own family, and would pay no regard to seniority, unless combined with other requisites for a due administration of the Government.*

The Constitution was framed in conformity to these enactments. *The three powers, Legislative, Executive and Judicial*, were united in the same person: there was indeed a Council of State, but it was without power or authority, and this from the very nature of the Constitution: there were two Ministers, one of Finance and the Interior, the other of War and of the Marine, with a Secretary of State.

Such a Constitution was a monster in politics. The Empire was an elective Republic, whilst the Constitution sanctioned, on the one hand, principles diametrically opposite to those of a Republic, and which could only agree at the most with a Government purely *despotic*; and again, on the other hand, by the most unaccountable confusion of ideas, the Constitution admitted principles the most *democratic*.

Alas! we were far from *then* possessing the judgement and experience we now enjoy; had it been otherwise, we should have established a *Constitutional Monarchy*, and have given ourselves useful institutions and a stable and regular government: what evils and calamities should we not have avoided. To err however in our first attempts in the difficult art of Government, was doubtless pardonable; since we see old nations with every advantage of knowledge and experience, guilty of mistakes as gross perhaps as ours. But here, as everywhere else, it was the people who suffered for the sins of their Legislators: they it is who always pay with their tears, their blood and their treasures, the forfeit of such errors; and since, thank heaven! we have abundantly discharged this debt, we surely may be allowed to deplore our past sufferings.

I have already remarked in several of my works, that the Emperor Dessalines, though a brave soldier, and an ardent patriot, animated with the most lively desire to promote the welfare and prosperity of his fellow-citizens and his country, was nevertheless deficient in those talents which are requisite in a good governor: and to this first misfortune he yet added that of surrounding himself with immoral and corrupt men in the pay of France, who enticed him to his ruin, as the Ex-colonists had done with respect to Governor Toussaint.

It is an ungracious task to speak of one's self, but there are truths which cannot be too often repeated when the safety of a country and an entire nation depends on them. The first duty of a political writer is to enlighten; the second to speak the truth without fear. He ought to consider nothing but what is just, salutary and beneficial to his country. He should not suffer himself to be biassed by any private interests, passions or prejudices whatever. He should generously devote his life to promote the happiness, the glory and the welfare of his country, and if he feel himself unequal to the task he has undertaken, he should wave every personal consideration, give up his attempts at writing, and commit his pen to the flames.

By an ordinance of the 26th of July, 1815, the Emperor appointed Henry Christóphe, General of Division, *Commander of the Haytian Forces*; Andrew Vernet, *Minister of Finance and of the Interior*; and Etienne Elie Gérin, *Minister of War and Marine*. The Generals of Colour Pétion, Geffrard and Gabart, were continued in their commands.*

At this period those Haytians who had expatriated themselves along with the French, sought the means of returning to the bosom of that country which they had already torn with civil commotions, in order to excite fresh troubles. The Emperor, acting more from liberal than prudential feelings, permitted their return, and directed the expences of their passage to be defrayed. We soon witnessed the return of Blanchet,

---

* Clerveaux, Gabart and Geffrard, three Generals of Colour, died nearly about the same time.

Dartiguenave, Fauhert, and David Trois, all adherents of the French and of Pétion, and the bitterest enemies of their country.

The Emperor received these treacherous and ungrateful men with the greatest kindness, and loaded them with favours; yet hardly were they landed before they joined Pétion, and directed every effort to the subversion of the empire and the revival of the flames of civil war.

The object of this faction was to raise Pétion to the head of the Government; for the accomplishment of which it was necessary to destroy the two Black chieftains, Jean Jacques Dessalines and Henry Christóphe, who, from length of service, no less than the wishes of the army and the people, had a right to the Government. Behold the methods taken by these factious wretches for the completion of their designs! Their agents were dispersed in every quarter: those who surrounded the Emperor, incited him to persecute those who were most attached to him, and who refused to share in the conspiracy: thus the conspirators gained the two-fold advantage of alienating from the Emperor his best friends, and preventing a knowledge of the truth from reaching him. Their accomplices, scattered throughout the provinces, secretly laboured to mislead public opinion; Papalier at Cayes, and Gérin at Anse-à-Veau, whither he had retired on the plea of indisposition; the younger Blanchet, who was at Gonaïves, made frequent journies from the West to the South; David Trois travelled over the country in the disguise of a pedlar, visiting the mountains from Rochelois to the Môle, Port de Paix, Gros Morne, and Cape Henry; to extend the conspiracy and render it general throughout the country.

Pétion was the soul of the plot: he was the mainspring of every movement. He affected the tenderest regard for the Emperor, who, on his side, was completely blind to his own personal danger, and reposed the most unbounded confidence in him. Pétion had all the arts of great conspirators : he exerted himself from day to day to increase his popularity : he flattered the people ; caressed the troops ; tolerated licentiousness and immorality : assuming the mask of philosophy he abandoned his duties, affected a total want of ambition, and an utter contempt of honours, rank and riches : beneath the rags of Diogenes, he concealed the most immoderate desires: and like another Sextus Quintus, this hypocrite marched boldly forward and in perfect security to the completion of his designs.

A general disorder pervaded the empire. The finances were disorganized ; the troops without pay or clothing ; the examination of titles to estates was conducted with extreme rigour, with a view to discover flaws to justify confiscation. The corruption which prevailed in the very highest departments ; the general discontent which silently manifested itself among the people and the troops, threatened an impending convulsion. All these evils were aggravated by Pétion's accomplices and the adherents of the French, who flocked together from all sides, and repaired to the West and South to open the prelude to the grand drama they were preparing for exhibition.*

To this inundation of licentious morals the Commander-in-Chief, Henry Christóphe, in vain endeavoured to oppose a barrier. He had maintained, as far as he was able, more order and regularity in the administra-

* It is to be remarked that every time the French meditated an attempt upon this country, they employed their spies and secret agents as precursors to it. The Priests were the instruments especially selected for the purpose, together with such *Indigénes* as were *Whites in principle*, and every other respect but complexion, as Milcent, Colombel, Labelinais, &c.

tion, and more discipline among the troops. His private conduct and regular morals led all to turn their attention to him, and he became the hope of every well-disposed person and fathers of families.

To these evils, from his perfect ignorance of their existence, the Emperor applied no remedy. He was blinded by his imaginary prosperity, and the flatteries of those who surrounded him, and studiously kept the groans of the people from his ears. These base adulators, these corrupt and profligate men, abandoned themselves to the most frivolous pursuits, as balls, intrigues and festivities. They were far from giving him such salutary advice as could open his eyes to his situation, save him from the impending danger, and strengthen his Government. The Emperor threw himself into the net spread for him by his enemies, who enticed him to a neglect of his duties, and the commission of acts unworthy of him, in order to deprive him of the respect and love of his people, and thus facilitate his downfall.

Nevertheless, Pétion and his adherents could not disguise from themselves the great and formidable obstacles to be surmounted in the accomplishment of their designs. On the fall of the Emperor the helm of the State would naturally devolve upon the Commander-in-Chief. This first step obtained, they yet had done nothing; they had every thing to fear from the people and the troops: they resolved therefore to use the name of the Commander of the Forces, as a means of effecting the meditated Revolution with less danger to themselves.

They fabricated a letter in the name of the Commander of the Forces, calling upon the people and the troops to revolt from the Emperor. In proceeding thus the conspirators gained a twofold object: should the Emperor escape their snares, they rendered him suspicious of the Commander-in-Chief. Thus they could not fail in one way or other either to destroy the Emperor, or effect the downfall of the Commander-in-Chief.

The plot exploded on the 10th of October, 1806, in the plain of Cayes, where the Emperor's friends were sacrificed to the vengeance of the conspirators. Gérin, the Minister of War, who pretended to be sick at Anse-à-Veau, put himself at the head of the insurrection of the South, and marched to Port-au-Prince. Pétion, to continue the Emperor in his false security, acquainted him that an insurrection had shewn itself in the South, and that he would set off to arrest its progress.

The Emperor, who had the greatest confidence in Pétion, depended wholly upon him, and directed him to take the necessary steps for quelling the disturbances.

Pétion departed for Port-au-Prince, with the troops under his command, in the intention of joining the Insurgents of the South. He took with him General Germain, of whom he was not sure, and gave orders both by land and sea, that no person should be suffered to quit the town, lest the Emperor should learn what was passing. Pétion left his troops at Grand-Goave, and repaired to Gérin at Petit-Goave, where they had an interview. The two divisions of the army effected a junction at Grand-Goave, whence, after putting General Germain under arrest, they marched for Port-au-Prince, which town they entered on the 16th of October, accompanied by Generals Yayou, Magloire, Ouagnac, and other leaders of the conspiracy

Meanwhile the Emperor continued at Dessalines. After issuing some orders preparatory to his departure he informed the Commander-in-Chief of the insurrection which had broken out in the South, and directed him to hold himself in readiness to march on the first notice. He left the command of Dessalines and the province of the west to Andrew Vernet, Minister of Finance, with orders to dispatch the troops in succession to join him, should he require their aid. He then set off for Arcahaye, attended only by a few Aides-de-camp and a weak escort of horse.

The Commander-in-Chief, on receiving the Emperor's letter, was filled with the greatest uneasiness, and instantly dispatched one of his Aides-de-camp to the Emperor for orders to march, advising him at the same time not to hazard his person without troops, and a perfect knowledge of the situation of affairs: but unfortunately the Aide-de-Camp was unable to reach the Emperor; for on arriving at La Source Puante,* he learned that he was no more.

An almost incredible fatality led to his death. On his route to Arcahaye he met one of his Aides-de-Camp, whom he had previously sent on a mission to the South, returning without having been able to penetrate farther than Miragoane. This officer gave him a faithful account of the state of affairs, and urged him not to enter Port-au-Prince without troops. But the Emperor, who had a blind confidence in Pétion, and whose intrepidity was superior to the suggestions of fear, spurned the salutary advice given to him, and dismissed the Aide-de-camp from his presence.

At Arcahaye he took for his guard six companies of men picked out of the 3d reg. and placed them under the command of Col. Thomas, and Lieut.-Col. Gédéon, with orders to march for Port-au-Prince, and wait for him without the gates, at a place called Pontrouge: for he halted himself to rest at the ci-devant plantation Labarre. It was at this place that, seeing the smoke at a distance in the mountains of the South,

* Six leagues from Port-au-Prince.

Ch. III.—OF THE EMPIRE.

he said to those about him, that *it was at this hour his comrade Pétion was to fire*; such was still his blindness with respect to that traitor.

The guard in question stationed itself advantageously at Pont-rouge, waiting for the Emperor; most of the officers dispersed themselves among the adjoining plantations; being on the point of entering a town which they supposed to be at peace with them, they entertained no mistrust or uneasiness.

Pétion, on learning the arrival of this guard, resolved to gain it over, and take advantage of it to lay a trap for the Emperor. For this purpose he dispatched Gen. Yayou, one of the blindest tools of the conspiracy, who succeeded in gaining over the officers and persuading them to enter Port-au-Prince with their men, when they were immediately replaced by a battalion of the 15th reg. of the troops of the South; and so far did Pétion carry his treachery as to place at the head of this battalion a commander of the same corpulence, and in the same dress as Gédéon, the better to deceive the Emperor; who seeing the troops at a distance entertained no mistrust.

Gérin, Yayou, Magloire and others, posted themselves with their troops in ambuscade on both sides.

From Port-au-Prince to Morne Drouillard, and even farther, ten thousand men, both horse and foot, had been so disposed by the conspirators, as to leave the unfortunate Emperor no chance of escape.

While all this took place without the town, Pétion remained peaceably at home awaiting the result. True to his accustomed maxims of hypocrisy, he did every thing privately by means of his confederates, in the two-fold view of profiting by the event in whatever manner it should fall out. Should the conspirators succeed in their undertaking, he was prepared to secure to himself all the advantages resulting from it: while, if the Emperor escaped their machinations, he reserved to himself the power of declaring in his favour, and throwing all the odium of the attempt upon the participators in his treason.

The life of this singularly deceitful man abounds in similar traits: he was in the constant habit of sporting with both friends and enemies for the attainment of his own private ends.

In the night of the 17th of October, the Emperor resumed his journey to Port-au-Prince, having but one and twenty persons in his train.

He traversed the whole plain of Cul-de-Sac in the most perfect security, without meeting an individual to apprise him of what awaited him.

On approaching Pont-rouge he saw the troops drawn up on both sides of the road, and conceiving them the same he had sent forward to wait his arrival, he continued to advance without suspicion. He was already deep within the ambuscades, without either discovering this circumstance himself or its being observed by any of his escort, till on reaching the troops he heard the word given to *make ready*, with cries a thousand times repeated of *halt, halt!* The Emperor now saw his mistake, discovered that he was betrayed, and found himself in the midst of the 15th regiment. This intrepid Chieftain, who had braved death amidst a thousand dangers, rushed amidst the bayonets and exclaimed, *Soldiers! don't you know me?* He took his cane, and knocked aside the bayonets opposed to him. The soldiers, struck with fear and respect, dared not to raise their hands against their Emperor, who continued to advance through their ranks. At length one of the boldest among them daring to level his piece, the Emperor immediately shot him with a pistol. At this moment Gérin, Yayou and the other conspirators who were concealed in ambush, gave the word to *fire*, when a general discharge took place. The Emperor's horse was killed, and he himself fell, pierced with a thousand balls. Thus fell the head of the empire, amidst the companions of his arms, his glory and his toils, after a reign of one year, ten months and twenty-six days. Col. Marcadier, the sole commander of his guards, fell bravely by his side defending him.

It was then that a white Frenchman of the name of Verret,* a favourite of Pétion's, whose life the Emperor had saved and promoted him to the rank of Adjutant-General, was seen to mutilate the body and take away his watch and seals. Then also Georges, of execrable memory, was seen to cut off one of his thumbs, which he sold to a stranger immediately after for ten Portuguese.† It was then that the dead body ———— but oh! climax of horror ———— they insulted and abused it even after death.

Thus did Pétion accomplish the destruction of his Sovereign, his friend and benefactor, in order to seize the reins of Government, and kindle anew the flames of civil war.

CHAP. IV.

OF THE CIVIL WARS.

HOW guilty are those ambitious and perfidious men who entailed upon their wretched country all the calamities of civil war! How criminal those wretches, who, with the evidence before their eyes of the disasters

* This Verret still holds a command in the South.
† The terms Portuguese, Johannes and Joe, are synonymous, and applied to a gold coin commonly current in the West Indies, and usually valued at eight dollars, or half a doubloon.—*Transl.*

resulting from it, and all the expenditure of blood which has taken place, persevere in using every effort to perpetuate it, in place of devising means for its extinction, and for destroying every trace of its pernicious effects! Our wounds are yet bleeding; should we not then rather pour into them the healing balsam, than madly strive to open them anew?

Never----never will I give to my countrymen the horrible and deceitful advice of Colombel and Milcent, those traitors paid by our enemies, who write only to excite civil dissension and animosity, and to stimulate their fellow-citizens to cut each others throats; but, actuated solely by the purest patriotism, I take up my pen in order to promote peace and harmony, with a mutual pardon and oblivion of injuries, in order to prevent the effusion of that valuable blood, which ought to be shed only in defence of our liberty and independence. If I retrace the misfortunes of our civil wars, it is contrary to my inclination; I have been driven to it, as we have been to the field of battle, in spite of myself, by my adversaries: and besides, I write more with a view of remedying these evils, and clearing our conduct from reproach, than to awaken painful recollections, which, were I able, I would most gladly bury in eternal oblivion.

The Emperor was no more! Had the abuses of his administration been the *true and only cause* of his downfall, the political commotion which produced it, would have had no further consequences. The reins of Government devolved upon his legitimate successor, and should have passed from the hands of the one to the other without further change in the Government. But, as I have already observed, Pétion's object was to seize upon the supreme authority for himself. In overthrowing the Emperor, he had removed but one obstacle; another yet remained, this was the Commander-in-Chief, whom it was likewise necessary to destroy in order to obtain the supreme command. But, as the Revolution which had taken place, had been effected in his name, it was necessary to bring about another, in order to obtain a similar result.

Before we proceed further, my readers will feel gratified by a sketch of the character of the two principal personages, who will occupy, though in a widely opposite manner, a conspicuous place in the history of our civil wars.

HENRY CHRISTÓPHE, from the earliest dawn of his public and private life, has uniformly shewn himself frank, upright, and honourable. An excellent father, a rigorous disciplinarian; strict in the discharge of his own duties; active, brave, and generous; lively in his disposition, incapable of fraud or dissimulation, he always speaks and acts with manly candour; just to the virtuous, and severe to the guilty, he is prompt to reward the one and punish the other: he carried with him to the throne all his virtues public and private; his frankness, his integrity, and his justice, his inflexible character and principles, have often been prejudicial to his interests, and his enemies have uniformly endeavoured to turn his very virtues against him.

ALEXANDER PETION was his opposite in every every thing: he was indisputably the most hypocritical designing, and ambitious man in the world: tolerating vice and disorder, kind to the guilty, caressing and flattering the people, in order to acquire popularity; a cheat, a traitor; effecting the assassination of his enemies in secret: he united to all the arts and talents of a conspirator, the most profound dissimulation; in a word, partaking of every vice, and equally corrup in his public and private character, he was singularly calculated to injure his country.

Henry Christóphe had the most indisputable claim to the Government, as well as the gratitude of his fellow-citizens, not only from his long and distinguished services as Commander-in-Chief, but also as the senior officer of the army;* and he had the voices of all good people in his favour; whereas Alexander Pétion had not the slightest pretension to the Government, since there were many other Generals whose claims were stronger than his both from the magnitude and length of their services. Pétion was only known in Hayti by the number of his treasons; and even the popularity he had acquired was purchased by his toleration of every kind of profligacy and licentiousness: nevertheless he succeeded, as I am about to shew, in producing a schism in the country, usurping power, and exciting a civil war.

From the moment of the Emperor's fall, the country became virtually divided; though this unfortunate separation was not at once perceptible, it nevertheless actually existed.

The troops of the first division of the West, who had been sent to join the Emperor under the command of Martial Besse, halted at Arcahaye, filled with grief for the tragical end of their chief. They were impatient to march to Port-au-Prince to avenge his death, but their General reluctantly dissuaded them from their design and besought them rather to return to their cantonments, and there remain peaceable and obedient.

The province of the North, and the first division of that part of the West which had no share in the bloody tragedy, acknowledged no authority but that of the Commander-in-Chief, and refused obedience to any orders but his: while the province of the South, and the second division of the West, which had brought

---

* Dessalines left no legitimate posterity behind him.—*Transl.*

about the Revolution, refused submission to any orders but those of Pétion and Gérin. These two leaders made a show of obeying the authority of the Commander-in-Chief; but notwithstanding their professions, they only executed them as they pleased themselves. In this state of affairs, a civil war could not be slow in taking place.

The conspirators continued at Port-au-Prince.—After the death of the Emperor they held a council, at which the impatient Gérin urged their immediate march to the town of Dessalines, which contained, as he said, the treasures of the tyrant; but as this could not be atchieved without a battle, the wily Pétion, espoused a contrary opinion, and opposed him. He represented that as the Revolution had been effected in the name of the Commander-in-Chief, if they were to march against the troops which obeyed his orders, they would betray themselves, and commit an act of aggression, which might materially injure them in the estimation of the army and the people. Pétion, who had chalked out for himself the line of conduct he meant to pursue, preferred the employment of dissimulation and perfidy, to open force, to oppose to his enemy whom he hoped to entangle in a snare as he had done the Emperor, and then destroy him with equal facility.

Here are the means they employed, and the measures they pursued.

It was necessary to explain to the people, and report to the Commander-in-Chief, the causes which had produced the late events. Gérin, in consequence, addressed the Commander-in-Chief from Anse-à-Veau on the 12th of Oct. 1806, acquainting him with the insurrection at Cayes and its origin: his letter began thus:

" *My dear General; all the military and people have*
" *long regarded you as the successor to the Government*

"*of Hayti:*" and he concluded in these words: "*to acknowledge you supreme head of this empire, until the happy moment of proving it to you viva voce, has arrived.*"

On the 13th of October, the Chiefs of the army of the South wrote collectively to the Commander-in-Chief, to give him an account of their levy en masse. "*We will not conceal from you,*" say they, "*illustrious Commander-in-Chief, that we are convinced your indignation will at least be equal to our own, and we joyfully and unanimously proclaim you supreme head of this island, under whatever denomination you think proper to select. You have all our hearts; we will swear before God to be always faithful to you, and to die in defence of you and liberty.*" Further on we find these words, "*Acquin, Anse-à-Veau and Jacmel, are for you and us.*" And again, "*We await, Commander-in-Chief, your orders for the whole of our operations: be thou our protector and that of Hayti: God will, we trust, bless the good cause.*"

The morning after the Emperor's death, Gérin, Minister of War, confirms, in his letter of the 18th of October, that of the 13th.

"*The Tyrant is no more, public joy applauds the event, while it names you to govern. The people and the army doubt not that your Excellency will undertake the duties which the marked and spontaneous will of the public has imposed upon you.*"

Pétion himself—the wily crafty Pétion—wrote to the Commander-in-Chief after this event. His letter of the 16th speaks of the transactions of the 17th, and concludes as follows:

"*We should not have accomplished our task, General, had we not been convinced that there existed a leader formed to command the army with all that plenitude of power of which he has till now possessed but the* "name. It is in the name of the whole of this army, always faithful, obedient, and orderly, that we intreat you, General, to take the reins of Government and enable us to enjoy the fullness of our rights and liberty for which we have so long fought, and to be the guardian of those laws which we swear to obey because they are just."

The Generals assembled at Port-au-Prince published a Proclamation, entitled "RESISTANCE TO OPPRESSION," in which they expressed themselves as follows:

"*While waiting the moment in which it will be possible to establish it* (a Constitution) *we declare that unanimity, fraternal affection, and harmony, shall be the basis of our re-union. We will not lay down our arms, till we have levelled the tree of our bondage and debasement, and placed at the head of affairs a man whose valour and virtues we have long admired, and who, like ourselves, has been an object of the Tyrant's insults. The people and the army, whose organ we are, proclaim General Henry Christôphe, provisional head of the Haytian Government, until the Constitution, in definitively conferring this high rank upon him, has determined its nature.*"

Now, all these authentic documents clearly prove, that he employed the name of the Commander-in-Chief to excite the people and the troops; and that the public voice called the Commander-in-Chief to fill the vacant office of first Magistrate of the State.

Pétion, whose object it was to entice the Commander-in-Chief to Port-au-Prince, in order to entrap him, as he had done his predecessor, endeavoured to persuade him to go there; but, anticipating the failure of his efforts to lure him into his toils, he began to adopt measures for producing a revolt of the army and people in the provinces of the West and North. For this purpose he disposed his agitators in every direction by land and sea, to circulate his proclamations and incendiary publications, inciting the people to rebel against the Commander-in-Chief. Pétion no longer kept any measures: he enlisted troops and collected them at Port-au-Prince, he formed companies of artillery and cavalry, and prepared to raise the standard of revolt.

Pétion had recognized the Commander of the Forces as head of the Government, and yet this same Pétion exercised the functions of Sovereign authority. He broke and changed the civil and military officers, whom he replaced at will by others. He disposed of the treasures of the State, and the magazines. He decided causes, and sentenced to death, without submitting his decisions to the head of the Government, as the laws required. He put such of the officers, as he suspected, inhumanly to death.

Generals Moreau and Guillaume Lafleur, were beheaded at Cayes and Aquin. General Germain and the Adjutant Generals Boisrond Tonnére, Secretary to the late Emperor, and Mentor, were bayonetted at Port-au-Prince by his orders and under his eye. Colonels Bazil and Aoua, with a host of other Black Officers, were assassinated.

Colombel and Milcent, you who upbraid us with the horrors of a civil war, which you yourselves originally excited, and which you endeavour to perpetuate, answer me! Whilst your leader Pétion was thus busied in making Haytian blood stream in torrents through Port-au-Prince, was a single drop shed in the north, by orders of the Commander-in-Chief? No, doubtless. On the contrary, the Chief of the Government beheld with the deepest sorrow the irritation and violence which prevailed among the people, and used every possible effort to tranquillize their unruly passions and bring them back to the controul of reason.

To avoid every ground of civil war, the Commander-in-Chief, without censuring the causes which had produced this melancholy catastrophe, or giving offence to the actors in the tragedy, held a middle course, and endeavoured by his proclamations, and the measures he pursued, to restore tranquillity, and organize the Government upon a new basis. In a proclamation of the 2d Nov. he speaks thus:

"*It is nothing to have overthrown a corrupt administration, unless we substitute a better in its room, and guard against that anarchy and disorder which so easily arise out of the political transition from one Constitution to another. Remember that the Government which will henceforward guarantee your rights and secure to you compensation for your sufferings, demands from you obedience, observance of military discipline, respect to your superiors, and submission to the laws. These are conditions without which it is impossible for him to make the smallest progress in the new career which is opened to him.*" And he concludes with these words: "Government wishes for the maintenance of the most perfect harmony, and the the sacrifice of every feeling of animosity, ambition, or party spirit, and has no other object than the welfare of the State."

The head of the Government then directed the primary assemblies to meet for the election or the deputies who were to assemble for the purpose of framing a new Constitution. Pétion and Gérin were directed to convoke the assemblies of the province of the South, and the second division of that of the West.

The seat of Government was at the Cape, which was the residence of the Commander-in-Chief: it was in this city therefore, according to every rule of custom, that the Constituent Assembly should have met. But Henry, to give the Generais a striking proof of his disinterested integrity, and, to remove every suspicion of undue influence, consented, unfortunately, to its being held at Port-au-Prince, remote both from his presence and influence; far from imagining that Pétion would turn his integrity against himself and against his country.

To understand Pétion and Gérin peace and harmony were re-established; *they* had removed the only obstacle to the prosperity of the country; and yet they continued to keep the troops collected at Porte-au-Prince, contrary to the orders and proclamations of the head of the Government, who commanded them to be marched back to their respective cantonments, as were all those in the North and West. It was in this town alone, in which the Magistrates, entrusted with the formation of the Constitution, were on the eve of assembling, that they kept a numerous force in arms: does not this clearly demonstrate their ultimate designs?

The deputies from the North, and part of the West, would have commenced their deliberations at the appointed time; but those from the South, and the second division of the West, had not yet arrived. Pétion deferred opening the assembly from day to day, and even refused to name the place where its sittings were to be held: he wished to gain time to mature his plans, and perfect his intrigues.

At length the day for opening the Legislative Assembly arrived. On the verification of the powers, there were found to be *seventy-four* deputies, in place of *fifty-six,* of which it ought to have consisted: Pétion and Gérin having for their own ends perfidiously given a majority of *eighteen* deputies in the two divisions of the South. Independent of which the assembly was overawed by the large military force in the town, and *was not free in its deliberations.*

Ch. IV.—OF THE CIVIL WARS.

In vain did the deputies from the North and the first division of the West, represent that the assembly was illegally constituted. Their complaints were negatived by the majority formed by the deputies from the South, and the second division of the West. The deputies from the North entered their protest against this pretended constituent assembly.

After such proofs, insults, and aggressions, the head of the Government could no longer continue an idle spectator of the calamities of his country. He had, during the season of irritation, tolerated all that the welfare of the country would allow: but the crisis had now arrived; the laws were violated and despised; he could not suffer his fellow-citizens to be butchered and oppressed before his eyes; and he clearly discerned that Pétion's sole aim was to seize upon the reins of Government. He therefore marched against Port-au-Prince, and on the 1st of January, 1807, encountered in the plains of Cibert the army which Pétion had marched for the invasion of the first division of the West.*

I have now explained the origin and causes of our civil dissensions; and, from what has been stated, my readers can judge who were the authors and exciters of the diasters which followed; and they will doubt-

---

* Pétion was defeated here: he owed his safety to the generosity of Henry, who liberated a number of prisoners on the field of battle, and halted the march of his victorious army for Port-au-Prince, in order to save the effusion of blood. From the place where he halted he wrote to Pétion and Gérin generously offering them terms of peace. Thus he gave Pétion time to fortify himself, and rally his troops. Henry fell into the same error with Hannibal after the battle of Cannæ, with this difference, that Hannibal fought against strangers, towards whom delicacy was needless, while Henry was opposed to his own countrymen, which renders his error more excusable.

less see with indignation, how a nation of brethren linked together by the most perfect unity of interests, has been disunited and set at variance, the one part against the other, by the intrigues and unbounded ambition of one man.

CHAP. V.

CONTINUATION OF THE SUBJECT.—THE PRESIDENCY OF BOTH SIDES.

THE fatal moment was arrived: Haytian blood had been shed by Haytian hands. Civil war was kindled, and brought in its train all those horrors and misfortunes which yet afflict our wretched and unhappy country.

Henry Christôphe had been unanimously recognised and proclaimed head of the Haytian Government by the people and the soldiery, and the very Generals and Magistrates who had just questioned his authority, had themselves been the first to acknowledge it and to take the oath of allegiance to him; as a reference to their own acts attests.

Pétion had nevertheless succeeded, through his intrigues, in arming them against the chief of their own choice, and inducing them to violate their oaths.

The abuses of the Emperor's administration and his tyranny had furnished a colourable pretext for his overthrow: but what ground of complaint could possibly exist against the present head of the Government. Had he committed any act of oppression, or abuse of power, to warrant the assumption of arms against his authority?—of what maladministration, of what crime had he been guilty? Surely of none! for he had not yet been allowed sufficient time to exercise a single function of Government; and I defy my adversaries to disprove this assertion. Not an individual had been arrested, not a drop of blood had been shed by his orders. On the contrary all the acts of the magistrates and officers of the South-west incontestibly prove the firm reliance placed in his high character and known virtues both by the army and the nation. What then could authorize a refusal to acknowledge his authority, and induce the generals, the magistrates, the people, and the troops of the South-west, to violate their oath of allegiance?—those especially who had been *voluntarily* foremost in proclaiming and acknowledging him supreme head of the Haytian Government, not only without any solicitation on his part, but even without consulting his wishes. A man whose virtues and integrity had been universally admitted, who had been allowed to be the only person capable of conducting public affairs with skill, had, by an inconceivable fatality, in the short space between the 17th of October and the 1st of January, lost their esteem and respect, and was represented to the people as a tyrant who had forfeited all his rights, and lost all talents and virtues: and this by the very persons who had not three months before declared their conviction that he was the only person capable and worthy of governing. What a change? How could they so suddenly deny his authority, and take arms against him? What could be the real grounds for this disastrous and unnatural war? What motives could be sufficiently powerful to induce a nation of brethren thus madly to deal destruction among one another? The very same which produced the civil war between Rigaud and Toussaint. These were the real motives, and none other ever existed.

Henry, like Toussaint, was dragged against his inclination into the field of battle. Pétion proved, like Rigaud, ambitious, unjust, and ungrateful; he was the blind instrument of the Whites. Had he consulted the true interests of his country, had he but listened to the voice of justice and of reason; had his heart been open to considerations of humanity, would he not have shrunk with horror from the prospect of the incalculable evils he was bringing on his country? Did he not know that the first authority never could devolve upon him, and that by endeavouring to seize upon the reins of Government he must inevitably kindle the flames of civil war? Did he not know all the calamities which must result? Could he be ignorant of them? He who had been a witness and participator in Rigaud's war against Toussaint. Why then attempt a similar war which must be productive of similar results? Does not all this clearly prove that Pétion sacrificed every generous and patriotic consideration to the gratification of his own ambition, and that the generals and magistrates, the people and the troops of the South-west, were blindly led to become subservient to the interests and passions of an individual?

In this civil war, disastrous and unfortunate to the Haytians, the Whites, as in all our former wars, played their accustomed game; they intrigued and gave advice on both sides; aided to the utmost of their power both parties in doing each other all possible injury: they busied themselves in procuring for each arms, ammunition, ships and provisions. The moment one side appeared on the point of yielding, they made every exertion to support it so as to prolong the contest.

And how do they act at present? Can it be believed that they have renounced their favourite project of sowing dissension, and arming us against each other? What are Colombel and Milcent, with the French established at Porte-au-Prince, at Cayes, at Jérémie, and at Jacmel doing? Are they not labouring to corrupt the minds of the people, and to gain adherents to their views? Are they not the vipers whom the Haytians of this part nourish in their bosom? who are sent, under the mask of commerce to excite fresh troubles.*

After the battle of Cibert, on the 1st of January, 1807, all intercourse ceased between the two sides: the separation of the country, hitherto but nominal, became real; and both the unity of the Government and the army was dissolved. The enemies of Hayti gained the summit of their wishes, and they flocked together again in the foolish and barbarous hope of profiting by our dissensions, and employing one party to crush the other.

Meanwhile both sides were occupied in framing a new Constitution and remodelling the system of administration.

A Council of State, formed of the general officers and notables of the North and the first division of the West, was summoned to meet at the Cape on the 17th of February, in order to deliberate upon a new Constitution.

This Council legislated for the three provinces of the North, the West, and the South. The Government was called *the State of Hayti*, and its Chief Magistrate, *President, and Generalissimo of the Forces by land and sea*. This office was for life, and the President had a right to chuse a successor from among the Generals only. The legislative authority was vested in a Council of

---

* A French *merchant* of the name of Sureau, who has commercial establishments at Porte-au-Prince, Jacmel, and Cayes is *banker to the Republican Government!!!*

State; *and a superintendent was appointed to take charge of the departments of finance, marine, and the interior, with a Secretary of State, who was to draw up and countersign all public acts, and conduct all correspondence both foreign and domestic.*

The principles of this Constitution partook more of those of a Monarchy than a Republic: it was the best adapted to existing circumstances, and the stormy aspect of the times.

The civil and military authorities in the South-west also formed themselves into a deliberative assembly, and legislated equally for the three provinces of the North, the West, and the South.

In this state of affairs the *original* was the only *real* and *indisputable* right. The Commander-in-Chief had been acknowledged head of the Haytian Government by the inhabitants of the three provinces. The Sovereignty existed in the whole body of citizens: one portion of the people had no right to legislate for the remainder, nor could the chieftain, who had been once elected, be legally deposed without the *unanimous* concurrence of the people. Nevertheless the Government of the South-west assumed the title of *the Republic of Hayti: the Constitution was modelled after that of the United States of America; the office of President was to continue for four years, with a Senate entrusted with the legislative power.*

Contrary to every principle of honour, of justice, and of equity, Pétion was chosen *President of the Republic*, and thus attained the summit of his ambition.

Proclamations and publications appeared on both sides, reciprocally casting upon each other the odium of having occasioned the civil war: the keenest reproaches tended to inflame their mutual animosity, and were the precursors of the bloody scenes which followed.

Henry Christóphe, of a frank and energetic character, satisfied of the goodness and justice of his cause, proceeded openly to the execution of his plans, while Pétion aimed at accomplishing his dark designs by secret intrigue.

Henry, on taking the helm of the state, applied himself seriously to the duties of his post. He re-organised all the branches of the public service, and corrected the disorders which had existed under the preceding Government. His comprehensive eye embraced all the details of the administration, police, justice, finance, commerce, agriculture, and military discipline; throughout the whole he introduced that spirit of order which so eminently distinguishes his Government, and is the chief cause of our present tranquillity, strength, and power.

Pétion, on assuming the reins of Government did not swerve from his Machiavelian principles in the interior of the Republic. To increase his popularity he flattered and caressed the mob: he authorised every species of licentiousness, crime, and immorality: every thing was tolerated at Port-au-Prince, and the greatest enormities were perpetrated before his face. He took off his hat to every passenger in the streets; and at night the foreign merchants were obliged to barricade their stores, and employ fire arms to protect themselves from pillage. Had a man committed a rape, Pétion would only smile and say *let him alone:* had another robbed, *he is a poor devil*, he would say, *doubtless he was in distress:* had another committed murder, instead of applying the law of retaliation, Pétion would observe, *it is impossible, for then there would be a loss of two men in place of one.*

He had overthrown the Emperor for the abuses of his administration, while in his own he committed an hundred times more crimes and abuses than ever were perpetrated under the Emperor. In his proclamations and speeches he affected the greatest repugnance to shedding Haytian blood, while in his instructions to his Generals he ordered them to *destroy every thing with fire and sword, and to do all possible mischief.**

In the silence and meditation of his cabinet he devised and arranged atrocious and perfidious measures for shedding torrents of blood: he directed his Machiavelian plans particularly against the men of colour in the North, who were, alas! the victims of his treachery. Pétion knew by experience that through their partiality for his complexion, he should be able to gain over and deceive these unfortunate beings, who were weak enough to be misled by his perfidious advice and suggestions. Pétion knew, in his diabolical calculations, that from exciting them to revolt against the supreme head, one of three results must follow; either that they must take up arms to serve his cause or perish, or fly and range themselves on his side: so that, however it fell out, this traitor, more artful than even Machiavel himself, could not fail to profit. Should the men of colour whom he seduced, prove victorious, his party would be triumphant: should they be slain in their revolt, or compelled to fly and rally beneath his standard, he would in either case be a gainer; he would either weaken the force of his enemy or swell his own.

After the issue of the event he still knew how to profit by it: he affected to pity the lot of those unfortunate wretches who had fallen through his machinations, and deceitful councils; he affected to welcome with ardour those who had escaped his snares, and his massacres: he exhibited them in public; and, to fill up the measure of his guilt, the result of his own

---

* Such were his instructions to General Lamarre, the originals of which are now before me.

crimes still furnished him with materials for drawing a frightful picture of the public calamities, and representing Henry Christóphe as a monster and a tyrant. After these public exhibitions he played a widely different game in his cabinet. Was mention made of the existence of Men of Colour in the North, notwithstanding what had taken place, Pétion would reply *so much the worse, I wish he had exterminated them to the last, what business have they there?* His object in exciting disturbance and revolt among us, was to compel us to do all possible evil and adopt such violent and severe measures as could not fail to alienate the affections of our friends, and create partizans for himself. Was it observed that one of his party had been captured by our patroles, that these had done nothing to him, but had released him with good treatment, *so much the worse* would Pétition say, *had they cut off his head, another would not have let himself be taken so easily.* Such was the artful man with whom Henry Christóphe, frank and upright himself, had to deal: is it surprising then that we have sustained such grievous calamities? That, however, which ought to astonish, and which surpasses comprehension, is to hear us reproached by these very people, with the calamities they themselves occasioned. It is not from a few accidental occurrences but from the general tenour of their conduct that the heads of Governments are to be judged: and, from the analysis I am about to give of events, we shall see who was the aggressor and the true author of the public misfortunes.

Pétion had been the sole author of the civil war, and yet he had the art and assurance to attempt a justification, and throw the blame of it upon the head of of the Government.

In one of his publications of the 17th Jan. 1807, in which he endeavoured to justify himself, he exclaims, *why cannot I raise my voice like the last trumpet, to convey to the deepest caverns of our rocks the language of peace and consolation? This is the height of my ambition, this is the conduct I could wish to pursue, and not to behold the effusion of such torrents of the blood of my brethren, already too unfortunate.*

We shall see how his *actions* accorded with his *professions*.

In this very year he multiplied his attacks to an infinite extent. He sent General d'Artiguenave to Grande Riviere to excite revolt, and lay every thing waste with fire and sword. This General was taken and punished with death. He commissioned General Cangé to produce an insurrection in the West, but his designs were counteracted by Marshal Besse, who arrested him and punished him as he deserved. Pétion caused a mutiny in the 9th regiment at Port-de-Paix, and sent General Lamarre with a considerable force to aid the mutineers, and gave him orders *to destroy every thing, to do all possible mischief, to make himself master of the town of Môle, and to fortify himself there.*[*]

He made a simultaneous attempt upon Mirebalais, where he was vigorously repulsed. He got possession of Gonaïves by treachery, and was driven from it again after having pillaged the unfortunate inhabitants, and set the town on fire. He besieged St. Marc with a numerous army, but was obliged to raise the siege, and retire with disgrace. He sent a strong force against Sourde, in the heart of the North, where his troops were totally defeated, and the celebrated David Trois, one of his commanders, lost his life. How have the unfortunate Haytians, victims to the ambition of Pétion, been cut down in these unfortunate campaigns! And yet this traitor had incessantly in his mouth his love

---

[*] Gen. Lamarre's papers fell into our hands on the capture of this town.

for his country, his repugnance to bloodshed, and his want of ambition, while he was straining every nerve to obtain the supreme authority. He dispersed his emissaries far and wide to excite the people to revolt, made immense preparations, attacked us by land and sea, and shed the blood of his countrymen by wholesale. Henry made head against the storm, flew from place to place with the celerity of an eagle, and was everywhere victorious.

A powerful party in the South declared in his favour. Jean Baptiste Dupérier, sirnamed Góman, took arms, and maintained himself in the inaccessible mountains of Hôte, where he alike resisted the forces sent against him and the plots formed to entrap him.

Meanwhile the Generals employed by Pétion for the destruction of the Emperor, and the usurpation of his authority, began to discover that they had been the mere tools of his ambitious projects: they saw, when too late, into what errors they had suffered themselves to be led, and the misfortunes which resulted from them to their country. Repentance filled their hearts, they dared to murmur, and Pétion instantly decreed their ruin.

Magloire, a general and senator, was the first victim: he was assassinated at Jacmel, with a multitude of brave citizens: Bonnet and David Trois, who executed Pétion's orders, enriched themselves with their spoils. Soon after Yayou, likewise a senator and general, even Yayou the friend of his bosom, his *Seïde*, the blind instrument of his passions, whom he named the *Haytian Brutus*—he too experienced the same fate with Magloire, being murdered at Fort Campan among the mountains of Leôgane, by the emissaries of Pétion. Chervain, commissary of war at Port-au-Prince, with a multitude besides, was sacrificed by the ambition of this new Robespierre, who selected and struck off the noblest heads, in order to seat his power the more securely over their bleeding trunks.

And thou Gérin! thou his equal, his auxiliary and accomplice! thou who hast done and sacrificed every thing for him, thou who hast served as a footstool for him to attain to power, thou shalt not be exempt, thou too shalt be his victim : thou hast been unjust, ungrateful and a parricide, thou shalt perish, thou shalt be immolated in the same way in which thou hast immolated him to whom thou owest thy life, thy reputation and thy glory.*

Gérin, a general and a senator, had fallen into disgrace, had become a mere cipher, and his advice was no longer regarded: dissatisfied with Pétion's administration he meditated another revolution: he feigned sickness and retired to Anse-à-Veau, where he concerted measures for playing the same game he had done in the time of the Emperor.

Gérin and Lamarre had a high esteem for each other: they had been companions in arms, were united in the strictest bonds of friendship, and maintained a mutual and active correspondence. Lamarre beheld Gérin's disgrace with grief, and was unable to disguise the resentment he felt. Some hasty expressions which he dropped at the Môle were instantly reported to Pétion, who from that moment conceived a decided horror and aversion for the men of the South; and he resolved to set aside, or destroy all the leading men of that quarter who could possibly traverse his designs, or throw any obstacle in the way of his ambition.

He vowed the destruction of Gérin, and dreading

* In the first civil war Gérin commanded Petit Trou des Baradaires under Rigaud: he was made prisoner by Gen. Dessalines, who received orders from Gen. Toussaint, to have him shot: Dessalines avoided executing this order, and saved Gérin's life.

the return of Lamarre and the forces under his command, to their homes in the South, he hoped that the town of the Môle might prove their tomb. The correspondence of Gérin and Lamarre leaves no doubt on this head.*

*ced *Boucassin*, 6th *July*, 1809.
Et. ELIE GERIN, *General of Division, commanding the Army in the absence of the President, to the Senator* LAMARRE, *General of Brigade, commanding the Army of the Expedition.*

General, my dear friend and colleague,

It is but two days since the letter of the 26th ultimo reached me, and I know not whether one from me to you was delivered to you by citizen J. J. Dartiguenave.

I felt confident, my brave comrade, that I should receive your congratulations, as soon as you were apprised of my return to the service. Your attachment to me, and your enthusiasm for your country, could not fail to suggest to you a flattering hope, but alas! I had formed quite another idea, yet without attaching much importance to it. Meanwhile events have but too unfortunately justified my fears. My counsels are always misconstrued. A column sent into the North under the command of Col Lys, in opposition to all I could urge to the contrary, returned on the 3d, after sustaining an irreparable loss in our friend Colonel David Trois, a brave and virtuous citizen. In a word, the loss of this officer is more prejudicial to the Republic than that of an entire regiment. But what is to be done? Death is our trade, and I look upon those who have already fallen, as far happier than those who survive. But must not every thing have an end? In fine, my dear friend, we endeavoured to pass the river Artibonite, with a column of 2,500 men, two leagues above the river called Fer-à-Cheval, in order to fall upon the town of Mirebalais; but, owing to the rapidity of the current and flood in the river, I was unable to effect my purpose. On the return of the army I proposed going to Port-au-Prince for artillery and other requisites for the siege of Verrêtes, which would have enabled us to establish ourselves from that point to the town of Arcahaye; and the left bank of the Artibonite would have served us for a boundary from Verrêtes to Grand Bois, and a tract of nearly thirty leagues

Whilst Pétion abandoned Lamarre to his fate at the Môle, he took measures for the successive overthrow of the leading men in the South. It formed no part of his plan to have them arrested, tried, and condemned to death; for this would have led to a discovery of his intentions, and his disregard of shedding blood, and thus have weakened his popularity and power, which rested on the urbanity of his manner, or rather upon his extreme hypocrisy.

At Anse-à-Veau he opposed to Gérin, Bruny le

would have fallen into our possession. This plan was not adopted; and the column set off; I know not wherefore they marched the army first here, hence to Pois, from Pois back hither again, &c. In a word, seeing this indecision, I hinted to the President that if he wished, I would offer to embark with the troops, provided he gave me five battalions, and that I would make a feint of proceeding to Jérémy, but really make sail for the Môle, where I should land the sailors and soldiers of the squadron, and raise the blockade of that place. Having placed you in a condition to resume active operations, I should have re-embarked the troops, and gone to suppress the pestilential insurrection in Jérémy; this would have been an affair of three months: the month of February would still remain to cross the Artibonite with a force of upwards of nine and possibly ten thousand men. These excellent plans were not adopted: and I know not what will be done: the army becomes weakened by sickness, desertions, and furloughs.

The enemy means, I believe, to resume offensive operations, for, within the last two or three days, two of his regiments have shewn themselves at the old town of Mirebalais. In a word I cannot but lament the fate which threatens the country, whilst almost every six months opportunities offer for bringing this war to a conclusion. *Keep this to yourself, my brave comrade, and continue to hope for some favourable event, for there is an invisible genius which has hitherto watched over our destinies.* Adieu, my friend, I embrace you cordially.

(Signed)   Et. GERIN.

Blanc, commandant of the 16th regiment, of which Gérin had formerly been colonel. Bruny attacked him in his house; Gérin, who was surnamed *Côte de Fer* (Ironside) by his brother soldiers on account of his intrepidity, valour, and numerous wounds, shut himself up there with a company of grenadiers, and defended himself vigorously. The house being at length battered down by the fire of the artillery, Gérin, endeavouring to escape, was struck by a fragment of a stone and fell, when a sapper of the 16th regiment cut off his head: his brave grenadiers fell fighting valiantly by his side. His dead body was dragged to the market-place of Anse-à-Veau, by his former companions in arms, as he had himself caused the body of the Emperor to be dragged and insulted before his eyes.

In recompence for this exploit, Pétion promoted Bruny le Blanc to the rank of General.

Thus did the specious Pétion overthrow all, whether friends or foes, who stood in his way.

The regiment of *Eclaireurs du Sud* revolted and joined the army of Góman. Pétion employed his usual stratagems against the officers of this corps. He fabricated letters calculated to make them suspected, and had these scattered in the vicinity of Góman's posts, who upon seeing them, suspecting the officers of treachery, ignorantly sacrificed them to the vengeance and perfidy of Pétion. What hosts of victims has he not immolated? And yet this is he whom they have the assurance to represent to us as an angel of mercy, sparing of human blood. Wherefore must we lay bare our wounds? Is it necessary to lift the veil which covers them? How, alas! can we heal them, if we want the courage to probe them? Behold Colombel and Milcent, the results of the civil wars and crimes, engendered by ambition, of which you, by your inflammatory writings, provoke a repetition. It is you—your calumnies, and misrepresentations, which have reduced me to the hard necessity of drawing this picture for you. You have made a pompous parade of the public calamities of the North, and have preserved a dead silence respecting those which have unhappily taken place in the South-west: what then? the blood of the *William Lafleurs*, the *Moreaus*, *Germains*, *Mentors*, *Boisrond Tonneres*, *Magloires*, *Yayous*, *Gérins*, *Chervins*, *Delvarres*, *Henrys*, with a still longer catalogue, which I should never have done naming—was it of no value? Was it not that of your brethren and fellow-citizens? Cease then needlessly to upbraid us! Is the magnitude of our calamities to render them perpetual? Is our blood to flow to all eternity, because it has hitherto been shed in torrents? Let us rather seek the wisest and most prudent, the promptest and most efficacious, means of terminating our civil discords, and for ever preventing a recurrence of our public disasters. Let us make a nobler and more worthy use of the power which Divine Providence has placed in our hands; to regenerate ourselves, and let us labour in concert and with renewed vigour to consolidate our rights, our liberty and independence, and close the wounds of our deeply afflicted country.

The siege of the Môle proceeded with vigour; in vain did Lamarre write to Pétion to solicit permission to evacuate this town. Pétion in reply ordered him to maintain his ground. In vain did Lamarre ask for succours, and draw a frightful picture of the extremity to which the army was reduced. Pétion ordered him to hold out to the last. " *Citizen President*," this general wrote to him, " *if a situation, the bare idea of* " *which fills me with horror, be sufficient to apologize for* " *the frequency of my letters, you will find that I never* " *was more excusable than now, especially when in the* " *present you will find a faint representation of what*

" cannot fail to touch the sensibility of your soul. Yes,
" Citizen President, to tell you that after such signal
" successes the heroes who atchieved them sink daily
" before my eyes, and die of inanition; to tell you that,
" notwithstanding the constancy with which they have
" uniformly encountered danger, and submitted to the
" severest privations, they see themselves shaken, they
" shrink with regret from their duty, and seek, far
" within the enemy's lines, either inevitable death, or at
" the best but a scanty supply of ground provisions to
" eke out a miserable existence," &c. &c.

After giving an account of his operations, this general, worthy a happier fate, concludes his letter as follows:—" For it is impossible to behold without the
" keenest anguish those whom the murderous bullets had
" spared, expiring under their arms without the power
" of relief; and, as in such a situation despair may lead
" to any extremity, I should have every thing to appre-
" hend, did not the courage and noble resolution of the
" heroes under my command, convince me I have no
" ground for alarm. I should have nothing to complain
" of, for they possess these virtues, and I may say
" without vanity that their own officers are not behind
" hand in setting the example of patience under priva-
" tion. I give you but a slight sketch, Citizen President;
" were I to enlarge it I should never have done. My
" whole dependence rests on your paternal aid. Save
" then, by the earliest dispatch of those necessaries of
" which we stand so much in need, and those reinforce-
" ments without which we cannot possibly hold out
" longer, an army in every way worthy of your regard
" and admiration."

Pétion continued to flatter him with promises of succour, he waited for transports and ships of war to convey them, but they never arrived. He ordered Lamarre *upon no account* to abandon the important point of the Môle. "*Where the public service is concerned, a heart like yours,*" said he "*cannot hesitate.*"*

Both the besiegers and the besieged performed prodigies of valour. Lamarre was killed by a cannonball as he was visiting the lines. This gallant warrior was worthy of shedding his blood in a better cause. Henry, an admirer of merit wherever found, bestowed a just eulogy upon his virtues and his talents.† Eveillard, who succeeded to the command, fell a few days after in battle, and was instantly replaced by Toussaint Boufflet. Henry, commiserating the misfortunes of the besieged, proposed a capitulation, but his offer was rejected with indignation, and the bloody flag was hoisted in token of their neither giving nor receiving quarter. After a most obstinate resistance the town and forts were carried by assault. The besieged, driven from them, retreated and defended themselves most heroically, till at length surrounded and overpowered by the victorious troops they were compelled to lay down their arms and surrender at discretion. By the laws of war they might all have been instantly put to the sword, having obstinately refused to capitulate, and having hoisted the bloody flag at the very moment of being reduced to the last extremity, and no longer capable of defending themselves. Their officers had rendered themselves responsible for all the blood shed in consequence of this unavailing resistance. Toussaint Boufflet and Jean Gournaut, their two commanders, deserved, according to the laws of war, to be punished with death, and they were so. They were not however *assassinated after having* capi-

---

* Pétion's letter of the 5th of June, 1810, to Lamarre.

† It was this officer who defeated General Rochambeau's guard at Petit-Goave, where Netherwood, the Adjutant-Commandant, lost his life.

TULATED, as Colombel has falsely asserted; and had they prevented the effusion of the blood of numbers of brave men whom they sacrificed by their obstinacy, their lives would have been spared.* There is a wide difference between the death of these two commanders, and the *assassination* of Generals Magloire, Yayou, and Gérin. Was Pétion ignorant that, by sending Lamarre and the troops of the South into the heart of the North, he exposed them to certain and inevitable destruction? Or did he not know, that by making the 9th regiment carry arms against its own Government, he exposed both the officers and men to be treated as rebels.

And now that these public disasters have taken place, Pétion's accomplices affect to commiserate the wretches they have made, the victims they have sacrificed, by their perfidious counsels and unjust aggressions. Had Pétion, in place of sending Lamarre and his troops into the heart of the North, kept them for the defence of their homes, we should not have been obliged to combat them, nor would they have been the victims of his ambitious projects. The brave Lamarre would perhaps have been in the full enjoyment of his life. What do I say? He has died the death of the brave; at his own home he would have been

---

* This reasoning corresponds exactly with that of the Marquis of Hastings in his dispatch respecting the capture of the fortress of Talneir in the East Indies, and the execution of the Killedar, of which the following is an extract:—"The forfeiture of pretension to "quarter when troops stand an assault has been established by the "laws of war, to prevent garrisons from wantonly subjecting "besiegers to the heavy loss likely to be suffered by troops exposed "in advancing to breach: a garrison would *from false points of* "*honour* always be tempted to indulge in slaughter, if impunity "could be obtained by throwing down their arms when defence "proved ineffectual."—*Translator.*

assassinated like his friend Gérin, Magloire, and a multitude of others.

The troops of the South, both officers and men, were, after their surrender, formed into a corps under the name of the Legion of the South. This corps now forms the 30th, or the regiment of Sans Souci; and is constantly paid, cloathed, and provisioned, like the other regiments of the kingdom.

During these transactions an important event took place in the South.

Rigaud arrived from France on the 7th of April, 1810, and landed at Cayes, on a second mission from Bonaparte, to form a party for himself in Hayti: he was received with joy by the people of this town. The news came like a thunderbolt upon Pétion, who nevertheless, concealing his surprise and dissatisfaction, invited Rigaud to Port-au-Prince, where they had their first interview.

These two chieftains, equally ambitious and treacherous, found themselves in a most awkward situation.

Rigaud saw with mortification that Pétion, formerly his inferior, had, by his intrigues and the course of events, become his superior and all powerful. Rigaud's pride was wounded and his vanity humbled. He knew Pétion from past experience, he esteemed him unfit for the exalted situation he filled, and he already meditated in his heart how to overthrow him, and seize upon a situation which he conceived his due, and to which his ambition aspired.

Pétion, for his part, viewed, with fear and a secret foreboding, Rigaud his former chief; whom he knew to possess talents far beyond his own. He was aware of the extent of his influence in the South, and was convinced that the sole object of his visit was to supplant him. Pétion therefore proposed to defeat him by his usual craft; what was to prevent him? The humbled vanity of the one, and the wounded ambition of the other, the one founding his pretensions upon his antient, the other upon his recent title, formed a contrast perfectly original, and worthy the pen of an able historian.

Pétion, nevertheless received Rigaud with every demonstration of the most cordial regard. He loaded him with caresses, and, as though it were necessary to give him some employment, appointed him as a general of division to carry on the war against Góman in the South, and either to compel him to submit, or at least check his progress in the direction of Grande Anse.

No one was deceived by the interview between these chiefs, by their cordial greetings, and affected friendship. The ambitious, treacherous and ungrateful character of each was perfectly understood, and it was readily foreseen, that these two designing traitors, who had already inflicted such evils on their country, would not continue long in harmony.

Rigaud was Góman's godfather; he hoped to succeed either in persuading his godson to submit, or enticing him into some snare which would bring the war to a speedy conclusion. But Rigaud's efforts and stratagems were unavailing. Góman maintained his resolution, and understood how to baffle the artifices of his unworthy and treacherous godfather.

At this period the Republic of Hayti, sapped in all its foundations by the vices of its administration, seemed on the very brink of ruin.

The army of the expedition had surrendered the Môle; the reins of Government were held with a weak and trembling hand; the finances were embarrassed with debt, and public credit was annihilated. From the moment of his obtaining the Presidentship, Pétion had trampled the Constitution under foot, and disregarded the laws. The Legislative body had been dissolved: and the mock Senate had disappeared, part of the senators having been killed, and the remainder either banished or compelled to fly to foreign countries. Occupied solely with the care of his own personal security, Pétion beheld no Republic beyond the walls of Port-au-Prince; within these he had concentrated all his resources, collected all the troops of the second division of the West, to whom he directed his whole attention, while the remaining troops of the South, who had not been sacrificed at the Môle, and were carrying on the war in the South under the command of Rigaud, were destitute both of pay and cloathing, and in a state of absolute nudity. Pétion was intent upon exhausting all the resources of this department.

There was hardly the semblance of laws; and the few that did exist were without force or vigour: the citizens were deprived of justice, and the greatest disorder prevailed in the Republic.

The Constitution was nevertheless *good, wise*, and, above all, *Republican*, having been modelled after that of the United States of America!!! What an example for those who are attached only to an idle theory, and think nothing else necessary to promote the welfare of a nation, than to frame a good Constitution. But reason and experience teach us, that *the first requisite to national happiness and prosperity is to be found in religious principles, and a correct morality.*

In this posture of affairs Rigaud, on the 1st of Nov. 1810, resolved to effect a separation of the province of the South, from the second division of that of the West; he rested his determination on the dilapidated state of the Constitution. *The Sovereignty,* said he, *resides in the people, who can resume their rights at will.*

Poor people! thus it ever is that the factious employ your name and your rights as a mask for their own ambitious projects! Rigaud summoned an assembly of the notables of the Province of the South in the hall of the department, and caused himself to be named and proclaimed General-in-Chief of the department of the South, with power to enact laws, and appoint to civil and military offices, assisted however by a *privy council.* This was a *military despotism,* the most detestable of all Governments.

Thus was realized all that persons of discernment had anticipated seven months before. Thus were confirmed the fears of Pétion and the hopes of Rigaud. Ambition now evidently was the idol both worshipped; all were convinced that nothing short of absolute power could satisfy their inordinate desires. They had hitherto been constantly united in their views and interests, but from the instant that the same object inflamed their ambition, friendship was at an end. Is it then surprising that each of these chiefs disputed the authority of Generals Toussaint Louverture, Jean Jacques Dessalines and Henry Christóphe.

Here let us pause a moment and contemplate the melancholy effects of ambition! Let us shed tears of blood for the misfortunes of our unhappy country. Let us bewail the afflictions of the Haytians, a brave and worthy people, deserving of a happier lot.

Yes! it is ambition, that cruel and unfeeling passion, that insatiable lust of power and distinction which has produced all the crimes and horrors of our civil wars. It is through it our unhappy country has been torn in pieces, her territory and population dismembered: that a good, sensible and generous people have been rendered barbarous, cruel and ferocious : through it we have seen our generals, our senators, magistrates, thousands of our bravest troops, the bold defenders of liberty and independence, women and infants, inhumanly massacred, our plains laid waste, famine produced with all its horrors, our towns burned or pillaged, the country clad in mourning, widows and orphans, nay whole families, exterminated or plunged into the most frightful misery: in a word, it is through it that we have seen our national character degraded and insulted, our enemies exulting over our civil dissensions, and taking advantage of them to insult us, to make us the most odious and disgraceful propositions tending to enslave us!

Such, Haytians! have been the effects of ambition! Such the crimes of Rigaud and of Pétion. May this heart-rending picture of our past misfortunes tend to soften the hearts of my fellow citizens, and lead them to reflect calmly both on our present and our future prospects. May the chiefs who guide the helm of public affairs lay aside all selfish interests and personal animosities, and consult only the welfare of the Haytians, their countrymen, still wretched, because disunited; and may they be convinced that nothing but the re-establishment of *peace, union and brotherly harmony*, can contribute to their prosperity. Should we wish to see a return of those times of terror and disaster? Doubtless not! Should we wish to see the bosom of our country torn anew, and drenched with the blood of our fellow citizens? Who is the inhuman monster that would desire to see such horrors? Who but another Colombel or Milcent could entertain such a wish? or desire to see Haytian blood again shed by Haytian hands: a contest in which victory is impossible, and disasters inevitable, since, in civil commotions, the misfortunes of the vanquished are reflected back again upon the victors. For five years we have wisely rested upon our arms: let us from henceforth reserve them for the enemies of our liberty and independence, should they attack us. As for our internal dissensions, let us summon sound sense, wisdom, prudence, justice and humanity, to put an end to them: these arms are neither cruel nor dangerous, why then do Colombel and Milcent dread them so much? What is there so formidable in these words *peace, union and reconciliation,* to make them tremble so on hearing them? But let us not here interrupt the course of our reflections: in proper time and place I will tell Colombel and Milcent what are the real grounds of their terror

Let us then banish from our councils these turbulent spirits---these heated and restless heads. The remembrance of injuries, of hatred, and of passion, never has been productive of good; it closes the heart against affection and reason, produces asperity, widens breaches, and provokes revenge. Colombel and Milcent know this well, for it is the engine of the wicked.

Let us banish then, I say, these perfidious advisers, these promoters of civil war, who know how to protect themselves from danger, who clamour for battles, but who never yet fired a musket in defence of the liberty and independence of their country.

O! my beloved countrymen! I adjure you in the name of our country, that country which is so dear to us, that country which alone we can inhabit with honour, and enjoy all the blessings of our Creator! Let us blot from our recollection every hatred and every animosity. Let us bury in oblivion all our past errors and misfortunes. Let us cast them into the deepest pit of forgetfulness, and apply ourselves wholly to the *present state* of our affairs. Let us reason justly, prudently, and without partiality, on our true interests. This is the only object which animates me, the only end I propose to my labours. Heaven grant I may attain it!

It is evident that Rigaud and Pétion have been the sole authors of our public misfortunes: it is a truth as incontestible as not to need demonstration; but the crimes of these men are exclusively their own, and should not be charged to the account of their colour.

Had Rigaud and Pétion been *Whites* or *Blacks* instead of *Men of Colour,* their cause being essentially unjust and bad, both in principle and character, would not have been more just or reasonable, and surely no one would impute the crimes of these two individuals either to the class of *Whites* or *Blacks*. It would then be barbarous, foolish and unjust, to charge the *coloured class* at large with the consequences resulting from the ambition of Rigaud and of Pétion, since the Haytians of colour were not only perfectly innocent of them, but have been among the principal sufferers.

All nations have had the misfortune to see born within their bosom ambitious wretches who have disgraced their name, their character and their glory by unheard of crimes and misdemeanours. All nations have had their Cæsar Borgias, their Cromwells, and their Robespierres; but an entire nation cannot be accounted guilty of the crimes of a few ambitious men.

The Haytians cannot then be held responsible for the crimes of Rigaud and of Pétion, the Haytians of *both colours* have been equally deceived, and equally sufferers by the passions of these two factious men.

The *North-west* having always been commanded by *black* Generals, and the *South West* by Generals of *colour*, European writers, little acquainted with the real circumstances of the country, have been led into a considerable error, imagining that the population of the *North* was *exclusively black*, and that of the *South* as *exclusively coloured*. Hence they have spoken of the *Negroes* in the *North* and the *Mulattoes* in the *South*, when in fact the population of all the three provinces of Hayti, the *North*, the *West*, and the *South*, consists of an intermixture of *Blacks* and *Mulattoes* in the proportion nearly of *one fifteenth* of the *latter* to *fourteen fifteenths* of the *former*.

This admixture has constantly subsisted both in peace and war, nor could it be otherwise, for it is nature that forms the connections of families, and leads to this intermixture of colours. Neither of the colours ever separated itself from the other in order to join one side exclusively: but in our civil wars, whether with the Whites or among ourselves, the population sided rather according to the district in which it was situated than according to the colour or opinions of individuals. In the war of the Revolution, as at present, for example; there were some *black* and *coloured men* who were *Royalists*, and others who were *Republicans*; and a mulatto or black who was a *Royalist* at Port-au-Prince under the English, had he been at the Cape under the French, would have been a Republican; while another who was a *Republican* at the Cape, would have been a *Royalist* had he been placed at Port-au-Prince.

Not that I mean to say that there are no fixed principles in Hayti, or that the inhabitants are mere weathercocks: on the contrary, there were men on both sides most obstinately wedded to their opinions; but this was not a general rule. In every country the mass of the population follows the tide in whatever direction it sets: and it is a fact that in our wars, the mass of the inhabitants sided according to the districts they inhabited rather than according to their opinions or colour.

Hence it arose, that in the *North-west* multitudes of *Men of Colour* served with the most unshaken fidelity under Generals Toussaint Louverture, J. J. Dessalines, and Henry Christóphe, while in the *South-west* abundance of *Blacks* were to be found fighting with blind devotion and fidelity under Rigaud and Pétion.

Had the *fourteen-fifteenths* of *Blacks* who composed the population of the *South-west* chosen to oppose the ambitious projects of Rigaud and of Pétion, is it not as clear as day that the *one-fifteenth* of *Men of Colour*, could not have prevented them. Now the *Blacks*, as well as the *Men of Colour*, neglected their true interest, which was to remain perpetually united and indissolubly attached. They suffered themselves to be deceived: led astray by the delusions of ambition, they became disunited; inextinguishable animosities arose, and, as though there had not already been sufficient cause for disunion and civil war, an absurd antipathy and a ridiculous prejudice has been created between the Haytians of the North, the West, and the South, who think themselves each superior to the others only from their belonging to different provinces.

It is the duty of a wise and conciliatory Government gradually to remove all these causes of civil war and disunion. The King of Hayti cannot be King of a province but of a kingdom: and the head of a nation cannot be the leader of a faction; he is the chief of the nation. It is the interest of a *Government* to promote union, of a *faction* to sow dissension. A Government concentrates the whole strength of a nation, and has nothing to dread but from external enemies: the spirit of faction tends on the contrary to perpetuate disunion and civil war, which constitutes in every age and country the hope and triumph of a foreign foe.

The course of the Revolution having proved that our white enemies, however divided in political opinions among themselves, were perfectly unanimous whenever the destruction of the Haytians was under discussion; the cause of the white French being then, I say, *unique*, that of the Haytians, however divided in opinion, should be *unique* also for their preservation; their common security requires that they should be always united and indissolubly attached.

Now it was sound policy, that in a population consisting of *fourteenth-fifteenths* of *Blacks,* and *one-fifteenth* of *Mulattoes,* the reins of Government should be entrusted to a *Black* rather than a Man of Colour: the acknowledged interests of the whole nation, and even of the Men of Colour required it ; and here the urgency of the danger pointed out the reasonableness and soundness of such policy.

Had Generals Rigaud and Pétion been wise and prudent they never would have deviated from these fundamental principles, which can alone promote the welfare of their country, and secure tranquillity and safety to the Men of Colour, whom they have inhumanly and perfidiously sacrificed to their inordinate ambition. Had the Men of Colour acted wisely, instead of serving as instruments in the cause of Rigaud and of Pétion, they would have resisted the projects of these two ambitious men, who had no right to the Government, and, in acting thus, the Men of Colour would have become the firmest supporters of legitimate authority, and would have found that protection and security which they would seek in vain by taking an opposite course.

Had Rigaud been generally deserted at the time by his followers, Pétion would not have ventured to imitate his example.

Let us hope, nevertheless, that the Blacks and Men of Colour of the South-west will return to their true interests, that they will take the course which sound policy, reason, justice and humanity have traced out for them, and which they never should have abandoned.

Meanwhile Petion did not dare to employ open force against Rigaud, he dissembled his resentment, and proceeded, according to custom, to circumvent his rival covertly, and make partizans for himself in the South.

Rigaud, who was by no means his inferior in finesse and perfidy, was not idle on his side, but likewise sought to gain friends and supporters at Port-au-Prince.

Generals Bonnet and Lys were among the first to desert Pétion and join Rigaud at Cayes, where he received them most cordially. Pétion seeing the desertion of these generals and that a complete separation had taken place between the South and West, sent an army under Generals Delvarre and Gédéon against Rigaud. Rigaud on his side concentrated his forces at Acquin, and prepared to march to the bridge of Miragoane, the limit of the two departments, in order to dispute the entrance into the South, with the troops of the West.

Pétion, who always had the precaution to second his military operations by negociation, had sent a deputation of the principal citizens of Port-au-Prince in advance of the army. This deputation found Rigaud at Acquin, at the head of his troops: he wrote to Pétion that it was not his design to make war upon him, but that he insisted on his ordering his generals instantly to retire from the territory of the South; and he at the same time commenced his march against them, with a view of either compelling their retreat or engaging them.

Pétion saw the peril of his situation: his fate depended upon a single battle: he hastened to Pont de Miragoane to prevent the two armies from coming to blows. Here the two chiefs held a conference on the 2d of Dec. 1810, in presence of both armies. Rigaud made a show of the great superiority he had over Pétion, and spoke to him with great firmness and hauteur. Pétion betrayed extreme weakness and pusillanimity, he succeeded nevertheless in deceiving Rigaud: he pretended that he had received intelligence that the army of the North was in full march to attack them, and profit by their dissensions, and that, divided as they were, it would be impossible to resist it. Rigaud, imposed upon by this artifice, entered into an accommodation by which Pétion was to command the second division of the West, while Rigaud held that of the South, and all debts contracted prior to this division were to be divided between the two Governments in order to be liquidated. It was further agreed, that, in case Pétion was attacked by the army of the North, Rigaud should march with his troops to the support of Port-au-Prince.

From this arrangement it appears, that Pétion, *President of the Republic of Hayti*, found his command reduced to the town of Port-au-Prince and its *arrondisement*; and to complete his misfortunes, the office of **President** was on the eve of becoming vacant, by the expiration of the four years at the end of which a new election was to take place.

It was then that Pétion remembered he had dissolved the Senate, and should be unable to secure his re-election to the office of President without assembling the legislative body: he found himself in great perplexity; the members of the Senate, as I have already said, had been slain, dispersed, or compelled to fly to foreign countries: there were but a few senators in Port-au-Prince, where they vegetated in obscurity; those of the South had returned to their own department which was no longer under his command.

Pétion saw the impossibility of convoking the Senate without the aid of his competitor. On the 18th of December, he wrote to Rigaud to request him to call a general meeting of the notables of the West and South to deliberate on a new Constitutional compact suited to their situation. Rigaud joyfully hastened to accept this proposition, hoping to succeed in influencing the assembly and procuring his own nomination to the Presidentship, counting upon the large majority which the two divisions of the South had over the second division of the West, and being able to play off against Pétion the same intrigues which he had himself employed in the first constituent assembly.

But the wily Pétion, anticipating Rigaud's design, set aside, by a second letter of the 4th of January, the arrangements mutually adopted on the 18th of December. He appointed Léogane, a town under his own command, as the place of meeting; here he was assured of being able to influence the assembly by his presence, overawe it by his troops, and render himself master of its deliberations.

Pétion also knew that Rigaud would not dare to appear in person in this assembly, without running the risk of being arrested, or of falling into some of the traps he would not fail to lay for him.

To strengthen his plans still more, Pétion gave fresh instructions with respect to the proceedings of this assembly.

Rigaud now discovering Pétion's design resolved to circumvent him: he protested against his letter and arrangements; suspended the election of deputies to the general assembly, and continued his decrees and proclamations for the separation of the department of the South from that of the West.*

Thus were renewed between those two ambitious men the same scenes, and the same intrigues as had formerly taken place, and the crafty Pétion was seen acting by Rigaud in 1810, as he had by Henry Christóphe in 1807.

* Rigaud's decrees and proclamations of the 2d, 3d, and 6th of November, 1810, year 7.

The office of *President* having expired, Pétion, frustrated in all his projects, was reduced to the sad expedient of assembling the few members of the Senate who could be found at Port-au-Prince; and he had the assurance to get himself re-elected by this illegally and unconstitutionally assembled junta. Could a few men, without any delegated authority, character, or respectability, legislate in the name of the people? Bad faith, injustice and ambition, have then always been the basis of this Republic.

Thus it was that this specious Pétion, this *unambitious* man, caused himself to be thrice successively elected to the situation of President; thus did he insult the good sense of his Senate by thrice playing off the farce of his re-election to the Presidentship: and God knows if he would ever have resigned it had not death terminated the cares of this life, and torn him away from his dreams of ambition!

While these events were passing in Hayti, the war proceeded with vigour in Europe. The navy of Britain covered the ocean. Pétion dared not openly display his partiality for France, through fear of bringing down upon himself the vengeance of the English. Nevertheless he maintained a secret correspondence with Ferrand at St. Domingo, and with France by means of confidential agents. He sent a coloured man of the name of Tapiau to France, to negociate a treaty with Bonaparte;* and he received

* It was at the close of 1813, that Tapiau concluded the treaty in question, with Bonaparte, who was to have sent into the South-west *fifteen thousand French troops, sixty thousand muskets, two hundred thousand weight of gunpowder, together with all the white planters who were in France,* to attempt in concert with Pétion, to reduce the country under the French dominion. Pétion sent a brig to Bordeaux to receive part of the arms and ammunition, which were landed at Jacmel, as if from Portugal.

one Liot, an emissary from Décrès, the minister of marine at Port-au-Prince.

Pétion, who, to escape the death with which he was threatened by the French during Leclerc's expedition, had become a Haytian in spite of himself, had likewise, in the event of being obliged to fly the country, reserved a plank to save himself from shipwreck; and already rivalled Rigaud, who would have delivered the country to France, and dragged his fellow-citizens into the bonds of slavery.

Rigaud, on his side, did not lose sight of his private interests, and, in case of events happening to oblige him to leave the country, secured considerable funds in foreign countries. He sent two cargoes of coffee to France and the United States of America.*

Whilst these two ambitious men were quarrelling about the dismembered fragments of our country, and an authority which belonged to neither the one nor the other, the government of the North consolidated itself.

Henry employed himself in civilizing his subjects, and establishing good order and discipline: he inspected the administration of the finances, and resources of the State, promoted agriculture and commerce, and watched to see that justice was duly dispensed to his subjects at the smallest possible expence. He required that all the public functionaries should be established, and gave in his own person an example of propriety of behaviour.

The greatest tranquillity prevailed throughout the provinces: travelling along the highways was safe by night and by day, and in the towns one might sleep with all the doors open without an apprehension of being robbed, so well was the order and police of the country regulated.

* One of his ships laden with coffee, and bound to Bordeaux with a Frenchman named Servan, Rigaud's agent, on board, was captured by our cruisers.

It was something to have been able to establish good order in the heart of the population which had been so long exposed to the contagion of corruption, and the demoralizing effects of civil war: it was doing much to check those ignoble vices which disturb society, licentiousness, gambling, and drunkenness, which, during the progress of the revolution and our civil wars, had been productive of such a multitude of crimes.

These vices, inherent in the state of bondage from which we emancipated ourselves, and the growth of warm climates, had been augmented and confirmed by the example of the French army. Married women and young virgins had been either ravished or compelled through fear to submit to the brutal lusts of the French soldiery. Both officers and men in imitation of their leaders abandoned themselves to orgies too horrible to be described. Gaming tables had been established in every direction, drunkenness and debauchery of every description were carried to the greatest possible excess. Irreligion, rape, murder and robbery, were perpetrated with impunity before our eyes by men who boasted of their superior knowledge, and *called themselves* Christians! As nothing influences men more than example, I may truly say that we are indebted to the French for the greater part of the vices and evil dispositions, which during our civil wars, occasioned such an overflow of crimes and horrors.

A thorough acquaintance with the character, morals and habits of a people is the first requisite to forming a judgment as to the constitution and government best adapted to them: had our critics known us better, they would not have passed so hasty and erroneous a judgment.

The civil war had not diverted Henry's attention from that foreign warfare which we yet continue to maintain. From the North to the West he completed and placed in the most perfect state of defence all the fortresses situated on the summits of the most inaccessible mountains. His watchful eye traversed the map, and followed with anxiety the gigantic strides made by Bonaparte over the European continent.

He furnished supplies to his neighbours the Spaniards, to enable them to expel the French from St. Domingo: he sent arms and warlike stores at his own expence to the Spanish General Don Juan Sanches Ramirez.

His forces, both by land and sea, were perfectly organised, and his finances in the most flourishing condition. Thus happily circumstanced, there was nothing to prevent Henry from carrying the war into the South-west, which was torn by faction and menaced with ruin in every part. The moment was favourable, but civil war was always repugnant to his generous feelings, and he never engaged in it without regret, and when unavoidably driven in self defence to repel force by force.

Far from thinking of hostilities, Henry, on hearing of the deplorable situation of the South-west, felt for the misfortunes of the people, and resolved upon making an effort towards reconciliation. He sent a deputation to Port-au-Prince, accompanied by a dozen soldiers of different corps of the South, made prisoners at the Môle, to acquaint their fellow-citizens with the treatment they had experienced, and to propose conciliatory measures to Pétion for the re-establishment of peace.

On the arrival of the deputation at Port-au-Prince, Pétion was absent, having gone to Pont de Miragoane to confer with Rigaud. He laid hold of this circumstance to intimidate his rival, whom he persuaded that a *large army* was on its march from the North, and that in their present state of disunion, they should be unable to make head against the impending storm. By this falsehood he imposed upon Rigaud, with whom he concluded an accommodation, as I have already said.*

Thus it appears the tactics of Colombel and Milcent are not new, but copied from those of their master in hypocrisy, stratagem and deceit. Every time we have spoken to them of *peace* and *re-union* they have cried *to arms*, and overwhelmed us with abuse: the motive is clear and simple: it is their only means of preventing our coming to an understanding, of creating fears and mistrust, and averting our *re-union*. But the arts of the wicked avail only for a season; once unmasked they cease to be injurious: they become only a ridiculous stratagem which brings disgrace and infamy on those who employ it to cloak their guilty projects.

Had Pétion given battle to Rigaud he would have been lost without remedy: but he knew how to dissemble his resentment, and, by the aid of intrigue, he gained time, and triumphed over his rival.

Having satisfied himself respecting Rigaud; Pétion hastened back to Port-au-Prince, where he dismissed the deputation, without deigning to listen to, or discuss the proposals of *peace* and *re-union*, and he even carried his perfidy so far as to detain the twelve soldiers of the South, who ought, according to the laws of nations and every rule of honour, to have been sent back.

Henry, who had visited St. Marc† solely with pacific views, now returned to his capital fully determined not to continue the civil war, but to wait till time, fatigue, and the excess of calamity should bring the Haytians back to reason and their true interests, *unity of wish and government.*

* See pages 95 and 96.
† *St. Marc* is a frontier and sea-port town, delightfully situated in the western part of King Henry's dominions; it is strongly garrisoned, and contains a flourishing school.—*Translator.*

Far from meditating a continuance of a barbarous, impolitic and savage warfare, a totally different idea seriously occupied us; namely, the adoption of the most effectual measures for guaranteeing our security, and preventing a return of this frightful scourge. Our own experience had convinced us that Republics were only calculated to produce dissension, and kindle the flames of civil war. On every change of Government, ambitious men were always ready to seize on the helm of the State and tear out the vitals of their country.

Henry is mortal, and it was foreseen that his death might produce a total subversion of his institutions, and rekindle the flames of civil discord. Prudent people, fathers of families especially, and those who wished for stability in a Government from which they derived their security, prosperity and happiness, looked upon a Constitutional and Hereditary Monarchy, as the only means of preserving us from the calamities and revolutions of civil wars; because the succession to the throne being clearly defined in Governments so constituted, the reigns succeed each other peaceably and without convulsions, and thus close the door against all ambitious pretenders: the heir to the crown being known to all, serves as a rallying point round which all may assemble, and receiving besides an education and principles suited to a Prince who is destined to hold the sceptre, and trained up from infancy in the habits and duties of government, ought to be better qualified to manage the reins.

Besides, a Constitutional Monarchy gives the nation every security which can consolidate its rights, and promote its happiness. Hence the counsellors of state and the notables, in compliance with the wishes of the nation and army, resolved upon changing the form of government and establishing a Monarchy in Hayti

Happy should I be could I gratify my readers by a display of the blessings which a firm, upright, and paternal Government has bestowed upon the Haytian people. But alas! in place of this, I must yet awhile call their attention to deplorable events, and stain some pages of my next chapter with the relation of deeds of blood.

CHAP. VI.

OF THE MONARCHY AND REPUBLIC OF HAYTI.

ALL Governments are placed between two rocks famous for shipwrecks, DESPOTISM and ANARCHY, which are equally dangerous to the stability of the Empire, and the welfare of the people. In the one the *restraint* of liberty leads to despotism, in the other the *abuse* of liberty leads to anarchy.—Each form of government then, has its dangers and its inconveniences, on which account the most skilful legislators have endeavoured to steer a middle course, equally removed from each extreme.

Modern writers on the law of nations have said much respecting the nature and principles of the various forms of Government, and have given birth to a multitude of theoretic systems.

It being the mania of the age to reduce every thing to systematic rules, and mathematical calculations, the science of Government has been regarded as a machine, and a preference given to the representative, above every other form, because the three powers of the state are wisely distributed and balanced.

Could the moral, like the physical world, regulate itself by the laws of mechanics, every thing in nature would advance with an uniform and steady pace. But this uniformity of proceeding does not by any means belong to the nature of man, in whom the equilibrium is perpetually destroyed by the interests or passions of the moment, and the balance of power made to preponderate to one side or the other.

Already has a large and enlightened portion of Europe adopted the representative form of government, and established constitutional charters, which recognize more or less all the rights of the several members of the community. It would doubtless be desirable if all the nations of the world were adapted to this form of government.

But as there are no two nations in the world which resemble each other, so neither are there two constitutions alike. For all nations to adopt the representative form of government, it is necessary that they should possess an equal degree of learning and civilization, the same climate and language, nay even the same manners, the same habits, and the same wants.

The experience of all ages teaches us that the *name* and *form* of the goverment has little to do with the happiness of the people: the essential point, which sound sense teaches us is, that the *governors* should be wise, just, and beneficent, and that the *governed* should possess virtue, piety, and morality.

This is the point to the attainment of which the legislator should bend all his efforts: and in truth, for what end does that constitution serve, which, however fair in theory, is inapplicable in practice, and produces in its execution no satisfactory result. He must begin therefore, with the Athenian legislator, by correcting the vices of the people, and giving them a national character along with a just sense of virtue and morality, and think, with the celebrated Montesquieu, that the best constitution is not that, which is most specious in theory, but that, which is best adapted to the people for whom it has been framed.

It would likewise be an error, and one which experience overthrows, to imagine, that liberty flourishes more in republics than in monarchies. Never has a nation existed upon earth more free, and in fuller possession of its political rights, than the English, and it is governed by a monarchy.

The history of republics, both ancient and modern, demonstrates the reverse: they have produced multitudes of tyrants; and never did there exist a more frightful tyranny, than that of Robespierre, under the committees of public safety and general security.

In founding the Haytian monarchy, our legislators were guided by the experience of every age: they did not aim at forming a constitution, plausible in theory and impracticable in execution, but one easy of application, simple in structure, and adapted to our existing wants.

We abandoned the republican form, from a conviction of the defects of this unsteady system of government. We sought a safe harbour, to secure us from revolutionary tempests. It was experience, and the misfortunes we sustained, which led us from a republic to a monarchy.

By the constitution of the 28th of March, 1811, the President Henry Christóphe was declared KING OF HAYTI under the name of HENRY: this title, with its prerogatives and immunities, was made hereditary in his family, in the direct line of legitimate males, according to seniority, to the exclusion of females.

The royal spouse was declared QUEEN OF HAYTI, and the presumptive heir to the crown was named the PRINCE ROYAL.

The other members of the royal family, bear the title of PRINCES and PRINCESSES, and are styled THEIR ROYAL HIGHNESSES.

Fifteen years was fixed as the period, at which our Kings should be considered of age; and during their minority, the kingdom was to be governed by a *Regent*, chosen from among the Princes most nearly related to the King.

The government was composed besides of *a Great Council of State, a Privy Council*, and four Ministers, namely of *War* and *Marine*, of *Finance* and *the Interior*, the Secretary of State, Minister for *Foreign Affairs*, and a Minister of *Justice*.

On mounting the throne, or coming of age, the King takes, upon the Holy Evangelists, in presence of the grand dignitaries of the kingdom, the Coronation oath as follows.

" *I swear to maintain the integrity of the territory, and independence of the kingdom; never to suffer, under any pretext whatsoever, the revival of* SLAVERY, *or of any feudal measure inconsistent with liberty and the exercise of the civil and political rights of the people of Hayti; to maintain the irrevocability of the grants and sales of the national property; and to govern solely with a view to the interests, the honour, and the welfare of the great Haytian family of which I am head."*

This constitution contained but few articles, being adapted to our existing situation: besides a *constitution* is not *a code of laws*, but merely the basis of one, and our legislators, in attending to our existing wants, bore in mind, that in proportion as the nation advanced in civilization, our laws would require amendment and improvement; that they must change with our manners, our knowledge, and our refinement, and could not possibly attain at once that perfection which is the result of time and experience alone.

On the 6th of April following, the Constitution was proclaimed in the presence of the Council of State, the civil and military authorities, and the assembled people and army; it was received with transports of the most lively joy, and amidst repeated shouts of *vive le roi!---vive la reine!---vive le prince royal!* and *vive la famille royale!*

Immediately after, the several acts which organized the new form of Government, were successively published.

The edict of the King, which creates an hereditary nobility in the kingdom of Hayti, with titles and estates granted by the Crown, as rewards for their services to the State, contains the following declaration: "*We solemnly declare that it is not our intention to exclude from the order of nobility, any of our subjects, whose services to the state, whether civil or military, shall render them deserving of admission into it: and that virtue and talents are the only distinctions which shall have weight in our eyes or those of our successors.*"*

This creation of nobility consisted of *four Princes, seven Dukes, twenty-two Counts, thirty-one Barons, and fourteen Chevaliers.* The nobility constituted the essence of the Monarchy, the one could not exist without the other: "*no Monarchy, no Nobility—no Nobility, no Monarchy,*" said the celebrated Montesquieu, who further added, that "*Nobility is the chief support of Kingly governments.*"

The institution of Royalty and Nobility has offended some levellers, but these institutions are found

---

* Art. 12 of the "*Edit du Roi,*" &c. subjoined to the "*Relation des glorieux evenements, &c. par le Comte de Limonade,*" page 65.

among the freest, the most civilized, the most enlightened and happy people of the earth. As these institutions have received the sanction of experience, and as their excellence has been recognized and proclaimed by the most distinguished legislators, we feel little apprehension of going wrong while we tread in the steps of our predecessors, and taking for our model every thing great and good which the world ever produced. All that is old has been new, if then ancient nobility be respectable, so also is the new, for it will in its turn become old; the sneers and insinuations thrown out against our institutions by factious demagogues, cannot therefore inspire any other sentiments than those of the most sovereign contempt. If some of the revilers of Monarchy have said " *that nobility is a kind of base coin which becomes depreciated every day,*" with much more justice might the advocates for this form of government reply " *that the creation of nobility* " *is a coinage whose value is unalterable, and whose mine,* " *being seated in honour, is inexhaustible.*" Were I desirous of retorting upon our adversaries the Colombels and Milcents, these imitators of the Gracchi, I should have no lack of arguments; but I prefer abandoning them to their own silly fancies and chimeras. Can folly be carried to a greater height than the attempt to confound rank, and establish a system of equality in society? Can the rich and the poor, the feeble and the strong, the brave and the coward, the learned and the illiterate, can they be regarded as equal? Do not the simple dictates of common sense proscribe this imaginary equality? What then do our adversaries want, what do they mean by this term EQUALITY? Doubtless that *equality of rights which the law recognizes* —the *only* equality that can subsist on earth. Well, do not the inhabitants of the kingdoms of England, of France, and of Hayti, enjoy *equality* in this acceptance of the term? Are they not tried before the same tribunals and by the same laws? LIBERTY and EQUALITY, those most valuable blessings for which we have so long bled and fought—how! O! how have your sacred names been prostituted! Some have imagined that *liberty* implied the power of blindly following the impulses of inclination; while others have supposed that *equality* required a confusion of ranks and fortunes. It is by the magic of these words, which have gained so much influence over the heart of man, that the factious of every country succeed in deluding and misleading the people; and it is always by declamations respecting their rights, and their welfare, that they succeed in enslaving them.

Equally the foe of anarchy and of despotism, I believe with the divine Plato " *that there is no state that can be happy either under the yoke of tyranny, or under the unbridled licentiousness of inordinate liberty. The wisest plan is to be subject to Kings who are themselves amenable to the laws. Excessive liberty and excessive oppression, are equally dangerous, and produce nearly the same results.*"

After the edict which creates the order of nobility, appeared that which established the royal and military order of St. Henry.

The King is declared the Chief Sovereign, Grand Master, and Founder: the order was composed of the Prince Royal, *sixteen grand crosses, thirty-two commanders*, and an indeterminate number of *Chevaliers*: the endowment of the Order is 300,000 livres per annum.

The civil establishment of the King and Queen, with that for the education of the Prince and Princesses Royal, was next organized.

The *Maison Militaire du Roi* was likewise created and organized at the same time. For this purpose soldiers of tried merit were selected throughout the army, and formed into five regiments of cavalry and infantry, under the names of the *Body Guards*, the *King's*, *Queen's*, and *Prince Royal's Light Horse*, and a regiment of Grenadiers called the *Haytian Guards*, to which were afterwards added the *corps of Royal Artillery*, and that of *Chasseurs of the Guard*.

On the 30th of May, the grand dignitaries, with the civil and military officers of the kingdom, took the oath of *obedience to the Constitution of the Kingdom, and allegiance to the King*, between his Majesty's hands: and on the 2d of June following, their Majesties HENRY I. and MARIA LOUIZA were consecrated and crowned KING and QUEEN of Hayti.

The King, in ascending the throne, preserved his original character unaltered. Neither his public nor his private morals underwent the slightest change; he was not, like most men, dazzled by his good fortune, but looked upon royalty rather as a burden which imposed fresh duties and obligations for him to fulfil towards his people, than as a title which elevated him to the splendour and majesty of power.

Here I deeply regret the necessity which compels me to terminate my work with all possible dispatch, lest I should lose the opportunity. It is this which obliges me to circumscribe myself within the narrowest limits, and to retrench a multitude of facts and proceedings which would have heightened the interest and animation of my narrative: I should also have been able, but for this, to dwell more at length upon the more remarkable traits of the heroic life of Henry, and to paint the physical and moral character of this extraordinary man, who has been so variously represented I should have been able to have described the characteristic traits of the principal personages of the Roy Family and Court of Hayti, as well as of thos Haytians who are more distinguished for their labour whether in war, in literature, or in the arts and sciences; but alas! time flies before me, the time so precious, so necessary, so indispensible for meditation and the arrangement of my ideas. I write from memory, and in haste, without leisure to make researches, and examine with sufficient attention the materials which surround me, and often even in the midst of the most cruel pain and suffering: can it then be strange if my pictures should prove but feeble sketches? Perhaps, nevertheless my readers will feel displeased at learning that they are weakly pencilled, but men of letters will be able to understand the efforts I have had to make, and the difficulties I have had to surmount in order to complete my task: I claim their indulgence towards the literary defects of an islander unversed in letters, and who writes from necessity, and from the impulse of that affection which he bears to his country, for the triumph of justice, of truth, and of humanity.

I resume my subject.

Henry, originally from the island of Grenada, is now of the age of *fifty-one years*, tall, well proportioned, of a majestic air and penetrating look: in his private character he is a good father, an affectionate and attentive husband. During an union of *twenty-five years*, the Queen, his august spouse, has always been an object of his tenderest regard; and he bears towards his children the most ardent and paternal love.

Yet it is this tender father, this affectionate husband, whom they have dared to calumniate so unjustly. He it is whom Colombel———But let me not anticipate.— A prudent man, and a generous friend, his advice and purse have always been at the service of his friends and dependents.

As a public character, as a magistrate, as a warrior, and as a citizen, Henry has given repeated proofs of his talents, his patriotism, and his valour, fearless in battle, his blood has been often shed in the cause of liberty and independence.

Quick and energetic, he has unhesitatingly exposed his person in the hour of danger: but, in the conduct of public affairs, and in the command of the army, his prudence never deserted him, nor did he ever leave any thing to chance.

Henry sleeps little, and eats quick; is active and indefatigable: he rarely consults physicians, being acquainted with his own constitution and the remedies which suit it.

Like other great men who have made their own fortune, his habits and manners are peculiar to himself: a great admirer of truth, and an enemy to falsehood and flattery, his principles of honour and integrity are invariable.

Henry has not received a school education, but possesses, in a high degree, that of the world. He has acquired information from reading, from travel,* and from his great enterprises. His long experience, joined to a frequent intercourse with enlightened men, a retentive memory, sound judgment, and strong powers of discrimination, have enabled him to acquire a vast fund of general knowledge, and render him a man truly extraordinary.

The Queen is about *forty-one years* of age, middle sized, with expressive eyes, and a pleasing physiognomy, indicative of mildness and benevolence. She is a wise and virtuous wife, an excellent mother, endued with a sensible and humane character, and a compassionate disposition, in short, worthy in every respect of the exalted rank, and the throne she fills.

Victor Henry, Prince Royal of Hayti, is in his *six-*

---

* The King served in the wars of the United States of America, and was wounded at the siege of Savannah.

teenth year, and already nearly as tall and corpulent as his father, with his mother's expression of countenance. His character appears to be composed of a happy admixture of that of both his parents. His mind, cultivated and improved by the writings both of the ancients and moderns, together with the study of languages and the various branches of science, affords the Haytians a promise of his becoming an accomplished, a just, and a benevolent prince.

Mesdames Première and Athenaïre, Princesses Royal of Hayti, the one *twenty* and the other *nineteen years of age*, are equally endowed with wit, talents, grace and beauty: they are the most rare and lovely models of filial piety, that Hayti can boast.

Such is the picture of the royal family of Hayti. Never has there been seen a more lovely assemblage of virtues, a more perfect specimen of domestic harmony, better parents, or children more tender, more obedient and more respectful.

I check myself, least I should be suspected of flattery; but all who have the good fortune to be acquainted with the royal family will do me the justice to acknowledge that I have paid but a feeble homage to truth.

Hardly had Henry completed the organization of the several branches of the royal government when, wholly devoted to public affairs, he placed himself in a new sphere, which was to add the reputation of a legislator to his military renown.

To attain this end, Henry cast his eyes upon the wisest and most enlightened men of the kingdom, whom he called together in the capital, and formed into a legislative commission charged with presenting drafts of laws, whose merits were afterwards to be discussed in the privy council and the great council of state.

This commission entered upon its legislative labours on the 31st of July, 1811. I was one of the secretaries, a circumstance which I notice, not out of ostentation, but for the purpose of adding more weight to my testimony.

Henry assiduously attended this council. However early we could be in our daily attendance, he was always at the place of meeting before us. The debate was opened in his presence, and he frequently explained the subject with the most profound discernment, and the most admirable justice and impartiality: and I have more that once remarked that Henry was one of the most zealous advocates for the rights of the people.

Towards the close of 1812, the laws relating to commerce, prizes, civil proceedings, the correctional police, agriculture, and the military, were completed, and these, collected together, formed the *Code Henry*, so called to perpetuate the memory of its immortal founder.

From the instant this code was promulgated, the old French laws, which awakened the recollection of our former oppressors, were immediately repealed, and all reference to them in judicial proceedings was strictly forbidden.

Thus the establishment of the Monarchy led us to the greatest undertakings. We made efforts which are hardly credible, to organize the royal government, and frame fixed and regular laws. We had indeed among ourselves immense resources, but we were ignorant of them; the mine was abundant, but hitherto it had been unexplored. Animated however by the genius of Henry, impelled by necessity, the hardest and most imperative of all laws, we dared the attempt.— Suddenly our intellectual faculties and ideas developed themselves with a force and rapidity the most surprising; we saw with equal joy and gratitude, that the

Creator who had endowed us with the physical force wherewith we had reclaimed our rights, had equally furnished us with the moral means of governing ourselves, like other civilized nations, in a state of society.

Toussaint Louverture was the chief founder of liberty; Jean Jacques Dessalines, of independence; Henry, after having powerfully assisted these two chiefs in establishing their authority in Hayti, became the first legislator of the Haytian people, the creator of their political and warlike institutions, and the reformer of their morals. It is also from his glorious reign that our civilization and learning are to be dated. So many claims to glory merit our gratitude and the admiration of our latest posterity.

Whilst the kingdom was consolidating itself, the republic fell more and more into decay. We have seen in the last chapter that Pétion had secured to himself a renewal of the *Presidentship*, for another period of four years, and that his territorial command was limited to the town of Port-au-Prince and its *arrondisement*, while the province of the South was under the immediate command of Rigaud. I shall now proceed with the events of this part of Hayti.

The republic was poor, burthened with heavy debts to strangers, and its finances were totally dilapidated. Hoping to extricate himself from his difficulties, Pétion had recourse to the dishonourable measure of debasing the coin. By an edict of the 27th of June, 1811, he ordered that all the silver coins current should have a piece cut out of their centre, and continue nevertheless current at their former rate.* The piece

---

* Clumsy as this method of mutilating the coin must appear to English readers, it has long been familiar in most of the West Indian islands, both British and Foreign, where, as might have been expected, it has increased the mischief it was meant to remedy.—*Translator*.

of silver thus cut out went to form an alloy from which a multitude of smaller coins were manufactured, and sent into circulation at above ten times their intrinsic value. This was a manifest robbery, to avoid levying a tax upon individuals.

Rigaud was far from idle in the South: he saw that, to make himself master of the supreme authority, he must drive Pétion from Port-au-Prince. He made his council draw up an address to the citizens of the department of the West, in which he accused Pétion of having occasioned the loss of the Môle; complained of his maladministration, of his suffering the finances of the republic to become dilapidated, his having dissolved the senate, and *annihilated the constitution,* which he *had never attempted to revive* (I use his own words) *except for his own convenience, in order to get himself renamed to the Presidentship.* In conclusion, Rigaud and his council stated that Pétion was the cause of all the misfortunes which had befallen the republic, and explained the motives of the step they had taken in declaring the department of the South independent of that of the West, in order to escape being dragged down the same precipice.

Pétion, who equally saw the necessity of overthrowing his rival and expelling him from the South, replied by an address from *the citizens of the department of the West, to their brethren of the South.*

Pétion, in this address, reproached Rigaud with his ambition and ingratitude to him, and charges him with being an agent of the French, as though Pétion himself was free from similar imputations. He even carried his assurance so far as to cite a passage from the New Testament against Rigaud, though the passage equally condemned himself.

" The Scriptures" said Pétion, " describe to us a " man who saw a mote in his neighbour's eye, but was "unable, nevertheless, to discern the beam in his own "eye." Pétion then goes on to reproach his *ci-devant* accomplice, and to expose their former villainies.

"*The administration of General Rigaud,*" said the Gazette of Port-au-Prince of the 9th of July, 1811, 8th year of Independence," *is not free from censure. We "remember well the arrest of General Montbrun, and "the perfidy used towards him; the insurrection of "la Valée protected by the soldiers of the 2d regiment "disguised as cultivators, and led on by Bouchard, for "the purpose of expelling General Beauvais from his "command at Jacmel.*"

Thus Pétion, in his blind rage against Rigaud, forgot that all these censures recoiled upon himself; forgot his own treason, perfidy and ingratitude to all his superior officers, and to all parties; forgot that Toussaint Louverture, J. J. Dessalines, and Henry Christóphe, had experienced all the effects of his excessive ambition and treachery: in his delirium he could distinctly see the mote in his neighbour's eye, while he was blind to the beam which darkened his own: thus was his citation from the Bible much more applicable to himself than to Rigaud.

Meanwhile Pétion undermined his rival in secret. When he was assured that he had a strong party in the town of Cayes, he excited a mutiny in the 17th regt., by means of his agents: Pétion's partisans in the town of Cayes, united with this corps, and attacked Rigaud in his own Government: an obstinate conflict took place, when Rigaud would have been overpowered by the number of his assailants, had not Borgella hastened to his relief from Acquin, with his corps of cavalry: the partisans of Pétion were cut to pieces by the victors. Had not Gen. Borgella arrived thus opportunely to his succour, Rigaud would have shared the fate of Gérin, and have been sacrificed by those under his command, to the vengeance and ambition of Pétion. Such of the insurgents as had escaped during the action, were searched for and put to death by order of Rigaud.

Such has always been the result of Pétion's plots; thus it is that this artful and wicked man has caused the destruction of his partisans from the extremities of the South, to those of the North, by exciting them to revolt against their chiefs; and yet he has the hypocrisy and effrontery to commisserate them and bewail their unhappy lot.

After this disaster, Rigaud, being attacked with a languor, retired to the *ci-devant* plantation Laborde in the plain of Cayes; his illness filled all who were attached to him with alarm, grief, and consternation; they feared that after his death they should fall victims to Pétion's vengeance, and time shewed their suspicions to be but too well founded.

Rigaud, perceiving his end approach, assembled his council and the generals under his command, amongst the more distinguished of whom were Borgella, Francisque, Vaval, and Wagnac, the two first, men of colour, the others black. Rigaud chose as his successor Borgella, who had been of such signal service to him, and whom he judged more capable and worthy of commanding than Francisque who was his senior. As for the two black generals their colour was long a ground of exclusion from supreme authority in the South-west.

Borgella did not, by his conduct, justify the confidence reposed in him by Rigaud, he had the weakness to submit with his followers to Pétion's discretion.— Gen. Francisque would possibly have conducted himself with more firmness and vigour, and have acted differently. Gen. Borgella did not understand his true position: he might have become all at once one of the worthies of Hayti by extinguishing the flames of civil war, and proving himself the benefactor of his brethren and country. In a word, he could, by listening to justice and reason, have acknowledged the royal government, which would have hastened to maintain him in the command of the South, by furnishing him with supplies of troops and money. But this general, being deficient in wisdom and policy, suffered himself to be led astray by an erroneous prejudice, and acted upon by a false fear.

After languishing for some time, Rigaud at length expired notwithstanding all the efforts of art, and with strong suspicions of having been poisoned: a suspicion which gained the more credit from the circumstance of Pétion's having already endeavoured to destroy him by arms, and because, from his well known character for treachery, he was deemed fully capable of so base a crime. What must strengthen this surmise still more was, that on receiving the news of Rigaud's death, Pétion affected the deepest concern, through which however the internal joy he felt at having got rid of so formidable and dangerous a rival, involuntarily betrayed itself. On Rigaud's decease, Borgella seized with a trembling and feeble hand the yet unsettled reins of the government of the South. The generals under his command were, as I have already observed, Francisque at Jérémie, discontented at having been passed over by Rigaud; Bruny le Blanc at Anse-à-Veau, of a doubtful character, and upon whom little reliance could be placed; Vaval at Acquin, who was a perfect cipher, a mere tool, one of the accessaries to the assassination of his own brother Gen. William Lafleur; and Wagnac, who was sick at Cayes, without holding any command.

Such being the state of affairs in the South, the wily Pétion found it no difficult task to sow dissention among these generals and gain over partisans, so as eventually to overthrow Borgella. Francisque was the first victim. He was powerful at Jérémie; in order therefore to accomplish his ruin, Pétion employed the same manœuvres he had used against Gérin and Rigaud, raising up a rival against him in Col. Henry. A bloody combat took place between the two regiments composing the garrison of Jérémie. Francisque, being defeated, was obliged to fly for safety to Cayes. Henry, his rival, was promoted by Pétion to the rank of general, which he did not long enjoy: he gave umbrage to Pétion who opposed a new rival to him, and he fell by the hand of Col. Titye, who, in his turn, was destroyed by Col. Bruneau, now commander of the thirteenth regiment. At the same time that Pétion drove Francisque from Jérémie, he gained over the troops under Bruny le Blanc at Anse-à-Veau.

While these unfortunate events were passing in the South-west, the greatest tranquillity prevailed, as we have seen, in the North-west, and the royal government was consolidating itself upon a firm and durable basis.

Pétion saw with grief our prosperity, which had progressively increased ever since the fall of the Môle. The foundation of an hereditary monarchy had blasted all his hopes, he could no longer count upon those revolutions or changes which might give him a chance of concentrating the whole authority in his own hands.

The situation of the republic was critical. A royal proclamation had placed all the ports of the South in a state of blockade. Our navy was infinitely superior to Pétion's: our ships were cruising off his ports, and prevented the entrance of foreign traders. In this state of things, the King had the strongest hopes of seeing a speedy termination of the civil war, and with it, of the miseries of the Haytians. His plan was magnanimous, noble, and worthy of his generous heart. He wished, by the maintenance of tranquillity and the dominion of law and justice in the kingdom, to enable the inhabitants of the South-west to judge from our state of happiness and prosperity, whether it would be more for their advantage to range themselves beneath a just and paternal government, or continue for ever involved in a deadly anarchy. " *Leave them to them-* " *selves,*" said Henry, " *the magnitude of their own* " *sufferings will recall them to reason and their true* " *interests. All we need do to reduce them is to remain* " *at rest, to be wise and prudent, and we shall not be* " *reduced to the sad necessity of shedding the blood of* " *Haytians, our brethren and fellow-citizens.*"

Petion felt the imminent danger of this wise policy. He perceived that this state of peace was a thousand times more fatal to him than civil dissensions and war, without which he could not maintain himself: he resolved therefore to extricate himself from this critical situation, and compel us to change our system of policy, by driving us to act on the offensive.

To effect this, at the same time that he expelled Francisque from Jérémie, and gained over the troops of Bruny le Blanc at Anse-à-Veau, he corrupted the sailors of our squadron and laboured to produce fresh troubles, and kindle the flames of civil war in the heart of our own country.

Major-General the Baron de Papalier, a man of colour and a native of Cayes, who possessed the King's fullest confidence, was one of the principal conspirators selected by Pétion for the execution of his guilty projects.

This Papalier was the same who commanded at Cayes at the time of the insurrection against the Emperor Dessalines, who had placed every dependence upon him. Papalier could have stifled this insurrection in its birth: his troops, who continued faithful to the emperor, petitioned to be led against the insurgents, but Papalier, by his refusal, afforded the insurrection time to spread, and was thus the primary cause of the emperor's death.

Taken prisoner afterwards at the battle of Cibert, on the 1st of January, 1807, Henry retained him in his rank of Major-General, employed him, and admitted him to his intimacy. On the foundation of the monarchy he was created a baron; previous to which he had married a friend of the queen's, and had, through the munificence of the king, amassed a considerable fortune, which now furnished him with the means of enlisting followers, and betraying his benefactor.

Artful, plausible and insinuating, the charms of his conversation, and suavity of his manners, captivated all hearts: he quickly gained over a multitude of adherents; and exerted himself to corrupt the sailors of the fleet, among whom he distributed, by means of his agents, cloathing and money, masking his designs beneath the cloak of generosity and patriotism.

In this state of affairs, part of the squadron sailed on a cruise off the south-west coast of the island. This was what the conspirators wished. The government, plunged in the most perfect security, was wholly occupied with the completion of the laws which form the *Code Henry*. Nothing of the conspiracy had yet transpired, nor was the smallest attention paid to what was passing. About this time a number of the partisans of the French had introduced and established themselves within the kingdom, among them Bunél, Montorsier and Viart, the two first white Frenchmen, the third a man of colour in complexion, but a white Frenchman in principle. Bunél had been treasurer under Governor Toussaint: to improve his fortune, and ingratiate himself with Toussaint, he had married a black woman. He returned to Hayti along with a Chevalier Lacauve, who had been sent to this country by the Comte de Willot, now governor of the island of Corsica, for the purpose of intriguing against the government.

This Bunél, after having contributed to the unjust seizure of a considerable sum, belonging to the royal government, in the United States of America, entered into the conspiracy with Papalier and Grandjean both father and son; these two last were relatives or connexions of Bunél's.

Montorsier had, along with some other Frenchmen, been captured by our cruisers. Henry distinguished him, loaded him with favours, and enabled him in a little time to accumulate a large fortune; in return for all which he soon gave us proofs of the basest ingratitude.

Viart had been secretary to the central assembly at Port-au-Prince, under Governor Toussaint, when this general completed the constitution which brought down upon him the vengeance of Bonaparte. Viart, on the arrival of the French, basely betrayed Governor Toussaint, to whom he was deeply indebted for the favours he had shewn him.

He arrived from France by way of America, and was coldly received by Henry as he deserved. The recollection of his treason was yet strong on Henry's imagination. *There is an unwelcome guest*, said the King, on first beholding Viart. Owing nevertheless to the urgent solicitations made in his behalf, his Majesty some time after, named him to the high situation of *Procureur General du Roi*, for the province of the West, whither he repaired to discharge his duties: we shall soon see the effects of this condescension.

The French could at this time, establish themselves like the subjects of other nations in our towns: they had commercial establishments at Cape Henry and at Gonaïves, in this last town a Frenchman named Belcour, was established in partnership with Caze and Montorsier; he made frequent journies to the South, and was one of the conspirators who disturbed the province of the West.

A multitude of foreign merchants, English, American, German, Dutch, &c. likewise inhabited our towns, and, peaceably occupied in their commercial transactions, lived in the most perfect harmony with the Haytians; while *only half-a-dozen Frenchmen*, at most, directed all their efforts to disturb the country and rekindle the flames of civil war. What an instructive lesson for the future.

Notwithstanding what had befallen Governor Toussaint and the Emperor Dessalines, in consequence of their welcoming and favouring the partisans of the French, we already fell, without perceiving it, into the same snares which had proved their ruin; so true is it that hatred and mistrust are not the most durable feelings of the human heart. Time had effaced every thing: animosity was extinct, and confidence established: the lessons of experience were forgotten, and a strange fatality led us to do all in our power to effect our own ruin.—There is nothing stable or lasting but those principles of government which are founded on a sage policy.

Hence results the necessity of permanent councils, in which all the learning and wisdom of the nation might be concentrated: in these all public affairs should be discussed with coolness and deliberation. Prudence is a foe to precipitation; and frequently measures of apparently the greatest insignificance, have proved the source of distraction and revolutions in the state.

Montorsier had returned from one of his voyages to Jamaica, and brought an account of what had happened.

in the fleet. The conspiracy first broke out on board the Princess Royal Amethyste frigate. The conspirators having seized the Admiral Pierre Saint Jean, Comte de la Presqu'île, and the other officers who refused to participate in their treason, immediately entered the harbour of Miragoane.

The commandant of this place, after landing those whom he suspected on board the frigate, embarked in her Colonels Bigot, Gaspard, and Monperous, with a number of the 16th regiment, to go in pursuit of the rest of the squadron, which was also taken and betrayed in the most shameful manner.

Some days after, this frigate fell in with the English frigate Southampton, commanded by Sir James Lucas Yeo. On being hailed by this vessel they refused to answer, and these inexperienced men had the folly to engage the Southampton, by which they were captured and taken to Jamaica, after a loss of ninety-six men killed and wounded.

When the news of this transaction reached us, which it did almost as soon as the event, Papalier was highly enraged with Montorsier, whom he treated as an idle gossip. Government had in fact been for som days very uneasy at receiving no tidings from the squadron. There is no doubt that Papalier hoped that government, anxious respecting its fate, would have sent the remaining ships in search of it, by which means we should have lost these also: thus Montorsier's report was far from agreeable to Papalier, whose projects it foiled by putting us upon our guard, and totally defeating the effects of the conspiracy.

Prior to the occurrence just mentioned, Papalier and Montorsier had been united in the closest bonds of friendship and interest. Papalier had employed the latter to transmit letters to Port-au-Prince by way of Jamaica: the mischief then which Montorsier had done in his eyes, arose from the precipitancy with which he communicated the intelligence of an event equally advantageous and interesting to both: but Montorsier in his impatience could not resist the pleasure he felt in communicating news so painful and distressing to us.

Such then is the depravity of the human heart, that the greatest penetration is necessary to fathom its depth, and to discover the blackness of crime in actions which appear indifferent to the vulgar, but which serve as a clue to the man of genius to penetrate the crooked labyrinth of wickedness which they conceal. Papalier made a shew of indignation at hearing news, at which nevertheless in the bottom of his soul he rejoiced, his only regret being to find it not sufficiently bad! and Montorsier, in his eagerness to publish intelligence at which he was inwardly overjoyed, carried his duplicity so far as to feign the deepest interest in our welfare By his assumed sorrow he expressed his goodwill towards us, insinuated himself into our confidence, and acquired in some degree the right of offering advice; of this he availed himself by urging our immediate march against Port-au-Prince, in order to further his vindictive projects of rekindling the flames of civil war.

It is thus that the French have always deceived us, and that they yet count upon deceiving us. "*To reconquer St. Domingo,*" says M. le Comte Beugnot, Ex-minister of the Marine of France, now Member of the Chamber of Deputies, "*there is but one method to be pursued, namely to make a shew of being kindly disposed towards the Haytians;** that is, in other words, to employ treachery to lull our suspicions asleep, and then entice us to the precipice. "*Few words and much apparent candour,*" says another Ex-planter of distinction in a letter to his friend, "*are the best means of success.*"

* Letter of M. le Comte Beugnot to M. Leborgne de Boigne.

Such are the principles, the logic, and the morality of the Comte de Beugnot and the Ex-colonists.

Nevertheless the conspiracy was far more extensive than had at first been imagined; it had spread throughout the kingdom. Papalier, Bunél, Montorsier and their accomplices, were commissioned to revolutionize the North, while Viart, Malvoisin, Belcour, and others were doing the same in the West. In a word, it was the French faction which, armed with the poignard of treason, and concealed beneath the mask of hypocrisy, raised these new commotions in our bosom, and exerted on both sides the most incredible efforts to rekindle the flames of civil war.

Since these unfortunate events we have learned that persons whose rank and official situations raised them above suspicion, had taken but too active a share in the conspiracy.

Nevertheless, Papalier, being the only conspirator who had yet openly shewn himself, was arrested and imprisoned.

The King was distracted with a variety of feelings: civil war was repugnant to his heart, and he saw himself driven to it by an unavoidable fatality. In this dilemma he called together his privy council to take their opinion. The majority, indignant at the treachery which had taken place, voted for marching immediately against Port-au-Prince, before the enemy could take advantage of the event. The advice of the council coincided with the wishes of the factious, who reckoned upon availing themselves of circumstances as they arose. They foresaw that the King could not be everywhere, and must necessarily be absent either from the army or from the interior, and in either case they trusted they should succeed in their designs, either in the army or in the interior of the kingdom. These hopes were, alas! too fully realized.

It was then unanimously resolved in council to march forthwith against Port-au-Prince.

The preparations for war were carried on with incredible activity. The event of the fleet had taken place in February, and by the middle of March the army was in the field.

The main body of the army directed its march by Mirebalais, previous to *debouching* into the plain of Cul-de-Sac through the defiles of Pensez-y-bien, and the King with his *maison militaire* took the high road of Arcahaye which led direct to Port-au-Prince. The second division of the army was to form a junction in the plain of Cul-de-Sac.

The fleet, laden with provisions and every warlike store requisite for the campaign, coasted along the shore. Notwithstanding the desertion of part of our ships our navy was still superior to that of the enemy.

Pétion had been previously informed of all our movements by the conspirators and spies he had among us: he knew we had made preparations for attacking him, but learning meanwhile that his affairs had taken a favourable turn in the South, he hastened with some troops to Pont-de-Miragoane to assist his partisans. On his departure he left the command to General Boyer, with orders to be expeditious in putting the fortresses of Cibert, and la-Croix-des-Bouquets, in a state of defence to check the first efforts of our army, and gain time for him.

This was the first time since the revolution that the name of General Boyer was seen to figure in our military annals: he had always been secretary to General Pétion; he mounted rapidly to the rank of general, and is the same who is now President of the republic. When we look to his career and the high rank he has attained, we should be tempted to believe, with the antients, that there exists an unjust, blind, and whimsi cal fatality which presides over human destinies, were we not thoroughly convinced that God governs the world by a just providence, and by ways impenetrable to weak mortals.

On the news of our march Boyer took post with his army at the *ci-devant* plantation Santo, in an intermediate position between the forts of Cibert, and la-Croix-des-Bouquets. He thus intercepted the two roads which led to Port-au-Prince, and covered this town which was in his rear. In front he had the savannah Houblon, while his right was strengthened by the fort of la-Croix-des-Bouquets, and his left by that of Cibert.

The king designedly slackened his march, to give time to the army, which had made the long circuit of Mirebalais, to enter the plain of Cul-de-Sac at the same time with himself.

Already our view extended into the plain, and we were not above two short leagues from Cibert, when the roar of artillery and musketry announced to us the battle of Santo. We quickened our march, and in a little time the *tirailleurs* were engaged with the enemy who hastily retreated into the fort of Cibert.

On the same day we communicated with the army, and learned the result of the battle of Santo.

Boyer, after a vigorous resistance, was defeated, and retreated precipitately to Port-au-Prince, with the remains of his army which had been cut to pieces. Our troops, irritated by the resistance and loss they had experienced, made but few prisoners in the heat of battle, these being sent to the King, he dispatched them immediately to the North, where they yet continue.

After the battle of Santo, the army took up a position in front of Port-au-Prince.

The fort of Cibert could not be taken by storm: it was necessary to lay regular siege to it. We made our approaches under a shower of balls, and raised our batteries within musket shot of the place. Already were the ramparts shaken by our artillery, and tumbling in ruins: nearly the whole of their guns were dismounted. Henry, commiserating the melancholy situation of the besieged, seeing that they could no longer hold out, and had already sustained a most severe loss, repaired in person to one of the nearest batteries for the purpose of addressing them and exhorting them to surrender.

The king stopped the firing; he signified to the besieged that he was going to speak to them; they equally ceased their fire; and instantly the most profound silence prevailed on both sides.

Then Henry, wishing to show himself to the besieged, the better to persuade them, accompanied by his aides de camp, mounted the trench: he wore his military decorations, in order that he might be recognized by the officers and men of the garrison of Cibert: the king gave his orders to the Comte de Limonade, who explained his majesty's intentions in a strong and intelligible voice as follows:

"*Generals, officers, subalterns, and soldiers! I
"address you in the name of the king our beloved sove-
"reign, who is here present. Surrender; you shall be
"continued in your respective ranks and offices; you are
"in error, you have been deceived; cease to maintain an
"unjust and barbarous war; you are reduced to the last
"extremity, you cannot defend yourselves longer. Sur-
"render, then! no injury shall be offered to you. We
"conjure you, for your own sakes, and in the name of
"the country, to surrender!*"

This address, which had been heard with the most profound silence, made a deep impression upon the garrison. Already were the best disposed anxious to surrender, but they were opposed by the more mutinous. General Metellus, their commander, finding himself unable to subdue their spirit, to end the dispute, ordered the firing to re-commence. The captain of our battery was pierced with a thousand balls within a few paces of the king. The contest was then resumed with increased fury on both sides, and continued till night.

The enemy availed himself of the darkness to evacuate the fort: he endeavoured to force our entrenchments, and open himself a passage through our lines, but was vigorously repulsed in every direction. The soldiers then separated, and mixed with ours; in this confusion, and under cover of the darkness they made their escape as well as they could.

The dawn of day disclosed to us the disasters of the night, and the horrors of war. General Metellus lay dead at some distance from the fort, having fallen, the victim of his temerity, in the flower of his age. Had he surrendered, he would have served his country, and spared the blood of his brethren and fellow citizens.

The fort of Cibert commanded the plain, and cut off the high road, from the North to Port-au-Prince: it was of importance to us to possess this point. To render it healthy and habitable it was necessary to purify its vicinity, for which purpose the dead bodies, which had begun to putrify, both in the fort and ditches, were burned. Colombel has availed himself of this circumstance to calumniate us, as though similar means were not employed in every part of the world to prevent contagion and pestilence.

After the capture of Cibert, the king with his *maison militaire* joined the army before Port-au-Prince, and immediately made arrangements for commencing the siege of that town.

Pétion, as we have already seen, had gone to Miragoane, to second the efforts of his partisans in the South.

Borgella was at Acquin, with a few troops, in an embarrassing and critical situation. Cayes, Jérémie, and Anse-a-Veau had declared in favour of Pétion, who employed the same stratagem he had played off against Rigaud, to induce Borgella to submit. *" The " army of the North,"* said he, *" is on its march, already " is it in the plain of Cul-de-Sac. How shall we be " able to oppose it, if divided among ourselves?"* Nothing more was wanting to determine Borgella to submit. The more effectually to persuade him, Pétion hastened to send to him his old friends Fremond and Panayoti who confirmed his resolution to surrender with his troops.

It is worth while to observe by the way, that every time the North has endeavoured, either by war or negotiation, to terminate our civil dissensions, the South and West, however divided, immediately became reconciled: hence we must conclude that their fear of the North exceeded their mutual animosity.

Pétion hastened to rally the troops of the the South, and repair with them to Port-au-Prince, which he reached before we had time to form the siege of this town.

It is impossible for me at this moment to detail the operations of this siege, since it would lead me too far from my subject. I shall therefore content myself with saying that prodigies of valour were displayed on each side. Our entrenchments already touched those of the enemy; the town was reduced to the last extremity, and could not have held out at the most above eight days, when an unfortunate event changed the aspect of affairs.

Pétion, during the siege, maintained a secret correspondence with the army, and secretly made every effort to corrupt our troops. Reduced to the most critical situation, in order to extricate himself, he had recourse to his favourite weapons *treason* and *perfidy.*

The king had gone to St. Marc, whither affairs connected with the service called him: in his absence he had left the command of the army to Field-marshal the Prince of Limbé, and that of his *maison militaire,* to his brother-in-law Prince Noël, colonel general of the Haytian guards.

The moment was favourable to the conspirators: they waited the king's absence to execute their designs. Henry received intelligence by a courier while at St. Marc, that the troops of the division under the command of the Duke of Plaisance, had revolted, made their general prisoner, and marched with him into the town of Port-au-Prince.

The king instantly set out to join the army, and on his arrival, summoned a council of war of his generals. The event which had taken place might be productive of still greater mischief: our interior was far from tranquil; the conspirators were active both in the North and the West. It was therefore resolved in the council to raise the siege of Port-au-Prince.

The departure of the army was effected in the greatest order, the enemy not daring to molest it in its retreat. The siege had continued two months and fifteen days.

It was time for us to return to the North-west: all the country was in a flame; the conspirators only waited the signal of the event which had taken place before Port-au-Prince, to strike a decisive blow. Already the mountains of St. Marc were in a state of insurrection through the intrigues of Viart; those of Great and Little Cahos were in commotion. Some days after Mirebalais revolted, and General Almanjor, who commanded the arrondissement for the king, was assassinated; and troubles had also broken out in the North. Pétion, apprised of all these movements by the conspirators, prepared to march in order to second the revolt.

It is an universal principle to chuse the least of two evils. The state was now on the brink of a precipice, and we had no alternative but to save, or perish with it: what do I say? it was no longer the preservation of Henry's *throne* that was at issue; it was the preservation of his life, with that of his family, his attached followers, and his fellow citizens, whose welfare required the consolidation of that order of affairs which he knew how to establish. In this emergency the council was compelled to take prompt and energetic measures for the public good. The generals commanding the several districts received orders to check the progress of sedition, and re-establish tranquillity by every means in their power.

During this calamitous period excesses doubtless occurred, as usually happen in civil commotions; when hatreds, jealousies, vengeance, ambition, lust, rapine, and plunder---what do I say? at a time when all the most hideous passions are let loose, it is difficult to curb their excesses.

Henry was afflicted with the most poignant distress; as each new treason was communicated to him I have heard him exclaim in accents of grief, *Ah! the barbarians! what then have I done to merit this?* O ye who calumniate this unhappy prince, who possesses nevertheless a generous, noble, and virtuous heart, do ye know him? Have you, like me, heard the expressions of sorrow which so forcibly displayed what passed in his mind? Have you surprised him in his closet shedding tears in secret for the sufferings of his country? Have you been placed in a situation similar to his before you judged so severely? What would you have him do? Should he have suffered himself to be dethroned and butchered with his family, and all who were most devoted to him?

As for myself, whatever judgment contemporary writers, or posterity may pass upon the events of his reign, I will bear testimony to the truth, I will declare, from the thorough conviction of my heart and conscience, that Henry is perfectly guiltless of the evils of the civil war, which arose wholly out of the unhappy period in which he was placed, and were not occasioned by any fault of his.

Like Augustus and Henry iv. of France, Henry mounted a throne reeking with the blood of civil wars. Never was a prince more unfortunate. Scarce had he taken hold of the reins of government when he found their possession disputed by an ambitious man: all at once he found himself surrounded by plots and treason, and deceived by intriguers and the ungrateful creatures of his bounty. He saw his throne and his life, together with that of his family and friends exposed to the most imminent danger. Encircled by difficulties, he was to be seen opposing to them the most heroic constancy and courage: he was to be seen persevering in every exertion capable of promoting the welfare of his country. In the midst of troubles he created laws, and made order to prevail in the midst of disorder, peace in the midst of war. From what Henry has accomplished during a season of such trials, we may easily conjecture how much he would have done for the welfare of his country, had he attained the government without opposition, had he not encountered traitors and ungrateful wretches, and had not his mind been harrassed by misfortune.

Pétion, building upon the success of the conspiracy put his army in motion to assist the revolters; but, learning, on his arrival at Verrettes, that the king was advancing in person against him, and that his partisans had either fallen or been defeated in all their attempts, he hastily retreated to Port-au-Prince.

The storming of Fort Boucassin at Arcahaye in 1813 by our troops, was the last military event of this disastrous civil war: from this period all hostilities ceased on both sides.

This year we witnessed the completion of the palace of Sans Souci, and the royal church of that town. These two structures, erected by the descendants of Africans, shew that we have not lost the architectural taste and genius of our ancestors who covered Ethiopia, Egypt, Carthage, and Old Spain, with their superb monuments.

On the 25th December of the same year died at the age of seventy-two, universally regretted, Andrew Vernet Prince of Gonaïves, Grand Marshal of Hayti, and Minister of Finance and the Interior. He had served under Governor Toussaint whose niece he married. He was afterwards Minister of Finance and the Interior both under the Emperor Dessalines and King Henry. He closed a long and useful life in the discharge of the high duties of his office, leaving him behind the reputation of an upright minister and a virtuous citizen, full of honour, and of rigid integrity. Henry mourned him as one of his old companions in arms, and gave him a splendid funeral. His body, after having been embalmed, was deposited in the Haytian Pantheon under the royal church of Sans Souci. Upwards of six thousand persons attended his funeral obsequies.* This is the same whom Colombel and Milcent affirm to have been put to death by the King's command.

After his death his widow, Eleanor Chancy, mar-

* I was principal secretary to the Prince of Gonaives in the department of finance and the interior for seven years.

ried Prince John, Duke of Port-Margot, (nephew to the king) who is likewise dead; and his widow is now one of the ladies of honour to the queen.

At the period of which I am speaking the war was carried on in Europe with the utmost fury. We saw with satisfaction the triumph of the allies, and the restoration of Louis xviii. to the throne of his ancestors. During our civil dissensions we had lost sight of France, and she also appeared to have forgotten us. She was not long however in reminding us of her existence and that from henceforward she was to become a prominent object of our attention.

Neither the restoration of Louis, nor the consequent change of government, could alter our political relations with France. We continued at war with her, as on the first declaration of our independence; we could then only suppose that Louis xviii. would have acted towards us with more justice, generosity and humanity than Bonaparte had done. But, on the other hand, we had reason to expect, with the restoration of the ancient *regime* in France, a revival of those prejudices which the revolution had abolished; and, above all, that the influence of the Ultra-colonists with the new government would prove highly prejudicial to our interests.

The change of government had produced no alteration in the politics and interests of the people, and experience shewed our fears to be but too well founded. Hardly had Louis xviii. mounted the throne of his ancestors, when the same men who had misled Bonaparte by their treacherous advice, and brought him to send out his famous expedition to St. Domingo; the Ex-colonists, I say, surrounded and assailed him with their clamours.

The portfolio of marine and the colonies was, at this period, confided to M. Malouet, an old man and an Ex-colonist, bigotted to all the colonial prejudices. This minister's first idea was to suggest measures for reducing St. Domingo anew beneath the yoke of France, and the restoration of *slavery* as in 1789. A *Malouet* was incapable of divesting himself of the influence of past recollections, and his project was the very climax of folly and absurdity.

He commenced by sending three emissaries with secret instructions to St. Domingo, to sound the disposition of the chiefs, and gain intelligence respecting our internal situation: it was indeed a perfect system of *espionnage*.

He selected as chief of this expedition one Dauxion Lavaysse, formerly a *Terrorist*, an agent of Robespierre's under the committee of public safety: and one of those immoral and degraded wretches, who, on their return to France, had been sentenced to twenty years confinement to hard labour in chains for the crime of *bigamy*. The second was a renegado Spaniard named Augustino Franco Medina, formerly employed at Bannique in looking after smugglers, afterwards appointed adjutant-general with the command of the district of Cibao by Ferrand; he signalised himself by his cruelty, in causing a massacre of defenceless women and children in his attack upon the village of Ounaminthé: the third was an old man of Bourdeaux named Dravermann, chosen in consequence of his connexion with Borgella in the South.

This plan of *espionnage* being organised, these three individuals set off: they embarked at Boulogne, landed at Dover, visited London, re-embarked at Falmouth, landed at Barbados, next at St. Lucia, afterwards at Martinique, whence they proceeded to Curaçoa, and at length reached Jamaica, where they were to wait for intelligence, and to arrange their plan of operations with the French refugees resident there.

The arrival of these emissaries was a source of joy

to all the French; they made an address to Louis xviii. soliciting him to resume possession of St. Domingo.—In their phrenzy they imagined themselves once more in possession of their former plantations and their slaves.

Dauxion Lavaysse chose as secretary Lafond Ladebat, an *Ex-colonist*, formerly a *member of the convention*. Montorsier who was at Jamaica, was the traitor who furnished him with information respecting the situation of affairs in the North-west.

When Dauxion Lavaysse had gained all the intelligence he desired, he drew up a pamphlet which he printed under the assumed name of H. Henry, entitled " *Considerations offered to the inhabitants of Hayti with* " *respect to their present situation and future prospects.*"

The pamphlet was drawn up with a view of preparing the way, and was to precede the arrival of the emissaries in Hayti.

Meanwhile Dauxion Lavaysse was by no means blind to the hazard of the game he was playing. Not being furnished with letters of credence to produce to the Haytian chieftains, he was desirous of accrediting himself, least he should endanger his person. He therefore addressed Gen. Pétion* from Jamaica on the 6th of September, and the King of Hayti†, on the 1st of the succeeding October, in conformity with his instructions, which directed him to make his first communication to Gen. Pétion: and in the twenty-five days which intervened between these two letters, he had time to receive an answer from Pétion and frame such a letter as he ought to address to the king, in order to produce the results he desired.

Pétion having given a favourable answer, Dauxion Lavaysse prepared to go immediately to Port-au-Prince, having first dispatched Franco Medina to the Spanish

* See Appendix B. No. 1. p. xiii.   † See Appendix F. No. 2.

part of Hayti, whence he was to enter the North, and he intrusted his dispatches for the king to Montorsier.

Hitherto we had no mistrust of Montorsier; but on the contrary he possessed our confidence; in Papalier's conspiracy he had exhibited a candour and good will by which he deceived us and furthered his own projects; we could not read the treachery of his heart; the king had loaded him with favours, and he was beloved by every body.

On his return from Jamaica he assumed an air of consequence, and declared himself the bearer of dispatches of the first importance to the country, which he refused to deliver except into his Majesty's own hands. The king was at Sans-Souci; Montorsier was directed to give the pacquets, of which he was the bearer, to the Baron de Dupuy, by whom they were forwarded to his majesty.

The King immediately summoned a privy council to take them into consideration. Ten years had elapsed since we had any communication whatever with France. A host of contradictory conjectures, as to the object of the French, was instantly afloat. What did they propose? Did they mean to recognise our Independence, or to re-enslave us? Did they mean to offer compensation for the injuries they had done us? Had they not injured us sufficiently without wishing to do us further mischief? The pacquets were yet unopened, and we already viewed them with horror.

At length the minister of state broke the seal, and read aloud Dauxion Lavayasse's letter; we heard a tissue of insults, sophistry, and falsehoods. The pamphlet of H. Henry was couched in similar terms, and to sum up all, they offered us the alternative of SLAVERY or DEATH!

The deepest indignation was depicted in every countenance; many of the members of the council, unable to suppress their feelings voted for an immediate call to arms, while others were anxious that the most energetic measures should be adopted on the instant. Henry curbed his feelings; perfect master of himself he listened in silence to their several opinions. One of these opinions the truth of history requires me to relate. "*Before*," said he, "*we reply, would it not be prudent to learn how Gen. Pétion and the inhabitants of the South-west propose to act?*" Henry then broke silence and said, "*No! let us begin by doing our duty. If General Pétion and the inhabitants of the South-west do theirs, they will act as we do. If they mean to disgrace and ruin themselves, would you wish us to follow their example?*"

Henry then informed the council that he had no secrets to keep from his fellow citizens; that it was his intention that all proceedings with the French which related to the liberty and independence of the Haytian people should be always publicly discussed, as being the only method of preventing French intrigue, and of making the people acquainted with their true interests. "*Such*," he said, "*has been the invariable rule of my political conduct. I am resolved not to deviate from this principle, but to adhere to it more rigidly than ever.*"

The council then immediately proceeded, without adjournment, to dispatch confidential letters to all the civil and military authorities of the kingdom, directing them to convoke without delay a *general council of the nation*.

Meanwhile Montorsier persisted in demanding an audience of the king, in order to speak with and endeavour to gain him over.

Henry repaired to the capital and complied with his request. At this audience the wretch, already fancying the French masters of Hayti, and flattering himself the dispatches he bore had intimidated the king, boldly avowed all the plans and projects of the Ex-colonists.

"*You shall have*" said he "*the sovereignty of the Island of Tortuga, where you may reside, or you will be allowed to retire either to France, the United States, or any other place that suits your wishes. The favour of Louis* xviii. *will follow you.*"

Henry checked his anger, in order to give him time to develope the whole of his projects.

"*I set no value upon my throne or crown,*" replied he, "*I shall descend and renounce it without regret, if I can flatter myself that my days will pass with tranquillity in the bosom of my family.*" "*And this*" added Montorsier, interrupting the king, and forcibly grasping his hand, "*this is the very thing they desire, this was the most formidable obstacle we apprehended, and behold you have already removed it.*" "*But,*" resumed Henry, "*what will my general officers, members of council, ministers, and secretaries, say to this? They are constantly with me, and will infallibly oppose such a plan.*" "*Destroy those who embarrass you,*" rejoined Montorsier, "*you must rid yourself of them as soon as possible ! ! !*" At this horrid declaration, which disclosed all the depravity of this Frenchman's soul, Henry could no longer contain himself, but raising his voice he called aloud, "*Come hither my officers! He wants to rob the Haytians of their freedom; he has dared to propose to me to destroy you, my best supporters, the firmest defenders of your country.*"

On hearing his majesty, the officers, who were in an adjoining room, rushed tumultuously in: Montorsier stood pale and trembling, and confounded----the first impulse of the officers was to throw the wretch headlong from the balcony into the street, but Henry checked them; "*No,*" said he, "*let him go, his frightful* "*projects are disclosed.*" Montorsier confused, with terror, despair and death in his heart, retired in silence.

This single historic fact speaks volumes; and the train of ideas to which it leads cannot fail to strike every reader of refletion.

On the 21st Oct. 1814, the general council of the nation met in the council chamber at Sans-Souci.

It is impossible to describe the indignation which filled the members of the council when they heard Dauxion Lavaysse's letter and the pamphlet signed H. Henry read. Among the members there were some who had borne the yoke of the French: the marks yet visible on their mutilated limbs attested the length and cruelty of their sufferings, and the barbarity of our tyrants. Others remembered to have seen their *fathers, mothers, brethren, sisters, relatives, or friends hung, drowned, burned, or torn in pieces by dogs,** and it was to such men, old warriors seamed with many an honorable scar, whose valour had driven before them the sanguinary hordes of the Leclercs and the Rochambeaus, that the proposal was made of returning beneath the yoke of tyrants, and choosing between the horrible alternative of DEATH or SLAVERY!!! In an instant all the hatred and animosity which had slumbered for years, was awakened with the most incredible violence. The members of the council rose spontaneously and swore on the point of their swords, in the name of the Haytian people, *that they would be exterminated to the last man rather than renounce their liberty and independence, or submit to France.*

An address to the King was instantly voted, in order

---

* See details of these atrocities in the second part of the *Systeme Colonial devoilée*, and also at pages 72, 73, &c. of the translation of the Baron's *Reflexions sur les Noirs and les Blancs*, published by Hatchard, Piccadilly.—*Translator.*

to manifest to his majesty the sentiments which animated them, and the resolution they had adopted.——This address,* strong in facts, in principles, and in arguments, ought to convince France of the spirit, the energy, and the determination of the Haytians.

But soon the indignation of the council gave place to enthusiasm when the king appeared in person with his son, the prince royal, by his side, to give his *viva voce* sanction to the address of the council.

Hardly had Henry terminated his speech when the room re-echoed with shouts of *Vive le roi!——Vive le prince royal!——Vive l'independence !——Liberty or death!——A war of extermination to our tyrants!*——and these shouts were repeated by crowds of people and troops who beset the avenues to the palace.

To enter into the feelings of holy enthusiasm which animated all ranks upon this occasion, it is necessary to peruse the noble, magnanimous, and ever memorable resolution sanctioned by the king, in which the nation preferred burying itself beneath the ruins of the country, to bowing its head beneath the yoke of tyrants.——This resolution struck terror and affright into the hearts of our enemies; they were from that moment convinced that every hope of re-enslaving us was forbidden to them for ever. What a gratifying day! What a day of glory and triumph for Henry and the Haytian people! The day on which we adopted this immortal resolution disclosed to us the full measure of national energy, spirit, and patriotism, which characterised us, and fully convinced us that we should be invincible.

Hardly was the resolution of the general council of the nation known in the provinces, before the people were prepared for war: from every side they ran to arms ; it seemed as if the French were actually landing

* See Appendix, F. No. 4.

on our shores. Some were preparing brands to burn their own houses; others were whetting their swords, pointing their spears, cleaning their muskets, and getting their knapsacks ready. Already had the industrious and provident housewife begun to secure her household linen and other valuables, putting aside those superfluous articles which were no longer necessary, and were destined to become a prey to the flames.

My readers will pardon these details which exhibit the manners, the character, and the spirit of the nation. All these preparations were chearfully made; the Haytian viewed with unconcern the probable destruction of his house and property; liberty alone was the object he prized; this was to him the first of all blessings, without which all others were valueless. The very children caught the inspiration of their mothers, each gaily made up his little bundle, and pointed with his finger to the mountain tops as the last refuge of liberty.

The letter of Dauxion Lavaysse and pamphlet of H. Henry had acquainted us sufficiently with the atrocious designs of the French; when, by an almost miraculous interposition of that divine providence which always aids the weak and the oppressed, and defeats the projects of the wicked at the very moment when their success appears most certain, Franco Médina, one of the French emissaries, fell into our hands. The secret instructions* of the minister of marine and the colonies, which he had with him, furnished the most incontestible proof of the perfidy of the French cabinet with respect to the people of Hayti.

Henry, whose paternal solicitude extends equally to all the Haytians in general, those of the South-west no less than those of the North-west, caused these secret instructions of M. Malouet to his three emissaries,

---

* See Appendix C. No. 1. page xxxiii.

Dauxion Lavaysse, Médina, and Dravermann, to be printed, to give them all possible publicity, and declare to the Haytians, the projects of their enemies. Henry accompanied these instructions by his proclamation of the 11th of November 1814, announcing the arrest of the French spy Franco Médina.

The king next repaired to the capital along with his court to attend a TE DEUM and thanksgiving to the ALMIGHTY for his divine mercy in thus fully unmasking the guilty projects of our inveterate enemies.

Médina was present at this TE DEUM: he was placed standing on a bench, so that his face might be seen by the people and the troops; and whilst we were addressing hymns of gratitude to The ETERNAL, he was suffering the penalty of his crimes. He heard the instructions of which he was the bearer, together with the letter of Dauxion Lavaysse, the pamphlet of H. Henry, and the replies to them, read aloud to the people. After the TE DEUM, printed copies of these documents were distributed to the army and the people.

Let any one figure to himself the situation of this spy, in the midst of a vast crowd, surrounded by an host of warriors who regarded him as a wild and curious savage, that came to propose to them SLAVERY or DEATH, CHAINS or ANNIHILATION *even to children of six years of age!!!* Where is the country of Europe in which, thus situated, he would have escaped being torn in pieces upon any other plea than that of insanity? yet here he did not receive so much as a scratch! Say now, the French, on which side the barbarians are? those who *would exterminate a whole nation for wishing to be free,* or those whose humanity* led them to spare the life

* I employ the term *humanity,* though not perhaps strictly appropriate, for such a feeling cannot exist towards a *spy:* but it is always painful to shed human blood, and we were desirous of

of a wretch whom they would have been justified in putting to death as a spy.

Meanwhile our whole attention was given to the transactions in the South-west. Notwithstanding our conviction that the mass of Haytians in this district never would consent to renounce their independence, we were not without some uneasiness respecting the machinations of the French and their adherents, who might by their perfidious counsels draw the people into some false step. Our fears, alas! were but too well founded, since Pétion was at this very time bartering away the civil and political rights of the people with a vile *spy*.

In this state of affairs we were informed that Dauxion Lavaysse, one of Médina's accomplices, had reached Port-au-Prince, where he had been received with every military honour. At this intelligence we became indignant.

Henry resolved to open the eyes of the Haytians of the South-west to the dangers they were incurring. The perils of the country, and the interests of the nation, obliged him to adopt expeditious measures for effecting a general reunion of the Haytians in order to repulse the common enemy, who offered us the alternative of DEATH or SLAVERY.

In vain did many persons represent to the king that since General Pétion had been so forgetful of the most sacred duty which he owed to his fellow citizens and countrymen, as not to have communicated to us the propositions which had been made to him, we ought not to acquaint him with what had taken place in the North-west. Henry replied, " *No affront which*

shewing our enemies that we arrested Medina, not for the barbarous gratification of punishing a *spy*, but from motives of self-preservation, and to prevent his doing us a manifest injury. How different is this mode of acting and reasoning from that of our enemies!

"*General Pétion can offer to me should prevent me from
discharging my duty by giving my fellow citizens the
necessary information to prevent their falling into the
snares laid by our tyrants: they are Haytians like
ourselves, and are equally my children. I should
therefore forget every thing but the obligation I am
under of studying only how to extricate them from the
impending danger.*"

Henry immediately ordered dispatches to be prepared for Port-au-Prince, and sent them off by three soldiers of the 20th regiment.

Whilst these transactions were passing in the North-west, and Henry was acquiring immortal glory by shewing himself a father to his people, and the most active defender of their rights, Pétion was wallowing in the mire, and covering himself with eternal infamy in the South-west, where he committed high treason against humanity and his country, and was guilty of a political suicide, a crime more horrible and detestable than even the murder of his sovereign with which he was already stained: he desired the enslaving, the murder, or the destruction of an entire nation.

But before I relate the proceedings in the South-west, it is important to make some preliminary observations, in order to introduce my readers to my subject: they will not forget that I write for the instruction of the great mass of my fellow citizens, too long vilified by traitors sold to the French; to refute their calumnies, enlighten public opinion, and render truth and justice triumphant.

My foreign readers will pardon the method I have adopted, and the manner of my expressing myself: in these I have adapted myself to the genius, the character, and the learning of my countrymen; of a people yet young, which has not been long enough civilized to possess the knowledge of letters. Hence, in works designed for the edification of my countrymen, I am obliged to suit my style to the level of their capacities, to use repetition, to make myself clear and intelligible to them, and to give, if I be allowed the expression, a *Haytian turn* to the grammatical structure of my language.

I write then solely for the information of the mass of my fellow-citizens. Such of them as possess more information than myself have no need of it: they know as well as myself all that has passed in Hayti: they, like myself, have before their eyes the writings of Pétion and his French accomplices; they can satisfy themselves of his perfidy, and his shameless treason against the Haytian people. If Colombel, Milcent and their fellows, feign ignorance of these matters, it is because they are themselves traitors and accomplices of Pétion, who are deeply interested in concealing the truth from their fellow-citizens, in order to mislead and replunge them in the horrors of slavery.

This digression is not irrelevant, it acquaints my foreign readers that motives directly the reverse of those which lead me to make myself clear and intelligible to my countrymen, operated in leading General Pétion to labour to render himself, in his writings, obscure and unintelligible to the people, in order to conceal the truth, and deliver them, without their knowledge, into the hands of the French.

Yes, in truth, it was the perfect knowledge Pétion possessed of the genius, the character, and the learning of the people, which induced him to employ in his writings *ambiguous phrases conveying a double meaning, equivocal words, elliptic expressions, and scientific allusions and comparisons* which have no reference to the moral and political situation of the Haytians, but which are nevertheless perfectly intelligible to his accomplices, though unintelligible to the multitude, to well-disposed readers who peruse them without reflection, and even to learned and enlightened strangers, who cannot be initiated in this infernal machiavelism, this mystery of iniquity. Pétion's diabolical plan was the same with that of the Ex-colonists, the same which they proposed employing against us: to profit by our want of knowledge, to impose upon our confidence and re-enslave us, by employing a system of perfidy and falsehood, a tissue of hypocrisy disguised in plausible language to perplex matters, entangle the unfortunate Haytians in the net and to blind them.

If on the one hand Pétion promoted the cause of the French, on the other he feared openly to appear their partizan, and commit himself too far with the people; he knew also that Henry watched his proceedings; therefore he feared to shew himself too openly; hence results the obscurity which prevails in his writings, and renders their translation* perplexed and difficult: to one page of reasoning on the Haytian side, succeeds another of reasoning on the French side, and from this amalgamation of contradictory principles and opinions, of hopes and fears which mutually repel each other, results that confusion which pervades his writings, which makes you lose sight for a moment of the thread of the conspiracy, but which you shortly recover again. This I have always observed in Petion's productions, as often as I have applied myself to their examination.

His treason is not of to-day; from the earliest dawn of the revolution he shewed himself a traitor to his country and his fellow-citizens. Though he belonged

---

* The word in the original is "*rédaction*," which the Translator thought he could not render better than above.

to the party called that of the *pompons blancs*,* and, as such, served under Colonel Mauduit,† he changed sides, and enlisted himself under the banners of the emigrant great planters, whom, as a member of the *pompons blancs*, he was pledged to oppose. Again we have seen him betray Gen. Touissant, accompany Rigaud in his flight to France, and return again, with the expedition under Leclerc, to make war upon his fellow-citizens; we have seen him, in the war of independence become a Haytian against his will, in order to escape the death which menaced him: we have seen him betray the Emperor Dessalines, plot the death of his chief and benefactor, kindle the flames of

---

* Among the numerous conflicting parties in St. Domingo during the first revolution was one, distinguished by the appellation of *pompons blancs*, from the white feather which they wore in their hats as a symbol, or avowed signal of the *royal*, in opposition to the *republican* party which wore the national cockade—as we learn from Bryan Edwards' " Historical Survey of the French " Colony in St. Domingo" (a work which exhibits a very partial, and, in many respects, a very erroneous view of the revolution there) and from the Report on the troubles in St. Domingo, published by order of the national convention in France.—It appears from this report that the members of this party acted a conspicuous part in that dreadful struggle.

From what can be collected respecting the principles of the *pompons blancs* they seem to have been opposed equally to the aristocratic party (that of the opulent planters) and that of *les petits blancs* or *white mob*, and they were at one time acting in concert with the government to oppose the excesses of both, and maintain public order.—*Translator.*

† This unfortunate officer whom even Bryan Edwards allows to have been " a man of talents, brave, active, and enterprising," fell a victim to the bigotry of the Whites and the fury of the republicans, and was massacred with circumstances of peculiar horror by the *white* troops of his own regiment.—*Translator.*

civil war, and disunite the territory and population of his country solely for the furtherance of his own ambitious projects: we have seen him successively destroy all the senators and generals his companions in arms, who had served as footstools for him to attain to power: even Rigaud his former chieftain and accomplice, he did not escape his perfidy and vengeance: we have seen him use all his machiavelian art to excite civil war, and make the blood of his fellow-citizens flow in torrents: we have seen him enter into criminal leagues with the French, correspond with Ferrand at St. Domingo,* receive Liot at Port-au-Prince, and send Tapiau* to France to negociate with Bonaparte; we have seen him, when Europe was in arms against France, and the navy of England covered the seas, afraid to declare openly in favour of the French, lest he should bring down upon himself the forces of England in conjunction with ours; hence he has been hitherto obliged to conspire the ruin of his country secretly and in obscurity.

We shall soon see the vile plots of this guilty wretch exposed; we shall behold this fierce republican, this angel of mercy, this father of his country, as Colombel and Milcent style him, prostrate before a vile spy, conspiring against the state, and incurring the guilt of high treason.

Pétion was incapable of seeing, in the restoration of Louis xviii. any thing but a favourable opportunity for executing his design of bringing Hayti back beneath the yoke of France.

Europe was at peace; he had nothing more to apprehend from the English, he could communicate freely with France, and strengthen himself, if necessary, with her forces; he beheld then with joy the

* Appendix C. No. 2. page xli.

arrival at Jamaica of the French envoys, who came to facilitate the means of accomplishing his purpose.

Pétion and the French were already agreed on the principal point, namely, the return of Hayti under the dominion of France, but they differed on some other points, as well as with respect to the means of execution. The Minister Malouet and the Ex-colonists desired that as soon as the act of independence was repealed, slavery should be instantly re-established as in 1789. Their distance from the country, twenty-five years of absence, the obstinacy of their colonial principles, their prejudices, their pride, and their avarice, would not allow them to see otherwise.

Pétion, on the contrary, who was fully acquainted with the exact state of affairs, was terrified at the danger to himself, and the impossibility of the attempt to replunge the black population into a state of slavery; he wished to have granted to the Haytians *the rights of French subjects and citizens*, and as to the restoration of slavery, that was to be gradual, without violent shocks, and with the aid of time: he saw with sorrow and uneasiness on reading the pamphlet of H. Henry, that the French had taken a wrong step, and strayed from the true road which would have led them to success. To put them into the right road again, he replied to this pamphlet by another entitled *Columbus*.* The reply was delicate, it was necessary to borrow a foreign name to speak thus, to lull suspicion to sleep, and yet gain the object he had in view.

By this publication Pétion had a double end to accomplish, the first was to prepare the people to receive the French emissaries, and to sacrifice their

---

* The pamphlet named Columbus is official; General Pétion has acknowledged it to be a government publication. See Appendix A.

independence without a murmur: to effect this he began with corrupting the public feeling, and endeavouring to revive our ancient attachment to France.

It is thus that I formed my judgment of the public feeling in Hayti, when the arrival of a delegation at Jamaica, sent by his Majesty Louis xviii. *to treat with this government, was announced. This news created no unfavourable impression among the Haytians; their eyes have been often turned to the shore to see the arrival of the deputies: honourable preparations have been made for their reception, and an electric feeling of sensibility, of regard, of prepossession, and every thing which the laws of nations hold most sacred, shot through every heart.**

Thus did he mislead public feeling. His second object was to make the French acquainted with his intentions, and demonstrate to them the error of the step they had taken, and that it was impossible, dangerous, and contrary to the interests of France, to precipitate the restoration of *slavery:* he proceeds as follows: " *This expectation has been hitherto disappointed, and I regret it after the impression made by the writing of M. H. Henry.*" " *In that I have seen,*" says he, " *an act little calculated to conciliate their minds, more especially under existing circumstances.*"† It is in this publication, a *chef-d'œuvre* of treachery on the part of Pétion under the assumed name of Columbus, that he traced out for the French and the Ex-colonists, the line of conduct they ought to pursue: through fear of their straying from it Pétion took them, as it may be said, by the hand, initiated them in his infernal policy, and gave them such counsel as none but the genius of evil could invent, to replunge his

---

* Appendix A. page 2. † Appendix A. page 3.

fellow citizens and brethren insensibly into the horrors of slavery.

"You do not possess," said Pétion to them, "you do not possess a thorough acquaintance with the true state of our present affairs; you cannot have a certain omniscience of all that has passed, after a long series of years of absence, and the interruption of two thousand leagues from the country: you should then begin by learning from the bottom all you have to do, in order that you may not be deceived; otherwise you will be perpetually subject to commit great errors, and will apply remedies often worse than bad, as has uniformly been the case with the French government through the whole course of the revolution of the colonies, especially during the expedition of Leclerc. If you had not been so precipitate in adopting hostile and premature measures; had you used the precaution to display frankness and kindness, to avoid with diligence hatred and prejudice, and above all every idea of slavery; had you not burned, hung, drowned, and torn the indigénes to pieces by dogs, you would have succeeded in bringing back the ancient order of things by degrees: trust then at the present day to my long experience: leave to me the power of acting and employing the most suitable measures to bring the Haytians back beneath the dominion of France: be satisfied with this; and for the present, suffer the indigénes to enjoy liberty provisionally."

Remark, that in order to make himself more intelligible to the French emissaries, Pétion employed the word OMNISCIENCE, *a term used by theologians to express the infinite knowledge of God*, while at the same time he rendered himself obscure and unintelligible to the multitude who could not possess sufficient erudition to comprehend the force of scientific terms. All those with which he has interlarded the work I am analyzing, of *political crises, be wise, be united, let us have confidence in ourselves, in the justice of our cause,* &c. &c. are introduced solely for the purpose of perplexing the meaning, and rendering it unintelligible to the people, who were not sufficiently enlightened or discerning to see that Pétion was bought by the French, publicly, and even by writing. Unfortunate Haytians of the South-west! my brethren! had it not been for the energy and the patriotism of the King of Hayti, for the genius of this great man who has saved the people, and has on this account become an object of hatred to the French and their adherents, you would not have known the depth of Pétion's wickedness, till you found yourselves again under the chains of the French: yes! you would have been enlightened only by the flames of the piles, since you were unable to see in his writings and in his conduct, that he was no more a Haytian but a Frenchman, that you were sold, and that he had nothing more to do than to deliver you up to your butchers, and to punishment!

Throughout the whole of the writing of Columbus, the word *independence* was not once noticed, a corroborating proof that it was sacrificed, and put out of the question.

To sum up the whole, in the month of September, 1814, Pétion desired,

1st. The reunion of Hayti with France as a French colony.

2d. That the Haytians should enjoy the rights of French subjects and citizens.

3d. And the French desired the restoration of the antient *regime,* the prejudices of colour, and slavery, as in 1789.

We had left Dauxion Lavaysse at Jamaica on the 1st of October, preparing for his departure for Port-au-

Prince; he had at that time received Pétion's reply*
to his letter of the 6th of September.

In this letter Dauxion had introduced a monologue insulting to Pétion, and the whole nation; speaking of Louis xviii. he put these words in his mouth; " *he will extend to us the rights of French subjects and citizens; which is undoubtedly better than to be treated as barbarous savages, or hunted as Maroon negroes.*"† On the 24th of September, Pétion replied to Dauxion Lavaysse, and in return for his insults invites him to Port-au-Prince, where " *your Excellency,*" speaking of a spy, " *will experience that politeness, attention, and respect which is due to your person, and the distinguished character you bear.*"‡ Petion subjoined to his letter the pamphlet of Columbus, to enlighten Dauxion Lavaysse, and direct his conduct. Colombel and Milcent answer me? Had Pétion your chief, he to whom you have as it were decreed the honours of an apotheosis, and whom you have all but deified by your base and silly adulation, had Pétion, I say, no duties to fulfil on the receipt of the letter from Dauxion Lavaysse? The country was threatened with invasion, and was on the point of becoming the theatre of a destructive and barbarous war: the liberty and independence of the Haytians was about to be attacked anew by their implacable enemy: the nation had been abused and insulted, it ought to be *treated like barbarous savages and hunted like Maroon negroes:* the first magistrate of the republic, the centinel placed to defend the liberty, the independence, and the rights of the Haytian people, ought not he to display his just indignation? Ought not his patriotism and his prudence, alarmed for the fate of his fellow citizens, to lead him to adopt every

---

* Appendix B. No. 2, p. xvi. † Appendix B. No. 1, p. xv.
‡ Appendix B. No. 2, page xvii.

possible measure for the security and welfare of the public, and to avert from his country the disasters which threatened it? Should he have suffered an enemy of his country, a vile spy, to presume to insult and outrage his government and fellow citizens before his face? Should he have tolerated this daring affront? What do I say? He has even done more; after having in the most respectful manner invited this enemy of his country to Port-au-Prince, he has received and lodged him in the best house in the town; he has paid this base spy the same honours as those shewn to accredited ambassadors; he has plotted with him the subversion of the state, the slavery of the blacks, the ruin and destruction of his fellow citizens. Even after the discovery of their horrible plot, he made humiliating and disgraceful propositions to France which he was instantly forced to retract. After loading his accomplice with presents and kindness, did he not favour his flight? Did he not charge him to follow up in France the execution of their criminal projects? Colombel and Milcent! vile republicans! you must admit this, the force of truth drags this acknowledgement from you, confess then with me, that your abortive republic was governed by a magistrate *as faithful as he was honourable!!!*

Early in November, Dauxion Lavaysse repaired to Port-au-Prince, pursuant to the invitation he had received from Pétion. This spy arrived upon ground which had been prepared for him by his accomplice; he then possessed a thorough knowledge of the state of affairs, he could not err or run any risk: he had the head of the government for his protector, his guide, and accomplice; he could in perfect safety push his daring enterprise as far as he wished; they could understand each other, speak, write and barter away the Haytians by *half a word*, and before their very eyes, without fear of betraying and compromising themselves, as a reference to the correspondence they then had will readily prove.*

To mask this infernal conspiracy, they had entrenched themselves in diplomatic forms; it was the more easily to blind the eyes of the people towards their horrible attempts, that after having come to a thorough understanding in their private meetings, they took a fancy to negociate by writing; it was easy for them by using ambiguous phrases, and words previously agreed upon, to explain and understand one another in points adopted and discussed in secret in the cabinet.

Thus Pétion, by a crime hitherto unexampled in the annals of nations, sold the Haytians by his correspondence even before their faces, at the very moment of his pretending to defend their cause, and maintain their rights. What frightful depravity! what base hypocrisy!

In the course of time I gave the details of this conspiracy in one of my publications, entitled "*The cry of conscience.*" In an essay destined, like this, to furnish materials for a history of Hayti, I conceive myself bound to transmit facts of so much importance to posterity; happy, far happier than we have been, in not having witnessed crimes so horrible as those which have stained and disgraced our national character.

I resume my narrative.

On the 9th of November, Dauxion Lavaysse officially required Pétion to "*restore the French colony in "the Island of Hayti, and to constitute himself, with the "principal officers, president and members of a provisional "government of Hayti, in the name of his Majesty Louis "xviii.*"† In the same note this *spy* urged Pétion to

---

* Appendix B.   † Appendix B. No. 3. page xviii.

use his influence *to prepare the people to surrender their liberty and independence*; nay, he carried his audacity so far as to declare that such of the Haytians as would not submit to become slaves again should be sent to the *Isle of* RATAU,* *as violent and incorrigible men, whose prejudices were incompatible* with the tranquillity of the colony: even before their arrest he pronounced their death, and the nature of their punishment.

To whom would this vile brigand have dared to make such propositions, but to the partner of his guilt? To propose the restoration of the French colony in Hayti, was it not to demand the repeal of the Act of Independence? Nevertheless nothing was more clear. Could the president of the republic negociate for an instant upon such a basis? Ought he to allow of such propositions? Had he a right to do so? Surely not: he neither had, nor could have it: Pétion betrayed the republic. Here then is a solution of his conduct.

To this shameful note Pétion replied on the 12th of November.† He foreswore himself, violated the act of independence and the constitution, insulted the sovereignty of the people, and began by letter to barter away the liberty and independence of Hayti. He told Dauxion Lavaysse *that he was compelled to be an Haytian in despite of himself, from a necessity which left him no choice of acting differently.* And note well that *from the 6th of September to the 20th of November,* the day on which the conspiracy was discovered, Pétion had, in all his letters, studiously omitted the word INDEPENDENCE, a corroborating proof that he had already renounced this guarantee of our rights and existence, which we had purchased at the price of so much blood. Such a

---

* RATAU an expression invented by M. Malouet to designate *the bottom of the sea.* See Appendix, C. No. 2, page xliii.

† Appendix B. No. 4, page xx.

forgetfulness could not have arisen from any other source than treason. We have seen him on the contrary, soliciting from Dauxion Lavaysse, *the rights of a French subject and citizen for himself.* We have seen him demanding *a confirmation of power in his hands, an oblivion of the past, and favours from the French monarch.* We have seen him tell this spy that they were *not far from coming to a mutual understanding,* but that for this purpose they must accede to his demands: *for, if it be necessary to reduce the blacks to slavery again, the attempt will occasion a sudden and general revolution, in which his personal security, and even his life would be endangered, and this would be of no advantage to the political system they wished him to pursue,* that namely of M. Malouet. Such is the amount of what I have been able to make out from a close examination of the correspondence of Pétion with Dauxion Lavaysse, sometimes only implied, but often distinctly and explicitly expressed.

Meanwhile the people and the troops at Port-au-Prince murmured, and were indignant at the reception Pétion gave to a Frenchman, who traversed the streets and the town without molestation, inspected the troops on parade, and insulted them. A thousand times would they have immolated this enemy of their country, but for the restraints of discipline.

The English and American merchants, established at Port-au-Prince, enraged at these proceedings, circulated rumours which thwarted the projects of Pétion and this *spy.*

On the 19th of November Dauxion Lavaysse wrote an insulting letter to Pétion, filled with invectives against the strangers,* while he lauded Pétion himself up to the skies, and called him *Frenchman* and *fellow*

---

* Appendix B. No. 5, page xxiv.

countryman. "*We are all French,*" said he to Pétion, "*may then the august name of* BOURBON *be the signal "for our rallying: may the wisdom and firmness with "which you have so long governed this country amid the "revolutionary tempests, yet be her compass and her "anchor. May France and her excellent monarch "owe the possession of this country not to compulsion, "but to the genuine French feelings and the loyalty of "its inhabitants. Your excellency is worthy of accom-"plishing this great work. May you be entitled to the "gratitude of your sovereign and your countrymen of "both hemispheres.*"*

Pétion replied to this letter on the morning of the 20th of November,† and by his silence with respect to the insults and slanders of this base *spy*, he tacitly acquiesced in them.

The 21st was the day fixed on by Pétion for the completion of his projects, but in the afternoon of Sunday the 20th he received by express from the king the printed instructions of the minister Malouet‡ to his three emissaries, together with the resolution of the general council of the nation, and the royal proclamation of the 11th of November.

They say that on the perusal of these documents Pétion and Dauxion Lavaysse were struck as with a thunder-bolt: they were completely disconcerted, and their plots unmasked: Dauxion Lavaysse fainted away, and Pétion trembled at the danger in which his treachery had involved him. Had not his heart been corrupted beyond the possibility of change, his sentiments would have altered from that day forward. Seeing his designs unmasked by the king of Hayti, and laid open to the world through the medium of the press, he sup-

---

* Appendix B. No. 5, page xxvi.   † Appendix B. No. 6, p. xxvi.
‡ Appendix C. No. 1, page xxxiii.

pressed from the people a knowledge of Malouet's instructions, and adjourned the meeting of the generals, which was to have taken place on the 21st, to the 27th of November, for the purpose of gaining time for reconsidering his plans and adopting new measures.

On the 27th, notwithstanding his having been for seven days in possession of the most incontestible proofs of Dauxion Lavaysse's being in every sense of the word a *spy*, unprovided with any credentials whatever—on the 27th I say, Pétion had still the assurance to submit, to the assembled magistrates, Dauxion Lavaysse's principal proposition, namely *the abolition of their independence, and the formation of a provisional government in the name of his Majesty Louis* xviii. He wished to complete the attempt at any price; he imposed on the good faith of the generals and magistrates, and defeated their real intentions: he demanded for the Haytians from Louis xviii. *only the independence of their rights,* that is the *rights of French subjects and citizens,* instead of demanding, as they designed, and doubtless believed he had, *the independence of Hayti*. Thus he renounced, by an equivocation, *the real independence,* while he preserved only its *shadow*; that is to say, the *rights of French subjects and citizens,* for this is in fact what Pétion means by *the independence of their rights.*

After having thus shamefully deceived the generals and magistrates of the republic, by making them renounce the *independence of Hayti*, he made them offer to establish the basis of an *indemnity* which he engaged they should pay with every security which might be required: he offered France an exclusive trade as in 1789, which he said *would promote the welfare* of both countries, and he concluded this disgraceful proceeding by entreating Dauxion Lavaysse to support his propositions by his interest with his Majesty Louis

xviii. and assuring him he was without any feeling *of animosity or prejudice against France.**

Thus the long sufferings of the Haytians, the cruelties they had sustained from the French, all, all was unable to make the slightest impression on Pétion's heart, *he was without any feeling of animosity or prejudice** against a nation which had, not above twelve years since, *burned, hung, drowned and torn in pieces by blood hounds*, his brethren and his countrymen. The commerce of 1789, SLAVERY and the SLAVE TRADE, constituted, according to him, the *welfare of both countries*; and he had at the same time Malouet's secret instructions in his pocket; he knew the French cabinet desired the re-establishment of SLAVERY, and dared even to avow it. I ask then every impartial observer whether there can be any person more decidedly a Frenchman, or more thoroughly a traitor, than this Pétion was?

After this open consummation of his guilt in the eyes of the people, and deceiving the generals and magistrates of the republic, he gave Dauxion Lavaysse his secret instructions, in which he pointed out to the French government the means to be adopted for the subjugation of the Haytians, as we shall find in the sequel. He rewarded his accomplice with some thousand dollars, and sent him away in a Haytian schooner.

Was the crime of high treason ever more glaring, or more fully proved? Was it ever attended with circumstances so abominable and disgraceful?

From the arrival of Dauxion Lavaysse at Port-au-Prince, to his first opening, one could see the thread of this perfidious conspiracy which was to knit itself by those combinations of *words* and those ambiguous modes of expression by which our tyrants reckon upon de-

---

* Appendix B. No. 7, page xxix.

ceiving our good faith, and drawing us into their snares. This system of perfidy and iniquity originates in the colonial prejudices; is founded upon our ignorance, and upon the profound contempt in which the race of blacks is held by the ex-colonists.

It is to Malouet, this Nestor of the ex-colonists, that we owe the invention of this system of falsehood and duplicity. It is he who first said that " since the word " SLAVE conveys the idea of *a man in chains*, let " the appellation of *not free* be substituted for it. Let " them purchase the *bodily labour*, the *services*, and *not* " the *moral person* of the African."*

It was by a similar sophism that the ex-colonists, in the infancy of our liberty, pretended they could blind and seduce us. Their inventive and diabolical genius perfected this system, and, in proportion as they observed our advance in knowledge, they refined upon their plans of fraud and perfidy.

Bonaparte was the first who employed this system of duplicity against us. It was he who said to us " *you are all equal before God and the republic* :"† he knew how he was blaspheming, but he deceived us, and he cared for nothing more.

In 1801 Malouet had been one of Bonaparte's counsellors, and in 1814 Pétion and Dauxion Lavaysse followed the advice, and reduced the lessons of their illustrious master to practice. First we have seen Pétion employ the scientific term *omniscience*‡ to make himself understood by Dauxion Lavaysse, and render himself unintelligible to the multitude; next we have found Dauxion Lavaysse demanding of his accomplice *to restore the French colony in the island of Hayti*,¶

---

* Vol. iv. page 23, of his Memoirs.

† See his proclamation in the note at page 26.

‡ Appendix A. page ii.   ¶ Appendix B. No. 3, page xvii.

instead of purely and simply demanding the *abolition of the independence, and the re-establishment of the French colony in its original state*, which was what he wished and meant: for the word *restore* conveys the common idea of *repairing* and *re-establishing* the state, while his real design was to *overthrow* and *destroy it*. After this we have seen Pétion demanding for the Haytians the *independence of their rights*, while it would have been so simple and natural to demand the *independence of Hayti*: but Pétion was deceiving and abusing the people, and in using this ambiguous phraseology he really demanded nothing more than *the rights of French subjects and citizens*, whilst he made the people, the generals, and the magistrates believe, that he had demanded the independence of Hayti. Thus he renounced the independence of the country, *a real independence*, for one that was *merely fictitious*, an *independence of rights*; or, to express myself in clear and precise terms, Pétion wished the sovereignty of the country to belong to France, but that he should retain the internal administration, and that the people should enjoy *the rights of French citizens and subjects*, which would have gradually conducted us either to a total extermination, or to the same horrors which we had to encounter in order to establish our liberty and independence.

After such facts, such crimes, and a treason so notorious, what judgement will both contemporaries and posterity pass upon the generals and magistrates of the republic for omitting to depose Pétion, and put him on his trial for his crimes and treason, substantiated by his public acts and official documents under his own sign manual? What opinion will be formed of these generals and magistrates who suffered themselves to be so shamefully deceived? Will they be considered as traitors, or as persons of weak understanding? Let them shew us in ancient or modern history, any nation, or even any horde of the most uncivilized savages which was content to disgrace itself by suffering its government to continue in the hands of such a chief, after a full discovery of his plots and treasons! Let us run over the history of the world, so fertile in examples of crimes and enormities, where in it shall we find the head of a nation, or even of the most savage banditti, willing to conspire with the enemies of his country for the slavery and destruction of his fellow citizens? Cataline, Cromwell, and Robespierre sought to attain the chief power, but never desired to reduce their country beneath a foreign yoke, to plunge their fellow-citizens into slavery, and involve them in certain destruction.

Brave Coriolanus! unfortunate Barnevelt! and thou too generous Essex! you lost your heads on mere suspicion! for the error of a moment!—while Pétion died in his bed! The ashes of this monster have been accompanied by the tears and regrets of his fellow citizens! O! how humbled do I feel while tracing these lines! Haytians! shall we then be reserved to afford the world in our regeneration the most striking contrasts? On the same side with all that is great and honourable, must our eyes behold that which is most base and vile?

The treason of Pétion could not produce its effect; but his perfidious plots occasioned nevertheless a manifest injury to the Haytians; they strengthened the system of duplicity and falsehood pursued by the ex-colonists, who mislead anew public opinion in France. They have strengthened them in their guilty belief that they can succeed in deceiving us by adopting a system of treachery, and the use of ambiguous words and phrases, and to such a height has their machiavelianism with regard to us attained, that in order to comprehend them we must construct a perfectly new vocabulary: formerly *not free* was the synonyme of *slave*, this was sufficiently intelligible; but at the present day its meaning is quite the reverse: to *restore* signifies to *destroy*; *benevolence* is synonymous with *perfidy*; *candour* with *treachery*; *truth* with *falsehood*; *virtue* with *vice*; *civilization* with *ignorance*; *morality* with *corruption*; ah! even *religion! religion!* given to mortals to console them in their afflictions, that pure source of morality whence flows every thing good and every thing virtuous, *religion* herself is become in the hands of these perverse men an engine of guilt and seduction.

It is according to such interpretations, that those very persons who shew us frankness and goodwill, may presently tell us that France does not want to conquer St. Domingo, but that she ought to labour to give birth to *civilization* and *morality* there; together with a new order of things, more conformable to nature, to justice, and to humanity! It is in this sense that they count upon sending out priests to Hayti, to seduce and corrupt the population; as though we were so ignorant as not to know that nations may be conquered as well, and even better, by civilization, persuasion and seduction, than by force of arms.

The better to accomplish his designs, Pétion sent to France, along with Dauxion Lavaysse, a Frenchman named Pradére, who was in his confidence, and the traitor Colombel, the same whom I am refuting, a creole of the mountain of Rochelois, a Haytian of a complexion the nearest to white, but a Frenchman in principle, a pupil of Pétion's and his private secretary, a tool of the French, and initiated into all their guilty projects, an implacable foe to the liberty of the Blacks and the independence of the country. This base renegado, and the Frenchman Pradére, were sent expressly to support the propositions made to Dauxion Lavaysse, and to give such information respecting the situation of the interior of the country, as the French cabinet might have need of. *

At the same time that Pétion dispatched his secret agents to the French government, in order to mask his true designs, he sent to London one Garbage, likewise his secretary, and Méronné, his nephew: the first died in England, and the second returned to Hayti, where he fell into a state of idiotism.

Immediately after the departure of Dauxion Lavaysse, Pétion reflected on the enormity of the attempts he had been guilty of towards the Haytian people.— These people, whom it was impossible to deceive for an instant by terms of science and ambiguous expressions beyond their comprehension, were, upon learning the resolution of the general council of the nation, and the arrest of Franco Médina, the accomplice of Dauxion Lavaysse, ready to rise and burn the town of Port-au-Prince.

Pétion then saw how much he had erred, notwithstanding his thorough knowledge of the country, and how erroneous an estimate he had formed of the public feeling of the Haytians: he saw the imminent danger he would have incurred, had he had time to proclaim the authority of Louis xviii. at Port-au-Prince, as he had proposed before the discovery of the conspiracy: he saw that he would have been lost beyond recovery, since the people would have risen in a body to assert their rights, their liberty, and their independence.— This holy, generous and magnanimous insurrection, would have instantly changed the war from a civil to a national one; the Haytians of the North-west would

* See in Appendix C. No. 3, page xlvii. an extract from the *Columbian*, a New York paper, of the 19th of November, 1816, an article inserted under the direction of Pétion.

have flown to the aid, and into the arms, of their brethren and countrymen of the South-west. And could Pétion and a few vile satellites, partisans of the French, ranged under the white flag, fighting for slavery and the subjection of their country, could they have resisted a whole people?—*an hundred thousand* warriors, rallied beneath their national colours, fighting in defence of their rights, their lives, and their property, for the emancipation of their country, beneath the standards of liberty and independence? Had he *fifty thousand* French in his ranks, he would be conquered in the end and driven into the sea.

In this, as in a multitude of other instances, Pétion owed his safety to the heroism of the King of Hayti; to his energy, his patriotism, and his entire devotion to the cause of the Haytian people. His faithful attachment to them inspired him with alarm on account of the dangers to which his fellow citizens of the South might be exposed, and his frankness of character led him to place before their eyes their true interests, at that important crisis: not, indeed, that the danger he apprehended was real. It was an evil, formidable in imagination, but too great and obvious to be realized; for what Haytian chieftain, however powerful, could possibly induce the population of Hayti to resign their liberty and independence, in order to submit again to the yoke of slavery and of France. It is a thing morally and physically impossible. Equally hopeless will be every attempt that the Ex-colonists may suggest to the French government to divide, to deceive, to mislead, or to ensnare us. It is impossible that any such insidious expedients should succeed, for their object is, in its nature, impracticable; and, if the French government persists in following the counsels and the plans of the Ex-colonists, disappointment and disgrace will ever be, as they have hitherto always been, the results; and all the armed expeditions which France can send against Hayti, whether directed against the North-west or the South-west, can produce no other effect than a *national war:* and I can boldly predict, that France will reap no other fruit from it than she has already done from Bonaparte's famous expedition under the Leclercs and the Rochambeaus!!!

The sun of Hayti continues the same, its climate and temperature are unaltered, and her inhabitants possess far more moral and physical powers of resistance than they did then!

Pétion saw then the imminent danger into which his treachery was on the brink of plunging him, had not the events of the North opened his eyes, and disclosed to him the abyss about to engulph him. In order to justify in the eyes of the people his conduct in having negociated with a vile spy and favoured his flight, he felt the necessity of publishing his correspondence with Dauxion Lavaysse, which I have analysed, and which he accompanied by his proclamation* of the 3d of December, a *chef-d'œuvre* of duplicity and absurdity: his art being to shew the fair side of the picture, in order to mask his guilt and treachery.† It was necessary to deceive the people, and turn their attention from this shameful transaction; Pétion, therefore, represented this as an epoch which ought to be ever memorable in the annals of the republic. He had sacrificed the *independence of Hayti* for the *independence of rights,* and he told the people that "*without independence there was no safety, no security for our regeneration*; he had been so base as to render the

---

* Appendix B, No. 9, page xxx.

† I know not what could be retrenched in printing these documents, but from what appears we may judge of the remainder.— See Appendix B. page xiii.

people tributary, and said *it was a generous action which ennobled them*; and at the very moment he was disgracing the people and covering them with infamy, he told them, *you have done what you ought*; he sold his country, his brethren, and fellow-citizens to the French, he already alienated their property, yet he told them, *the right of arms has placed the country in your hands, it is your property*. In place of arresting Dauxion Lavaysse as a spy, as his duty, the safety of the state, and the laws of nations obliged him, he spoke of *his character and the law of nations*, as if there was any *law of nations* for *spies:* but in his confusion he stammered, and sung out his recantation as loud as he could. I will ask of Colombel and Milcent if, according to the principles of natural law and that of nations, *the welfare of the people is the supreme law*, how could Pétion prefer the welfare of a spy, to that of the nation? How could he violate the laws of nations, and his most sacred duties, to save a spy, to the injury of his country and of the safety of the people?

Pétion, on the departure of Dauxion Lavaysse, disguised his treason under a specious pretext, he spoke of nothing but the law of nations, he had nothing in his mouth but the respect due to the law of nations, and this because he had himself violated it together with the most sacred of his duties. But what then is the law of nations?—from what source is it derived?—what are its limits?—are not its rules written and graven in the heart of man? Since my adversaries have not thought proper to define it, in order to deprive them in future of the power of deceiving the people again by cloaking their treason beneath the mantle of this sacred law, I will take upon myself the task of discharging this duty. I again repeat that it is for the mass of my countrymen that I write, let me be permitted to enlighten them.

The law of nations is nothing more than the natural law, *do not to others that which thou wouldest not wish to have done to thyself*; here is its invariable foundation, and principle: but as the whole human race forms an universal society, distributed into independent nations who have not the power of imposing laws upon each other, it was necessary, for the maintenance of an indispensible commerce between them, to establish certain *compacts* either *expressed* or *understood* which should serve as reciprocal laws; these *compacts* are founded on natural law, and owe their existence to the general interests of all nations. Now both natural law, the general interests of nations, and the example of every age, agree not only in the necessity of embassies, but also, in granting to every public minister three sorts of prerogatives. 1st. *To be received and recognized as such:* 2dly. *To enjoy a perfect security not only for himself but his suite*; and 3dly. *to have those honours and distinctions paid to him which are due to his character and to the sovereign who sends him.*

Three legitimate causes may likewise give a right of refusing an ambassador or other envoy; the first derived from *the person who sends him*; the second from *the person of the minister himself*; and the third from *the nature of his mission.*

"It is not," say the most celebrated writers on the subject, "contrary to the law of nations to refuse "a minister who comes from an enemy in arms against "us, or from a prince whom there is reason to sus- "pect of treachery."

The Dutch refused to receive an envoy from the King of Spain, till he had recognized them as a free and independent republic. The United-States of America adopted the same principle with respect to England. The King of Hayti does the same towards France, and I dare to hope his government never will depart from this principle, on which the salvation of Hayti depends. We can equally refuse a minister who has formerly been our subject, hence with still greater justice should the Haytians refuse the Ex-colonists who had been their masters; and when the French cabinet last sent us, as select commissioners, men who were all Ex-colonists, accompanied by some refugee Haytians to signify to us the pleasure of the King of France, it was a twofold and direct insult offered to the Haytian people and its government, since the orders of the French government were commnuicated to us through men heretofore our masters, to whom we might object on this account, and through Haytian subjects whom we might reclaim and punish as traitors and deserters.

Such a choice was not rashly made by M. le Viscomte du Bouchage; those who received and welcomed these commissioners and their refugee companions have partaken largely of that insult.

But I antcipate the order of time.

A public envoy then may be refused who entertains any rancour against us; one who is taken from the dregs of the people, or is of a notoriously bad and profligate character, an adventurer, cheat, or impostor; in short an envoy who comes to protest against our rights and proceedings, or is commissioned to offer degrading propositions, to foment disturbances in the sate or do us any manifest injury. We cannot be said to violate the laws of nations with respect to such a person when we refuse to admit him into the country, and send him back on reaching the frontiers.

An envoy likewise loses his rights by violating his official character, since the same law of nations which gives security to the foreign minister, should likewise guarantee the sovereign or government of the country against any designs he might form against the person of the prince, or the authority which is recognized there. For what, again say the writers on the law of nations, what would become of kings, states, and nations if other sovereigns were at liberty to send *assassins, disturbers of the public peace, wretches capable of entering into plots against the welfare of the country,* clothed in the character of ambassadors, and enabled under this cloak to perpetrate with impunity the most heinous crimes, and to violate the most sacred duties. In such a case every sovereign is justified in arresting the envoy, and punishing him with the utmost severity that his conduct deserves. Such are the rules of the law of nations with respect to public ministers: let us now examine those for governments.

Diplomatic communications between governments are always regulated by the political situation in which they are placed. They are interrupted, relaxed or broken off, according to the good or bad understanding which subsists between the courts.

Now, at the period of the negociation in question no *political relation* could exist between the Haytian and French governments, since both countries, by the simple declaration of our Independence on the first of January, 1804, were in a state of open and declared hostility.

Hence the Haytian government could only view France as an hostile power, until she had, by a formal act or solemn treaty, recognized the independence of its own people.

The government, therefore, established by the Haytian people, possessed neither the power nor the right to alter one iota of the fundamental law of the state. It was, on the contrary, bound to maintain, defend and govern, according to the political interests of the people expressed in that law. The changes resulting from our civil dissensions, have made no change in the fundamental principles on which our respective constitutions are based.

The restoration of Louis xviii. produced no alteration in our political relations with France. They continued, as I have already observed, the same as on the first day of the declaration of our independence, and we are to this moment, in a state of open and declared hostility with France; nor, till she has recognized our independence, can she regard us in any other light than that of insurgents *equally incapable of sending or receiving a public minister.*— Hence no communication can be opened between the the two governments, till the French cabinet has first recognized our independence.

The French cabinet being unwilling to do this, and considering us as insurgents, was consequently unable to send us an accredited ambassador, since this would be a virtual recognition of our independence; for *every state or body politic which receives ambassadors, possesses an equal right of sending them.* The French cabinet being then unable to enter into a direct communication with the Haytian government can only employ *secret* and *unaccredited* emissaries, who must introduce themselves into the country under false pretences, in order to sound the people, and procure such information as is necessary to direct them in their preparations for war. Persons of this description are virtually considered as *spies*; and those who undertake so dangerous a game may, if detected, be arrested and put to death* without any violation of the laws of nations.

The French cabinet had yet another mode of pro-

---

* Such was the unhappy fate of the brave Major Andre, in the war of the American revolution: yet no one called that a violation of the law of nations!—*Translator.*

ceeding, namely, to send out commissioners to notify its orders to the government of Hayti, to return to its obedience. These, however, could not be received any more than the former, without a violation of the constitution of the state. It was this last method which the French cabinet adopted. But let me not anticipate.

Dauxion Lavaysse, as I have already shewn, was a man long and thoroughly disgraced in public opinion, and was moreover *utterly unaccredited* in *any manner whatsoever*, as the instructions of M. Malouet, the minister of marine and the colonies, prove.* These emissaries were *to appear in St. Domingo only as persons coming to make commercial arrangements, either on their own account, or that of some mercantile house. They were artfully to sound the inclinations of the chiefs, after previously learning the nature and extent of their internal resources, and the degree of influence they possess in the island. They could not sign any formal treaty, since that would be derogatory to the dignity of the king of France; but could only discuss with the chiefs a plan for the political reorganization of the colony, and the revival of the prejudices and slavery which subsisted in* 1789.* And this is precisely what Petion and Dauxion Lavaysse have done at Port-au-Prince.

According to every principle of the law of nations, I demand of Colombel and Milcent whether Pétion should have received Dauxion Lavaysse at Port-au-Prince? Since even had he been an *accredited* ambassador or envoy he had forfeited his official character, by the baseness of his mission, his own conduct, his insults and outrages: an envoy being always a minister of peace, while he was nothing more than a genuine

* See the instructions of the Minister Malouet to Dauxion Lavaysse, Medina, and Dravermann, in Appendix C. No. 1, p, xxxiii.

spy; and we are unacquainted with any law of nations which exists for such persons. It would be singular that in this republic a law of nations should exist for such culprits, and yet that it should not exist for the safety and protection of the people.

But his advocates may allege in his defence, that having once invited Dauxion Lavaysse, to Port-au-Prince, he could not do otherwise than receive him, and send him back. To this I will reply, that the first fault of the magistrate of the republic consisted in having answered insults and outrages in a manner as foolish as it was disgraceful. In this point of view then, the conduct of the first magistrate of the republic, exhibited unpardonable incapacity, want of foresight, and weakness. Ah! would to God it had been so, and that President Pétion had only erred through ignorance: but unfortunately he never has displayed in his conduct either incapacity, want of foresight, inadvertence, or weakness; his crime has always been that of high treason, with a full knowledge of the cause, and premeditation of the event.

I will again ask of my opponents, how, on the arrival of Dauxion Lavaysse at Port-au-Prince, Pétion discharged the duties of his office, and observed the regulations of the laws of nations?

Should he not, according to the usage established in diplomatic communications, have made Dauxion Lavaysse produce his credentials? Should he not, according to the uniform practice of all governments, have begun by satisfying himself that they were drawn up and addressed in the customary forms; that they contained nothing offensive in their terms, no odious and inadmissible propositions at variance with the laws of his country? Should he not, in fine, have satisfied himself whether the person sent to him had sufficient powers for entering upon a negociation so nearly affecting the interests of the state? Had Petion done his duty and studied the welfare of his country, he would have attended to the usual and indispensable formalities on the reception of a public minister: he would then have been convinced that Dauxion Lavaysse had no public character, and possessed no powers whatever, but was merely a secret emissary of the Minister Malouet, commissioned to procure information respecting the interior situation of the country; and that the French cabinet viewed him (Pétion) solely in the light of a leader of the insurgents of St. Domingo: he would not have entered into a negociation with Dauxion Lavaysse, nor would he have been exposed to the disgrace of seeing this mission of *espionnáge*, which will be an eternal source of shame and confusion to the minister who directed it, and to President Pétion for having so infamously participated in it, solemnly disavowed by his Majesty Louis xviii.*

Had Pétion not been a traitor, and had he been unwilling to put Dauxion Lavaysse to death, could he not have arrested him, to prevent his returning to France with the information desired by the French cabinet for the guidance of its operations against Hayti? Could he not have reconciled what he owed to the laws of nations and to humanity, with his most sacred duties, with the safety of the state, and the welfare of the people? Was it more humane to save the life of an individual, than to endanger the existence of a whole nation? Could he not, like the King of Hayti, have satisfied at once the laws of nations, and the safety and welfare of his subjects? Has not Franco Médina, the accomplice of Dauxion Lavaysse, been arrested and detained? Has he been able to return to France to communicate the necessary information respecting the

* Appendix F. No. 3.

state of the colony? Have we, by arresting him, violated the rights of nations, or been wanting in humanity, or in what we owe to ourselves? Who can blame us? Why has not the French cabinet claimed Franco Médina as its envoy? There is no medium or alternative in the question: it must either be the King of Hayti who has violated the laws of nations by the arrest of a *spy*, and thus securing the safety of the state and the welfare of the people; or it must be Pétion who has violated them, by favouring his flight, betraying the state, the people, and his own most sacred duties. But I check myself. I have said enough. I beg Pétion's accomplices to resolve the question. Let us now hasten to turn aside from scenes so disgraceful and afflicting, to direct our view to the North-west, to a theatre more gratifying and consolatory to the friends of liberty and independence.

We have seen that the French cabinet proposed to the people of Hayti, by its emissaries, *to choose between* SLAVERY and DEATH: never were more sanguinary and insulting propositions made to any nation upon earth! The ex-colonists published in France under the eye of his most christian majesty, *that the population of Hayti ought to be exterminated to infants of the age of six years, who were to be reserved as slaves.* These young victims might be safely allowed to live, as they could not yet have received the first impressions of liberty. It was in the bosom of a nation, old in civilization and knowledge, that such horrors were penned! It was under the sanction of the *most christian* monarch, under the censorship of *a polished* government and an *enlightened* people, that such *unchristian* propositions were printed.*

The king, indignant at such crimes and perverse-

---

* See the works of the Ex-colonists, the Drouins, de Bercy, de Charraults, &c. printed in 1814.

ness, at the hateful proposals of the French cabinet, and at the projects of guilt and destruction of the Ex-colonists, published a general plan of defence for the kingdom.

According to the principles of natural law which authorise the maintenance and defence of our rights, by means similar to those employed in their invasion, he could not have given them a better answer, or opposed to them more suitable arguments.

"The designs of our implacable enemies, says Henry, are known; they desire either to *re-enslave*, or to annihilate us: we have to fight for our liberty, our independence; we have to defend our lives, with those of our wives and children; we should employ against our enemies all the means of destruction which they mean to direct against us: we must adapt our system of defence to the nature of the attack, and to our localities, so as to bring all our force to bear, in order to defeat our tyrants."

Then, by article 1, Henry recommended to all generals commanding the several provinces and divisions of the kingdom, to keep themselves supplied from henceforward with candle-wood, made into torches, and other combustibles proper for producing a conflagration.

The 2d article directed, that, on the disembarkation of the French army, all *villages, towns, plantations, works,* and other establishments situated in the plains, should be burned to the ground, in order to deprive the enemy of every shelter from the inclemency of the climate and weather; that the whole population should retire to the mountains; that the bridges should be broken down; the banks of rivers, brooks, and lakes cut, and their waters turned over the highways; all the roads broken up and rendered impassable; the cattle and horses driven into the most inaccessible fastnesses of the mountains; carriages, carts, waggons, and every thing else, without distinction, which might be of use to the enemy, destroyed and rendered unserviceable; so that on landing they should find nothing but ruins, and a country completely laid waste, where towns, villages, and plantations formerly existed.

The 3d article directed a war of ambuscade and stratagem; to endeavour to lead the enemy's forces into the defiles of the mountains in order to engage them to advantage; to continue to exercise the troops in taking sure aim, and to direct their fire chiefly against the officers and guides; and never to fire a shot from an ambuscade without killing an enemy; to endeavour to do them all possible mischief, with the least possible injury to themselves; to watch their motions closely; to lay snare upon snare for them; to seize promptly upon every opportunity of surprising them; to harass them continually; to disturb their rest, especially by night; to keep them in a state of perpetual alarm; and, when, exhausted by useless fatigue and watching, they should have relaxed the vigilance of their defence, to fall suddenly upon their camp with ten times their force, and put them all to the sword. The Haytian troops were also to strive to weaken the enemy's force by cutting off their convoys of stores and provisions, &c.; all places adapted for ambuscades were to be marked out beforehand, and every one was to know the post assigned to him in battle.

The 4th and 5th articles directed, that all the militia of the kingdom should be formed into battalions and squadrons of *Royal Dahomets*.* Districts of the first rank to furnish, six battalions and one squadron; those of the second rank, four battalions and one squadron; and those of the third rank, three battalions.

* So named from the kingdom of Dahomy in Africa.—*Trans.*

Of the troops thus organised, the infantry were to fight at the foot of the mountains, in the entrance of ravines and defiles in ambuscade; while the cavalry were to penetrate into the plains to watch the motions of the enemy, fall upon their stragglers, and intercept their couriers.

The army of the line was to defend the forts, and form moveable columns to cover all points threatened or attacked by the enemy.

The 6th article recommended a concert of operations among the troops of every description, and to concert among themselves in order to obtain more complete success.

The 7th article directed centinels to be stationed on the most elevated spots, and loftiest trees, to discover the enemy's manœuvres, and, when discovered, to blow trumpets, and sound the *cararou*, which is to be repeated from mountain to mountain, so as instantaneously to announce the presence of the enemy to a distance of upwards of ten leagues round.

The 9th article stated, that as the bloody struggle on which the Haytians were entering was *a war of extermination*, his majesty ordered and directed all generals and officers, *not to give any quarter* to the prisoners whom the fortune of war should place in their power, whatever be their rank, age, or sex, but to put them to immediate death without the smallest pity or remorse; that it was a sacred duty imposed upon them to exert every means in their power to destroy and exterminate their enemies, in order to secure the triumph of the Haytian cause, and the security of their country.

The 12th article confirmed the arrangements of the 9th. All the generals and other officers were to inspire the nation with a proper sense of its dearest interests, and convince the Haytians individually of the necessity of rallying all their forces for the defence of the common cause, and that they should not hesitate to employ every imaginable method of destruction, even those forbidden by the laws of nations, for the purpose of exterminating an enemy who would replunge them into slavery: that every kind of punishment was allowable, since there did not exist another instance of a people situated like the Haytians. The generals and commandants should cherish throughout the nation a spirit of animosity against these tyrants, these base supporters of slavery; they should caution the people against the treachery of these sanguinary monsters, who will not fail to employ, according to their habitual practice, their favourite weapons of fraud and artifice, to mislead the people by fair speeches and treacherous proclamations as before, especially in the expedition of Leclerc.

By the 13th article, it was recommended to the aforesaid generals and officers, to encourage the highest degree of enthusiasm among the Haytians, and to shew them how little they need fear the enemy they were about to engage; and to demonstrate this to them in the plainest manner, said Henry, " you have only to remind " them of the glorious exploits performed in the war of " our independence; that then, when three-fourths of the " population and army of Hayti had submitted to the " French, the remaining fourth, this handful of heroes, " reduced to fight man for man, and sometimes without " other weapons than the stones they met with, made " head and baffled all the efforts of the French."

" That, in the last place, when the Haytians had " risen unanimously, they had been reduced to the " necessity of employing pikes, old arms corroded with " rust, and iron hoops in place of swords, to fight with: " at a time, when they were even obliged to depend " upon the supplies of arms and ammunition taken "from their slain enemies on the field of battle, to destroy the survivors, they succeeded in expelling these tyrants from their country; whereas, at the present day, they were abundantly supplied with arms of every description, &c. &c.; that the whole nation had but one and the same wish, that of exterminating their enemies; hence the contest could not turn out otherwise than to their advantage: that it mattered little how numerous the forces of the enemy were; the Haytians would make no account of their numbers, the more there were, the more they would kill."

Immediately after the publication of the general plan of defence of the kingdom, all the regiments of the line were made up to their full complement, and the whole of the population capable of bearing arms, was organized into an efficient militia; all the old and unserviceable arms were condemned, and replaced by new ones from the royal magazines.

Our arsenals were likewise filled with all kinds of warlike stores, and government made immense purchases to the amount of many millions of dollars, which were paid for in ready money.

All the citadels and fortresses of the kingdom, seated on the summits of the most inaccessible mountains, were put in the most perfect state of defence: immense magazines were filled with salt, provisions, and medicines of all kinds, for the hospitals and other urgent wants. Both the army and the whole population laboured with the most indefatigable zeal and inconceivable ardour. Cannon of the largest size were carried across precipices, and planted on the summits of the loftiest and most inaccessible mountains. The transport of cannon-balls, and other warlike and commissariat stores, was conducted with songs of joy. They toiled night and day in the arsenals, and often even upon Sundays and holidays. Henry went every where in sunshine and in rain he stimulated the exertions of the workmen, directed the works, and often shared himself in the labour. " My children," would the king say to the Haytians, " in the first war of independence we " had to encounter every sort of privation, this time we " shall be in want of nothing, I have provided every " thing. While you are engaged with the enemy, " your wives and children will be in safety, they will " be protected by the impregnable citadels with which " I have covered the country. You will have for " yourselves and families necessaries of every descrip-" tion, which I have collected for the wants of the " army and the people." " Heretofore," he would again say to them, " we were obliged to traverse the " mountains without a place for shelter; our warlike " stores, our treasures, and our booty, were all at the " mercy of the enemy. Now this is no more the case, " we can defend ourselves securely in impregnable " citadels."

What a difference between Henry thus sacrificing his rest, his life, forgetting himself, and thinking only of the welfare of his subjects, and Pétion, intriguing, and using every endeavour to drag them to inevitable destruction.

Whilst the population was thus engaged in making preparations for war, the writers of the North-west, indignant at seeing the people of the South-west deceived and led into disgraceful measures by their government, made the presses groan beneath their productions, in order to enlighten the public feeling in that quarter, and compel Pétion to change his system: he himself was so confounded and ashamed of the conduct he had pursued, that he was obliged, in despite of himself, his hatred, and his ambition, to pay homage to the patriotism of the King of Hayti.

At an entertainment which he gave at Port-au-Prince, he said with a faint satisfaction, " *gentlemen,* " *we are at peace with the king of Hayti.*" He even drank to the *re-union of the Haytians.* In shewing so fair an exterior his object was to produce an oblivion of his treacherous conduct, which had impaired his popularity: he lauded then *peace and re-union*; he soothed the virtuous and well-meaning Haytians by these sweet and flattering hopes. The traitor—his heart was far different.

A calm, the happy precursor of peace, prevailed; the threats of the French had appeased the waves and lulled the tempest; hostilities had long ceased on both sides: the King of Hayti had returned to his favourite plan of coming to an understanding, of making an union of interests, rather than see a barbarous and destructive war maintained contrary to the true interests of the Haytian people: a plan from which his majesty is resolved never to swerve, notwithstanding all the efforts and intrigues of the enemies of Hayti, both domestic and foreign, to lead him to act on the offensive.

Every thing seemed then disposed for peace and union; persons belonging to Petion's territory who had been captured by our patroles, had been instantly released, treated in the most hospitable manner, and furnished with the public papers to communicate to their fellow-citizens. One of our barges which had been taken and carried into Port-au-Prince, was likewise sent back by Petion, who gave the captain a supply of public papers, and assured him he desired nothing so much as peace and re-union. On our side there was nothing we longed for more.

Then Henry, ever guided by an ardent desire to promote peace and harmony among the Haytians, resolved a second time on making conciliatory overtures,

For this purpose he selected two men of colour, the Comte du Trou* and the Baron de Ferrier; and two blacks, the Baron de Dessalines and the Chevalier Edward Michaux, to carry the olive branch of peace to our compatriots of the South-west.

These four envoys were bearers of a dispatch from the Comte de Limonade, minister and secretary of state, to General Pétion, in which the minister proposed to him in the name of the king—1st, *A total oblivion of the past.* 2d, *A frank and cordial re-union.* 3d, *A continuance of rank and command to General Pétion.* 4th, *A continuance of rank and employment to all the civil and military authorities, as also to all the subaltern officers of the army.* 5th, *Admission into the hereditary nobility of the kingdom, according to the scale of rank:* and 6th, *A general guarantee of property to all Haytian proprietors.*

The king engaged to maintain the officers, civil and military of all ranks, in the situations and employments they then held: and Haytians belonging to the North-west, whom the events of the war had placed in the South-west, were allowed to return to their homes, a reciprocal indulgence being granted to such Haytians of the South-west, as chanced to be in the North-west.

In his dispatch, the secretary of state hinted to General Pétion that he was accused of aiding the cause of the French, and urged the necessity of his clearing himself from such serious charges.

The four envoys set out; on reaching the advanced posts at la Source Puante, the Comte du Trou, chief of the mission, wrote to General Pétion, to announce his arrival and the object of his mission. Pétion instantly replied, that the envoys should be received with all the respect due to his countrymen; and he dispatched one

* The Comte du Trou, is since dead.—*Transl.*

of his aides-de-camp to accompany the envoys to Port-au-Prince.

Thus far it appeared to be Pétion's intention at that time to negociate with us.

The envoys arrived at Port-au-Prince on the 18th of February, 1815. The people flocked in crowds outside the barriers of the town to meet them; they were received with a transport of joy and cries of *Peace! peace! we have peace!* The king's envoys augured favourably, from the disposition of the people, as to the success of their mission; but what was their surprise on the following morning to see Pétion, after opening the dispatch they brought him, perfectly outrageous: he discovered that the Comte de Limonade's letter was deceitful and insulting; he took it amiss that he spoke to him of *peace*, of *union*, and *oblivion of the past*: nay, he carried his scruples so far as to be offended at the deputation consisting of two men of colour, and two blacks.

What then did Pétion want? What did he desire? He asked for peace, and he rejected it when offered: he desired the reunion of the Haytians, and he became furious when it was proposed to him: he knew well that civil war could only be extinguished by a reconciliation between the two colours, and yet was offended at the deputation being so constituted as to reconcile the interests of both colours.

The policy of this crafty and deceitful man, is contained in a single paragraph. He deceived the whole world: he really desired neither peace, re-union, nor the extinction of the civil war: he wished for an accommodation indeed, but it was such an accommodation as suited the execution of his designs.

I shall now endeavour to lift the veil which cloaks the infernal policy of this man, which has been productive of so much calamity to his country.

The Haytian cause and territory being one and indivisible, the object of the King of Hayti in proposing peace and reunion, was to establish a *unity* of government as the national interests of Hayti required.

General Pétion, by retaining his rank and command would have continued to hold the internal administration of the South-west, and would have retained in his own hands all the security he could desire, and the King of Hayti would have been able to stipulate for the general interests of the Haytians.

This arrangement would have reconciled all claims and all interests, would have given every guarantee that was necessary, and removed every obstacle which could perplex the recognition of our independence. It would have taken away from foreigners every pretext for evasion, and for seeking to negociate with one side to the detriment of the other.

Such an arrangement would have been honourable and glorious to both parties, and valuable to the general interests of the Haytian people. Had General Pétion been really a patriot, a friend to his brethren and country, he would have joyfully hastened to accept a compromise *(mezzotermine)* to accommodate happily and to the satisfaction of all parties our deplorable differences: but this arrangement did not suit General Pétion, because it deprived him of the means of serving the cause of the French, and betraying his fellow-citizens; and the more so, because he was at this moment negociating in France, and expected the arrival of commissioners, and a system of colonial legislation, accompanied by the *brevet* of governor general of the colony. Now a *unity* of government and peace established on this basis could not suit the execution of his guilty designs; it is clear and manifest that the proposed peace and arrangement were different from what he wished or designed. He could no longer view otherwise than with horror, the peace and reunion, he but a few days before desired.

It is further evident that the civil war was cherished and fomented solely by the Men of Colour; it was therefore sapping the very foundations of his policy to employ Men of Colour to extinguish it; it is on this account that he was enraged; and he foresaw that in making the cause cease, the effects would cease also. It has always been his policy not to appear anxious about the Men of Colour, whom he considered as his own, and obliged to serve his cause, which he had made theirs likewise; while he caressed and flattered the Blacks, who ought to be his enemies, because he feared them, and felt the necessity of gaining them over; he also made them his *seïdes:* it is on this account that he abandoned the black population to licentiousness and idleness, and allowed them to act as they wished, and to follow the impulse of their own passions: he deceived his unfortunate fellow-citizens, in order to attach them to him, and acquire a reputation among them for good nature.

His country, glory, and the welfare of the state, he held in no estimation; the corruption of morals, the degradation of his fellow-citizens, disgraced and debased by mean vices, was all a matter of indifference to him, provided he could attain his own ends, which were the entire dominion of the country and the sovereign power.

Such was the policy of this deceitful man, it was based on perfidy, bad faith, ambition and hypocrisy.

In place of which, Henry, the friend of order, of justice, and of industry, pursued an opposite course; he censured without distinction all who deviated from their duty; maintained with rigour the administration of the laws; he neither wished nor looked for any thing but the welfare of his country, and the well being of his fellow-citizens; he proceeded straight forward, and without deviation, to his object, without regard either to colours or individuals, to circumstances, or to the time in which he was placed.

It is such conduct that has obtained for him from his detractors the reputation of severity; and his frank upright and rigid character, his virtues, his ardent patriotism, and the advancement of his compatriots in social order, morality, and civilization have, to the disgrace of humanity must it be said, often been turned against him, and proved injurious to his interests: the reason of this is plain; a young and ignorant people easily suffers itself to be seduced and misled by the hand which flatters, caresses, and conducts it to its ruin; but the day will come, when it will discover its error: the day I trust is not far distant, in which the Haytian people, animated by feelings of justice and gratitude, will bless and cherish the hero who has corrected the vices, and reformed the manners of his nation, preserved its national glory and reputation unimpaired, and promoted its welfare.

This is the policy of Henry; it is based on justice, honour, and probity!

A man like Pétion with whom the names of glory, honour, and patriotism, are but empty sounds, could not accept the conditions of a peace which, however it might have promoted the welfare of the people, would at the same time have set bounds to his ambition, and checked the execution of his guilty projects.

The presence of the royal deputies at Port-au-Prince incommoded him, he hastened to dispatch them, and replied to the honourable and generous proposals of peace by the grossest abuse.

Pétion saw that his treason had placed him in a

critical situation; the public feeling was daily changing at Port-au-Prince, and leaned towards reunion and peace; he resolved to give affairs another turn; to extricate himself from this painful situation by a master stroke; to rouse their spirits and dispose them to enmity and civil war.

He immediately employed all his old stratagems to effect a change, and entrap us in his new snares: to turn our thoughts from the present, which alone occupied them. To make us lose sight of his conspiracy with Dauxion Lavaysse, he revived all the bickerings of our civil wars, which had been for many years buried in oblivion. This traitor, wished only to live in the recollection of the past: the present was hateful, and pregnant with terror to him; he feasted his imagination only on the past calamities of the public, of which he had been himself the first mover.

On the 20th of February, 1815, he launched out, like a madman, a furious proclamation, in which he loudly called the Haytians to carnage and civil war, and provoked the King of Hayti by direct insults. His object was to make us march for the third time against Port-au-Prince, where he would again have sought to employ against us, his favourite weapons, treason and perfidy, which had already succeeded so well; and afterwards this would have furnished him with the means of bringing us into discredit with foreigners, by representing us as unjust aggressors, as absurd and foolish men who attacked him at the moment we were threatened by a common enemy, and offered the alternative of SLAVERY or DEATH!!!—He wished also to extort from the king a proclamation similar to his own, in order to make use of it hereafter: but all the arts, devices, insults and clamours employed by Pétion were treated with the most sovereign contempt by the King of Hayti, and Pétion appeared in our eyes to resemble the ass cloathed in the lion's skin, striving to frighten all other animals by his braying.

On the 9th of March, 1815, the four years of the *presidentship* having expired, Pétion had himself re-elected for the third time, and, as *he said*, without ambition! Many eye witnesses have informed me how these *demagogic* farces were got up at Port-au-Prince. I fear, were I to pass them in silence, I should disappoint my readers.

" The moment arrived in which Pétion was to lay
" down his everlasting dictatorship: each prepared to
" play his part well to please the tyrant. *Imbert*,
" secretary of state, who was to personate a president
" for twenty-four hours, *Imbert* also studied to pay his
" court to the hypocrite. At length the time came for
" Pétion's appearance on the stage, he made a feint of
" wishing to resign his authority in favour of *Imbert*,
" who instantly exclaimed, ' *No, no, I will not accept*
" ' *the office; there is none but yourself, president, who*
" ' *can save the republic.*' And instantly all those who
" had been stationed for the purpose, advanced, sur-
" rounded the hypocrite, and shouted unanimously,
" ' *Yes, yes, there is none but you, president, that can*
" ' *save the republic.*' And *Imbert*, on the watch for
" the opportunity, shouted ' *Long live the president,*
" ' *long live the republic one and indivisible, and impe-*
" ' *rishable:*' and the whole multitude repeated the
" same shouts."

Meanwhile, on the return of the king's deputies from Port-au-Prince, the Comte de Limonade replied to the invectives of Pétion, in an impressive letter addressed to his fellow citizens of the South-west: I accompanied this letter by a pamphlet entitled *Le Cri de la Patrie*, in which I began from that time to unmask the treason and excessive ambition of Pétion.

This crafty and perverse man, seeing that our publications against him were addressed to the people of the South-west, replied by a work entitled " *the people of the republic of Hayti, to MM. Vastey and Limonade:*" a work containing nothing but insults and extravagancies.

Petion desired to make us change our battery, he wished us to pass him by and reply to the people by similar insults, but he was again foiled in his attempt: in place of answering the people as he meant, I levelled against him another pamphlet, entitled " *Le Cri de la Conscience,*" in which I accused him of high treason; convicted him of being an accomplice with Dauxion Lavaysse, a French spy; of plotting and maintaining a criminal understanding with the enemies of Hayti, tending to subvert the state, and plunge the inhabitants into slavery and the prejudices of 1789; all which was proved by fifteen heads of accusation grounded upon legal and authentic proofs, and documents signed by General Petion's own hand: he was so amazed and confounded by these serious charges, that he preserved the most profound silence from that time; grief at seeing his plots detected, the disgrace and infamy which attached from henceforward to his life, conducted him in a little time to the tomb.

The *Cry of Conscience* has never been answered by our antagonists; in the last publications from Port-au-Prince they have confined themselves to calling it a foolish invective manufactured at Sans-Souci. I agree with them that it is much easier to bestow this epithet than to reply to it: but I think I should observe to Colombel and Milcent, that they were bound to refute such a work; the gratitude and affection they owed to their hero, imposing it upon them as a law; and a regard for their own honour, if they possess any, making it an imperative duty.

I have already had occasion to bring my readers acquainted with M. Colombel;* and it will not be improper to inform them in this place what sort of a man this M. Milcent is, who has occupied our attention so long. M. Milcent is a man of nearly the same kidney with M. Colombel; a Creole of Grande-Riviere in the North; a Haytian in complexion only, but French in principle; like Colombel, one of their tools, and initiated in all their guilty projects; an implacable foe to the liberty of the blacks, and the independence of the country; a base renegado, paid by the French cabinet, and lately sent from France to infest the republic with his writings; a corrupter of the national feeling and public morals; a free thinker; an atheist, who writes to the injury of the blacks, according even to the admission of the writers of Port-au-Prince themselves. †

This Milcent who has never done any thing for his country; who has never fired a shot in the cause of liberty and independence; this Milcent, I say, whose mind is unfortunately only an inflammatory brand, has erected himself into the *pedagogue* of the republic: there he has crushed all other writers beneath the weight of his science and erudition; with his lying and wanton pen he delights his friends the excolonists, and ridicules with the bitterest irony the productions of the Haytians, which he has the assurance to treat as mere rhapsodies.

These are the men who write against us—a Milcent and a Colombel!—these are the men who are appointed defenders of the republic; immoral men, without any regard or respect for their fellow citizens; enemies of the blacks, of liberty, and of independence.

* See page 169.
† See *l'Abeille Haytienne*, No. 3. p. 8. a Journal printed by Milcent, at Port-au-Prince, in 1818.

Just as I published *Le Cri de la Conscience*, the correspondence of Catineau Laroche, an excolonist, with Pétion, fell into the hands of government, and completed the developement of Pétion's conspiracy.*

According to these documents Pétion was to have been *Governor General* of the colony;† the excolonists were to have been put in possession of their properties;‡ slavery was to have been gradually re-established; France to have an exclusive commerce as in 1789;‡ shelter for her ships and cruisers in the ports of Hayti;‡ and, in the event of a maritime war, Pétion was to furnish a contingent of regular troops,‡ and co-operate with the French in making war on the King of Hayti, for the purpose of reducing the population to the yoke of France and slavery.

We then hastened to make this news public by means of the press, and dispatched a number of pacquets with it to the South-west, to enlighten our fellow citizens: but such was Pétion's vigilance, that it was almost impossible to get these papers introduced; as soon as they fell into the hands of his police-agents, they were committed to the flames.

While this was passing in Hayti, Dauxion Lavaysse reached France, along with Pétion's agents, in the course of February 1815. His letters of the 6th of September§ and 1st of October,‖ had arrived before him through the medium of the public prints, and had been laid before Louis xviii. by M. le Comte de Beugnot, successor to M. Malouet, as minister of marine and the colonies. This minister inserted in the Moniteur of the 19th of January, the following notice, *that the mission of Colonel Dauxion Lavaysse had for its sole*

---

*Appendix D.   § Appendix B. No. 1. page xiii.
† Appendix D. No. 1, page xlix. postscript
‡ Appendix D. No. 3, (B) p. li.   ‖ Appendix E. No, 2. p. xcv.

object to collect and transmit to government information relative to the state of the colony, and he was in no respect authorised to make communications so contrary to the object of his mission. The king, said M. le Comte de Beugnot, *has expressed his high displeasure, and ordered his disapprobation to be made public.**

Thus, in place of disavowing, M. le Comte de Beugnot confirmed the *espionnage* of Dauxion Lavaysse; since sending persons under false pretexts, without any official character, to collect and transmit information, was complete *espionnage*.

This procedure of the Comte de Beugnot covered Pétion with shame and ridicule; but he was amply compensated by the praises bestowed upon him by the French news-writers. The *Journal des Débats* of the 16th of January, 1815, contained the following passage. " The determination of Christóphe should not have any " influence upon the only plan which can restore St. " Domingo to France. It is the part that Pétion will " take, which will decide the fate of this colony. If " this chieftain, whom they represent as unambitious, " mild in his disposition, and more enlightened than " his rival Christóphe, consults the interests of the " coloured population, to which he belongs, he will " negociate with France. It will be easy to demonstrate " to the Men of Colour, that being, like the Whites, " proprietors, and unable to preserve their properties, " except as they are cultivated by Negroes, it is their " interest to attach themselves to the white proprietors " and the government which protects them. The " Men of Colour know their numbers are an insuffici- " ent protection against the Negroes, who will soon " exterminate them, unless the kingdom of Hayti be " overturned. To attach the Men of Colour to the

* Appendix F, No. 3.

"French government, it is only necessary to grant the "rights they claim as proprietors; and if the armies of "the provinces of the West and South were joined to "a division of the French army, Christóphe would not "exist six weeks."*

The ex-colonist Jean Reignier, editor of the French newspaper called the *Courier d'Angleterre,* for the 27th of January, 1815, apologises for the conduct of Pétion. "Conduct," said he, "*suited to the interests of St. Do-*"*mingo, and which justifies the opinion we entertain of* "*the moderation of Pétion's character, and the motives* "*which have induced him to emancipate one part of the* "*island from the yoke of Christóphe.*"

The French cabinet prepared to enforce these odious threats by arms; transports were fitting out to convey troops and commissioners to Port-au-Prince. "*They* "*have named,*" says the *Memorial Bordelais,* whence I quote the passage, "*they have named pacificators,* "*whose judgment, in concert with Pétion, should orga-* "*nize a system of colonial legislation, which will quickly* "*effect the reduction of the North.*"*

The escape of Bonaparte from the isle of Elba in March 1815, arrested the sailing of this expedition. Pétion again owed his safety to the greatest chance. Had Bonaparte waited but *one month,* the expedition would have sailed, and both its fate and that of Pétion would have been decided.

One of Bonaparte's first acts on his return to France was to abolish the slave trade. This traffic had been abolished in 1793 by the national convention, and was restored seven years after by Bonaparte, during the administration of Tallyrand; and in 1814 this same M. Tallyrand, minister of Louis xviii. raised the most insur-

* See the *Memorial Bordelais,* a political, literary and naval paper, No. 372, for Saturday the 1st of April, 1815.

mountable objections to the abolition of this commerce. According to him, it was *an idea altogether novel and unpopular in France.* In fine, by dint of the most urgent solicitations, he succeeded in obtaining from the allied powers a respite of five years for the continuance of the trade; and in 1815, Bonaparte, *in order to make himself popular,* abolished it. A hundred days after, Louis xviii. confirmed this solitary act of Bonaparte's, which was preserved, as a great act of morality and justice.

It is plain that in 1814 the cabinet of Louis xviii. at the instigation of the Ex-colonists, meditated either *the destruction or re-enslavement* of the Haytians. The reservation of five years farther continuance of the slave trade, was only made with a view of enabling them to replace the *indigéne* population, in case of its extermination, by other unfortunate victims from Africa.— When we consider the manner in which the various successive governments have sported with human life and liberty, our thoughts are painfully affected; might we not be almost inclined to say, that men are an accursed race, prone to evil rather than to good, and always disposed to mutual animosity, carnage and contention?

Bonaparte's return to France kindled anew the war in Europe. This was a thunder-bolt to Pétion, who found himself deserted by France and surrounded by enemies. On the first restoration of Louis xviii. he had laid aside the mask, and openly declared in favour of France. He now feared that this renewed war would bring down upon him the hostilities of the English and the King of Hayti. Had not Bonaparte been defeated at Waterloo, the war would have been prolonged in Europe, and Pétion, like the French, have been unavoidably crushed beneath the weight of our arms.

The Haytians of the North-west, and some even of the South-west, had, by their patriotic writings, rekindled the sacred flame of patriotism, of liberty and independence, which Pétion had endeavoured to stifle in the hearts of the people of the South-west. At our rallying cry of *liberty, independence,* or *death,* they had shaken off the torpor into which the treason of their chief had plunged them: they had as it were recovered that energy which had formerly characterized them in the war of independence: the shades of the Geffrards, the Ferous, and the Jean-Louis François, had appeared to reanimate their courage and chide their sloth. Pétion became every day more unpopular, and symptoms of insurrection manifested themselves in every direction: he had become an object of hatred and contempt to those Haytians who had not renounced honour and their country. In August 1815, a conspiracy was hatched at Port-au-Prince, the ramifications of which extended through the plain of Cul-de-Sac, and even as far as Jacmel. The plot was discovered on the very day that Pétion was to have been assassinated. Numbers of the conspirators, martyrs to the liberty and independence of their country, were shot near Port-au-Prince, at a place called Morne-à-Tuffe. Among them was Captain Celestin Maneville: Lieutenant-Colonel Louis Lerebourg, one of the leaders, was so fortunate as to escape from Port-au-Prince, and he proceeded to raise an insurrection in the mountains, from Fond Verrettes to Sale-Trou.

The conspirators had arms and ammunition, and even arsenals, in the very town of Port-au-Prince.

In the month of December following, Lieutenant-Colonel Louis Lerebourg was betrayed into Pétion's hands. This gallant officer was beheaded at Jacmel. I know not whether any confession was extorted from him: but within a few days after his death Pétion committed a horrible crime at Port-au-Prince.

I omitted to mention in its place that General Delvarre, the same who had marched against Rigaud at the Pont de Miragoane in 1810,* had been arrested and accused of a conspiracy against Pétion in 1811 : it was then rumoured that he had snapped a pistol at him, which had missed fire. I know not how far this is true, but it is undoubtedly certain that this General always expressed his opinion plainly on the necessity of the Haytians coming to a mutual good understanding and bringing their civil dissensions to a speedy termination.

Delvarre had been tried by a court-martial and condemned to death; but being a black, it was deemed impolitic to execute him ; and, at the instance of one Archibald Kane, a merchant of the United States and an intimate friend of Pétion, the capital punishment was commuted for five years imprisonment!

Delvarre had undergone his punishment, the period of imprisonment had expired, and Pètion had solemnly promised to liberate him. The unhappy man looked forward from the bottom of his dungeon to the moment of his restoration to freedom, to his beloved wife, and adored children, to his family and the extensive circle of his friends : he heard the doors of his prison opening, hope lighted up his heart, and reanimated his drooping spirits; he rose up, but in place of the deliverers he expected, he encountered only merciless butchers; he was killed, his body was dragged out of the town, and thrown into the cemetry without any funeral rites. His weeping widow and numerous friends, obtained with difficulty from the savage Pétion, permission to pay his wretched remains, those last rites which man is bound to pay to man. Pétion had retired to the

* See page 95.

plantation Letort, where he had fixed his residence. This was the new Caprea from whence he ordered these executions. While penning these lines, I almost fancy myself carried back to the reign of the cruel and hypocritical Tiberius.

After the death of Delvarre, it was rumoured in Port-au-Prince, that a conspiracy was to have broken out in this town, and that this general was to have been taken from prison by the conspirators, and placed at their head. I am ignorant how far this rumour was well founded or not; it is possible that Pètion circulated it, for the express purpose of giving himself a pretext, and lessening the horror generally inspired by this crime, especially among the men of colour at Port-au-Prince, who manifested their indignation: they foresaw that Pétion, by the sacrifice of the blacks, prepared the way for their own destruction.

The force of events had obliged Pétion to deviate from his usual line of policy; his character was so altered that his best friends could no longer recognize it; he was become a savage and a despot; he abused all who approached him; he lived in a state of ceaseless anxiety, tormented with fears and alarms; he saw nothing but conspiracies and conspirators ready to strike and punish him for his attempts against the liberty and independence of his country. Pétion weighed the magnitude of the danger in which he had involved himself; he saw that all the efforts he could make in behalf of France would be useless, and would bring with them a certain and inevitable destruction. He resolved therefore to become a Haytian again in despite of himself, to turn the current of popular opinion once more in his favour.

The anniversary of the 13th year of our immortal independence was at hand: Pétion seized with avidity on this happy circumstance, which gave him an opportunity of displaying to the people his patriotism, and his pretended love of liberty and independence.

Every thing was prepared for the celebration of this fête at Port-au-Prince, and throughout the whole of the South-west, with the greatest pomp and magnificence. Pétion appeared at the ceremony holding two children by the hands, a black on his right and a coloured child on his left, as a token of union between the two colours. Repairing beneath the tree of liberty, which he had so shamefully betrayed, the man, who had refused to mention the word independence in his acts, and had declared in his letters that he was *without any feeling of animosity or prejudice against the French nation,** this very man, I say, was seen boldly to pronounce the oath of *hatred to France, and to die rather than live under her dominion!*

After having thus played off this comedy, he affected to speak of the French with hatred and suspicion; he no more mentioned the independence of rights in his proclamations, but wrote in all his letters about the independence of Hayti.

To endeavour to retrieve the credit of his government, he planned a revision of the constitution, that constitution which he had so despised and abused: this revision was made on the 2d of June, 1816, in a desert place at Grand Goäve; in this solitude the legislators had nothing to interrupt their serious meditations; nevertheless it is only necessary to cast a cursory glance over the revised articles, to be satisfied of the chief motive which rendered this pretended revision necessary.

The 105th article of the constitution declared, that *The President is appointed for four years:* and this

---

* Appendix B. No. 7, page xxix.

article revised in the 142d of the new code declares, that *The President of Hayti is for life.*

Surely this was not a *revision*, but a total *subversion* of the republican form of government, established by the constitution of the 27th of December, 1806. In causing himself to be *named for life,* Pétion violated the principle of republican governments, which does not admit a permanency of the functions of the chief magistrate. To be convinced of this it is only necessary to cast our eye over the history of republics; that especially of the United States of America, upon which he wished to model himself. Had he been desirous of escaping the ridicule of getting himself re-elected every four years, as he had already done three times, he had a much simpler method, namely to follow the example of the immortal Washington, and resign his place to another; it was the same with the right which he caused to be given to him by the 164th article of the constitution, of chusing and appointing a successor: this again was an arbitrary, despotic, and *anti-republican* principle; a base adulation of the senate which surrendered to him the rights of the people.

In a *monarchy,* the right of succession is agreeable to the laws of nature; the son ought to succeed to his father; but, in a *republic,* to grant the first magistrate the right of appointing his successor, is to abandon the government of the state to the power, the will, and the caprice of an individual: it is no longer the people that elect and proclaim their chief; it is a man, an individual, who is governed in his choice by his taste, his partialities, and his private friendships.

Pétion, the demagogue, was not even a republican, which would never be credited, did not experience and observation demonstrate it. During his whole life, he followed the voice of his passions alone; he looked but to his own object, sovereign power. I am astonished that the apologists for this constitution have not anticipated me in these remarks; yet they are sufficiently obvious, and deserve well to attract the attention of the republicans of the South-west, who believe themselves in good earnest governed by an *arch-democratic* republic.

Some other articles of this constitution, thus pretended to be revised, have also appeared to me worthy of remark: every thing which interests our fellow-citizens, should also be interesting to us; every thing which can be injurious to them, ought likewise to trouble us: hence it is that I address the following observations to the Haytians of the South-west.

The 38th article of the revised constitution enacts, that *No white, whatever be his nation, shall be allowed to set his foot on this territory as a master or proprietor.*

Since the revision of the constitution was the question, it appears to me that you would have done well to revise this article thus: *No Frenchman, whatever be his complexion, shall be allowed to set his foot on this territory, by any title whatsoever, until the French government has recognized the independence of Hayti.*

In this way you would have excluded none but the French, blacks, mulattoes, and whites; and this for a determinate period; which would have been a measure at once just, politic, and natural; nor would you have given offence to the prejudice of colours; in place of which by the 38th article, such as you have preserved it, you have given a general exclusion to the whites of all nations, which is not only far from reasonable, but unjust, impolitic, and contrary to the laws of polished nations. We forbid the French to land on our territory, whilst they are our enemies: nothing can be more just and natural, for there is no law in the world which can oblige us to receive into our bosom enemies capable of doing us a manifest injury: but to extend this law to all whites in general; to confound friends and foes; would be even more than injustice, it would be an act of inexcusable folly and extravagance.

It may be said, in reply to my objections, that it is unnecessary to dwell upon this 38th article of the constitution, which is placed there, like others, only for form's sake; since it is true, that not only whites of all nations, but even French, both blacks, mulattoes, and whites, are admitted at Port-au-Prince without distinction; witness Louis Labelinaie, Colombel, Milcent, Pradére, Sureau, &c. &c.

To this I answer then, that the constitution of the republic is but a vain pretence; I can readily believe you do not adhere to it. I allow again, that all you advance is true; whites in general are received at Port-au-Prince, without distinction of nation: but this advantage does not counterbalance the injurious exclusion the constitution gives to whites, and the objection continues in full force.

The act of independence excluded none but the French peremptorily from the territory of Hayti. But, as it was repugnant to Pétion's heart to exclude them alone, he discovered that it was more just to extend the exclusion to all whites in general, without distinction of nation.

I cannot pass in silence the 44th, which necessarily follows from the 38th article, and is worded as follows: *Every African, Indian, or their descendants, born in the colonies or in foreign countries, who may come to reside in the republic, will be recognized as Haytians, but shall not enjoy the rights of citizens until after twelve months residence.*

This article is unconstitutional, it is a violation of the principles contained in the act of independence, which expressly forbids our disturbing the peace or the domestic economy of our neighbours directly or indirectly. This article is moreover in direct opposition to the fifth article of your Constitution, which maintains the principles established by the act of Independence.

Now by the 44th article, you make a direct appeal to the black and coloured population of the colonies or foreign countries, to come and settle themselves in the Republic : you offer them an asylum *in the Republic, which is sacred and inviolable,* according to the 3d article of the constitution, with the prospect of enjoying the rights of citizenship after a years residence: a measure which tends directly to disturb the peace and internal government of those foreign colonies or countries. This undoubtedly is not your intention ; but the fact is that the 142d, 164th, 38th, and 44th articles of this *soi-disant* revised constitution, are *unconstitutional, unjust,* and *impolitic,* and contrary to the general interest of the Haytian people.

This constitution neither consecrates any right, nor furnishes any security, internal or external. The 142d and 164th articles deliver the people and the state into the power and will and caprice of an individual : while the 38th and 44th offer nothing satisfactory to the foreign colonies and countries. I have explained myself sufficiently ; I should fear to say more. It is for the purpose of placing before the eyes of my fellow citzens of the South-west the defects of their constitution, which may occasion them so serious an injury ; it is for the purpose of replying to the remarks which have been made upon me, that I have felt myself obliged to make these observations from which I should otherwise have abstained.

Such is the difficult situation in which we find

ourselves placed, that we have only a choice of evils: if we preserve silence the mischief spreads, it can neither be arrested in its progress nor corrected; our very silence is tortured into evidence against us; if we speak we rouse up a multitude of interest, our conduct gives offence, and subjects us to censure; hence of two evils we have only the choice of the lesser.

Pétion then found himself recalled by the Haytian people, as well as by the force of circumstances, to the cause of liberty and independence; in the revision of the the constitution he even fell short of the mark at which he should have aimed, so powerful were his fears. He had been accused by the people of wishing to sell the country to the *French whites*. In order to exonerate himself from this charge, he extended the exclusion of the *French* to the *whites* in general: he was charged with being the enemy of the *blacks*, and by way of proving the contrary, he invited the *blacks* of *every country* to come and settle in the Republic. So difficult is it when we stray from the direct path to recover it again; one error always leading us into another.

Meanwhile M. le Vicomte du Bouchage, who had succeeded the Count de Beugnot in the ministry of marine and the colonies, reckoning upon Pétion's offers and promises, took measures for sending out commissioners to Hayti.

The events which had taken place in Europe, and the occupation of France by the allied armies, compelled the French cabinet to alter its original plans; and instead of sending an armed expedition to support its negociations, as had been formerly designed, it was obliged to content itself with dispatching commissioners only to notify the designs and pretentions of France, to the chiefs of St. Domingo.

We have already seen that M. Malouet, minister of

marine and the colonies, had selected as emissaries to Hayti, a *terrorist*, an agent of Robespierre's, notoriously infamous, and, to complete his character, sentenced to the gallies for the crime of bigamy; a *renegado Spaniard*, formerly a smuggler; and an old man equally unknown in Hayti and in France. Such were the persons chosen to execute his disgraceful projects.

The Viscount du Bouchage, entertaining the same prejudices, and schooled in the same principles as M. Malouet, likewise made an unfortunate choice when he sent us commissioners who were all *ex-colonists*: the French cabinet, always influenced and misled by the ex-colonists, imagined that these perverse and deceitful men still retained some influence in the country. The Viscount du Bouchage fancied then that he had made a master-stroke when he selected *six ex-colonists* to notify to us the orders of Louis XVIII.

My readers will doubtless not be displeased to learn the names and characters of these *ci-devant* masters, who were thus sent to insult, deceive and entrap their *ci-devant* slaves.

The Viscount de Fontanges, chief of the mission, is an old man, an *ex-colonist* of Gonaïves, *ex-colonel* of the regiment of the Cape, *ex-commandant* of the *cordon* of Marmelade, who had twenty-eight years before carried on hostilities against Generals Jean François and Biassou, the champions of freedom.

The Viscount de Fontanges, during the revolutionary war of St. Domingo, possessed great influence over the men of colour, whome he carressed and flattered, in order to induce them to make war upon the blacks under Generals Jean François, and Biassou; it was expressly on this account that he was chosen as envoy to General Pétion, being, from long experience *quite expert at such intrigues.*

The renowned Esmangart, an *ex-colonist*, an extensive planter of the plains of Cayes, now a counsellor of state, is said to be a man who shudders at the bare mention of *liberty*, and is reported to possess influence in the South-west.

George du Petit-Houars, an *ex-colonist* of Lower Limbé, was known in the country to be imbued with all the prejudices of the ancient regíme, and execrated the blacks and men of colour.

Laujon, was an *ex-colonist*, *ex-procureur du Roi* at St. Marc: he was selected in consequence of his having written memoirs in which he pointed out the course which the whites ought to pursue for the purpose of making the men of colour and the blacks mutually destroy each other.

Jouette, an *ex-colonist* of the mountain of Arcahayes, had been one of the satellites of Leclerc and Rochambeau.

In fine, the sixth, Cotelle Laboulatrie was an *ex-colonist*, *ex-procureur du Roi* at Port-au-Prince, a man deeply versed in the crimes, the stratagems, and the treachery of the ex-colonists.

These commissioners were likewise, in testimony of their good faith, sincerity, and kindness, to be accompanied by certain Haytian renegadoes.

The better to ensure the success of the commissioners, the Viscount du Bouchage collected from all parts of France those Haytian traitors and renegadoes who had followed the French army on its evacuation of St. Domingo, under Rochambeau; in order to send them to Hayti before the arrival of the commissioners, for the purpose of preparing the minds of the people to receive them favourably in the north-west as well as in the south-west.

These traitors reached St. Thomas's in a French

vessel. There learning the fate which they had to expect, if they dared to pollute the shores of the northwest with their sacriligious feet, they hastened to Port-au-Prince, to Pétion, their copartner in guilt. The right of asylum in the republic was sacred and inviolable, especially for traitors and spies. A crowd of these cowardly deserters, these most dangerous enemies, most cruel scourges of their country, was seen to arrive in this town; amongst them was to be seen the traitor Bellegrade, who had betrayed Governor Toussaint Louverture, Louis Labelinaie, a man barbarous and cruel even to an absurdity, the *Séide* of Rochambeau; a man who had in the course of one short day hung, in the presence of Pétion, twenty-five unfortunate females of the plantations Saint Michel and Madeline; a man who was guilty of the destruction of four or five hundred human beings, his brethren and fellow citizens, whom he delivered up to the French to be hung, strangled, drowned, burned at the stake, or torn to pieces by dogs. Such were the wretches, yet dripping with the blood of their compatriots, who were received and welcomed by Pétion at Port-au-Prince.

Notwithstanding their having been forewarned of the fate which awaited them in the kingdom of Hayti, there were found among these renegadoes, some bold enough to hazard the attempt, but they were arrested as soon as they entered, and experienced the punishment due to spies and traitors.

While these events were passing during the years 1814, 1815, and 1816, Henry lost not an instant in putting the kingdom into a state of defence, and we were fully prepared to receive both the French commissioners and army, in whatever manner they might present themselves.

Nothwithstanding our great preparations for war, the King did not cease to direct his attention to the public prosperity. War, agriculture, commerce, and public instruction, each claimed his attention; it was necessary, said he, that all should advance together, without interfering with each other: the more difficulties he had to encounter, the more courage did he display, and the more resources did he develope.

Henry watched with vigilance the designs of the French upon Hayti, and his chief study was to find out the means of counteracting them. He saw, from what passed in the south-west, that the French counted more upon subduing us by intrigue and corruption, than by force of arms. From this moment Henry saw more than ever the importance of making the people acquainted with their rights and their duties: and he determined upon diffusing the light of instruction throughout all classes of his subjects.

Next to a change of religion, a change of language is the most powerful method of altering the character and manner of a nation. It was resolved in council to found schools, academies, and royal colleges throughout all the towns and parishes of the kingdom: that instruction should be given in the English tongue, and after the English method: it was also resolved that public instruction should be given *gratis* in Hayti; at the national cost. Immediately after this the government considered about the means of obtaining masters from abroad, and issued orders for erecting suitable buildings to serve for schools.

In the course of the same year, 1816, we saw the national school opened in the capital; and in the succeeding years, the towns of Sans-Souci, Port de Paix, Gonaïves, and St. Marc, had schools established in them, and opened to the public *gratuitously*.

Printing, that precious art which diffuses human knowledge, has been of signal service to us. In less than six months government caused three printing establishments to be founded, at Cape Henry, Sans-Souci, and the Citadel Henry; it will be easy for us progressively to establish them in all the towns throughout the kingdom.

By means of these printing offices, the writers, and journalists of the north-west poured forth a deluge of papers into the country, especially into the south-west. The news of Europe circulated, and met the eyes of the people. All the writings of the ex-colonists were answered and refuted: all communications direct and indirect, which were received from the French, were immediately published and dispersed through the country; this publicity defeated their plans, and carried death to their hopes. Three months before their arrival, we had announced to our fellow citizens of the south-west, the approach of the commissioners who were to be sent to them, we had forewarned them to be upon their guard.

Pétion then anxiously looked for the arrival of these commissioners, at Port-au-Prince; he was reduced to such a state of weakness, as to be enabled to do any thing for them: he would doubtless have been well pleased not to receive them, but he had received and welcomed a spy; he could not therefore do otherwise than receive the commissioners. Had he sent them back, he would have condemned his own conduct with respect to Dauxion Lavaysse: he therefore decided on receiving them. He was already disgraced to the utmost, and could not make himself worse.

At length, on the 5th of October 1816, the frigate Flora appeared in sight of Port-au-Prince, preceeded by the brig Railleur, having on board this colonial and legislative commission, so long looked for, whose wisdom was, in concert with Pétion, to gain over the district of the north for France. The Viscount de Fontanges while yet at sea, acquainted Pétion with his arrival by his letter * of the 2d of October, in which he declared the end and object of his mission.

From this moment Pétion had no farther occasion for corresponding with the commissioners; he knew enough; he ought to have refused to see them, and forbidden their entrance into the ports of the Republic.

First, Their rank of *commissioners* implied a superior authority by which they were commissioned to notify its orders to its subjects.

Secondly, Their quality of *ex-colonists*, passionate, vindictive, and tyrannical; of *ci-devant masters*, the natural and implacable enemies of the Haytians.

Thirdly, The object of their mission, which was to procure a recognition of the sovereignty of France by the Republic.

These three reasons should have made Pétion refuse to see the Commissioners, and to order them away: but Pétion was unable longer to entertain a feeling of the dignity of a man; humbled and disgraced in his own eyes, every sentiment of honour, of justice, and humanity, was banished from his heart; he was hardened in infamy, and was no longer susceptible of shame.

The Viscount de Fontanges began his letter by acquainting Pétion that the white flag, which he had so long courageously defended, had been enthusiastically hoisted for more than two years in all countries which had formerly been subject to the dominion of the King: that *St. Domingo alone delayed doing so*.

* App. E. No. 1. page lvi.

The Viscount entertained no doubts respecting the reception which the commissioners had to expect, he was fully convinced of the loyalty of Pétion. " We "send you," said he to him, "Colonel the Chevalier de " Jouette, and the Chevalier Dominge, chef d'escadron, " who are the bearers of this letter, together with M. " le Dué, one of your countrymen, who has expressed " a wish to accompany them."

Wishing to recall again to Pétion's memory their former intrigues, when they fought against the freedom of the Blacks, this *ex-colonist* commissioner concluded his letter in the following terms:

" *Your old General, the Viscount de Fontanges, he* " *under whose command you and your countrymen so* " *honourably defended the royal cause, when perjured* " *subjects dared to attack it, is at the head of this* " *pacific mission.*"*

The Viscount de Fontanges proposed to Pétion to hoist the *white flag*, and betray his national colours; to receive commissioners who were all *ex-colonists*, *ci-devant* proprietors of men in St. Domingo, the natural and implacable enemies of the Haytians, who came to notify to them the orders of the King of France. What answer ought Pétion to have returned to such an overture? that the act of independence, the constitution of his country, and the duties of his station, forbade his entering into any negociation the basis of which was inimical to the liberty and independence of his country. That the Republic, free and independent, could not admit the commissioners of a foreign power who came to signify its orders to her. That doing so was an insult offered to the majesty of the Republic. That the Viscount de Fontanges, and

---

* Appendix E. No. 1, pages lvii. and lviii.

the commissioners who accompanied him, were moreover all *ex-colonists*, the natural enemies of the Haytians. The act of independence, and the 38th article of the Constitution, proscribed them from the country; that if they were not allowed to set their foot in the country as simple individuals, much less could they be suffered to do so, when they appeared in a character hostile and insulting to the Republic. That it was the greatest insult which the French cabinet could offer to the people of Hayti, to send their former masters to order their *ci-devant* slaves to return again to the dominion of France. That from the aforesaid considerations, the president of the Republic felt himself bound to order the French commissioners to withdraw; that the ports of the Republic were shut against them, and that with respect to the person named *Le Dué*, he should be arrested as a Haytian subject, and delivered as a deserter, to the sword of the law, to meet the fate reserved for traitors and spies.

Such is the answer Pétion ought to have given to these *ex-colonist* commissioners, had he understood what was due to his office and to the dignity of the Republic. But he was nothing more than a traitor sold to the French; he had already dishonoured himself by negociating with a base spy; he therefore experienced no difficulty in giving a favourable reception to the *ex-colonist* commissioners. Here is the substance of the reply which he *did* make to the Viscount de Fontanges.

We have in truth, (says Pétion) defended the *French flag* with abundant courage, and *an unbounded devotion*: he did not chuse to say the *white flag*, for this would he feared have roused the feelings of the people. Next, after indulging in common place remarks upon the events of the revolution, that revolution which Pétion hated, because it had given liberty to the Blacks,* upon the known character of his most Christian Majesty, his mild principles, his unheard of misfortunes and those of his family, the contest which had been maintained, as long as it was cruel and sanguinary, the uncertainty of his fate, &c. &c. &c. In fine, after abundance of trifling delivered in a flat and insipid style, he was compelled to come to the *espionnage* of Dauxion Lavaysse. I should be afraid of weakening this master-piece of villainy, were I to give it otherwise than in a literal copy, after which I shall make a slight commentary upon it.

" During this interval, General Dauxion Lavaysse
" arrived at Jamaica, and assumed the character of a
" royal commissioner. A work, published under
" his influence, appeared a brand of discord hurled
" amongst us to create disunion, to set the family at
" variance with its heads, and the heads with the
" family; a qualified slavery was there depicted in
" the most specious colours, and the people were
" called back to it in the mildest manner; while the lot
" of the leaders was to be that of mischievous savages,
" DEATH OR BANISHMENT TO THE ISLE OF RATAU,
" after having aided in seducing and reloading with
" chains their brethren, their friends, the companions
" of their arms and their glory. Notwithstanding all
" this, General Dauxion Lavaysse, dared to present
" himself at Port-au-Prince, where he was received
" with kindness: the acts of his mission were made
" public, his instructions were unmasked, and avowed
" by himself. In what point of view could his mission

* Appendix E. No. 2, page lviii. Pétion's hatred of the revolution betrays itself in every line; he boasts of having, under Colònel Maudit, defended the white cockade.

"be regarded?—as an *espionnage!* In this case, what risk did he not run? Nevertheless these instructions were signed and sanctioned by a minister in the confidence of the King, and thus bore the stamp of authenticity. What a subject of reflection for us. All these documents were, we are well assured, long under his most christian Majesty's consideration, and no doubt often carefully examined by him. The public prints of all Europe have resounded with them; and they have been repeatedly republished with remarks much to our credit; and in which our wisdom and moderation have been approved of. General Lavaysse has returned to France, *after having received every testimony of the most sacred hospitality.*"*

I appeal to all impartial men, even to Pétion's own friends and advocates, to Colombel and Milcent, does not every word, every line of this passage, contain a host of the most palpable falsehoods? But I must proceed to expose its sophistry.

"*During this interval*": of what interval does Pétion mean to speak? Is it of that which intervened between the dispatching of Dauxion Lavaysse to Hayti, and the return of Bonaparte from Elba to France? This is what Pétion means; and yet there was *no* interval between these two events. The first measure of the minister Malouet, had been to dispatch Dauxion Lavaysse to Hayti, and he had arrived in France in February 1815, *before* the return of Bonaparte from Elba. There was then *no interval* between the dispatch of this spy to Hayti, and Napoleon's return to France. This introductory falsehood, which appears nothing at first, was committed designedly, for the

---

* Appendix E. No. 2, pages lix. and lx.

purpose of lessening Pétion's guilt in the eyes of the people. " *General Dauxion Lavaysse arrived at Ja-*
"*maica, and assumed the character of a royal commis-*
"*sioner*": this again is an imposture. The minister Malouet in his instructions* calls Dauxion Lavaysse a *secret agent*; the Compte Beugnot calls him colonel.† This Dauxion Lavaysse impudently assumed at Jamaica the title of *General* and principal agent‡ of the minister of marine and the colonies; but it was Pétion himself who chose to style this spy in his public acts, *the deputy of his Majesty Louis* xviii, *king of France and Navarre*§; which is again another falsehood. "*A*
"*work, published under his influence, appeared a brand*
"*of discord hurled amongst us to create disunion, to set*
"*the family at variance with its heads, and the heads*
"*with the family; a qualified slavery was there depicted*
"*in the most specious colours, and the people were*
"*called back to it in the mildest manner.*" The work in question is that of H. Henry, the same to which Pétion replied under the signature of Columbus.‖ My readers will bear in mind that it is in this pamphlet that Pétion ascribes to the ex--colonists a certain *omniscience*¶ respecting the measures to be pursued for the reduction of the Blacks to slavery, and he had even the effrontery to speak of them. "*The lot of the*
"*leaders was to be that of mischievous savages*": another imposition, another perfidy on the part of Pétion! Read the letter of Dauxion Lavaysse, of the 6th of September, to Pétion,** together with the instructions of the minister Malouet;†† the chiefs were

---

* Appendix C. No. 1, pages xxxiii, xxxvii, and xxxviii.
† App. F. No. 3, page ci.   ‡ App. B. No. 3, page xvii.
§ App. B. page xiii.   ‖ App. A. page i.   ¶ App. A. page ii.
** App. B. No. 1, page xiii.   †† App. C. N. 1, page xxxiii.

to receive rewards for their perfidy, but it was the people who were to be "*treated as barbarous savages,* "*and hunted as Maroon Negroes.*"* Admire for an instant with me, the manner in which Pétion humbugged the people: he cut off the last member of the sentence, *hunted as Maroon Negroes,* because he feared rousing the fears of the Blacks, whom he had sold, but was unable to deliver up; and he referred these insults to the chiefs, while in reality they were meant to apply to the people: his motive is easily understood. More crimes, more falsehoods, "*death, or banishment* "*to the isle of Ratau, after having aided in seducing* "*and reloading with chains their brethren, their friends,* "*the companions of their arms and their glory.*" We have seen Pétion mutilate passages, employ sophistical quibbles, and write absolute nonsense, in order to confuse every thing: here he would make it appear as though these expressions, *death or banishment to the isle of Ratau,* belonged to the work of H. Henry, whilst they are found literally in the instructions of the minister Malouet,† and by implication in the correspondence of Dauxion Lavaysse with General Pétion; while it is Pétion himself who was to put the Haytians to death; and send to the *isle of Ratau* or *elsewhere,* those whom it might be deemed inexpedient to send back to slavery. How was his note changed? These *barbarous savages,* these *Maroon Negroes,* these *violent and incorrigible men,* had become the brethren, the friends, the companions of the arms and the glory of this traitor. I am at a loss for epithets strong enough to characterize avowals so shameful and disgraceful as these. "*Nothwithstanding* "*at all this, Dauxion Lavaysse dared to present himself* "*at Port-au-Prince, where he was received with kind-*

---

* App. B. No. 1, page xv. † App. C. 1, No. page xxxvii.

"*ness! the acts of his mission were made public, his in-*
"*structions were urmasked and avowed by himself.*
In "*what point of view could his mission be regarded?*"
and Pétion himself replies, "*as an espionnage!*" What
an admission!—he had the impudence to write and
subscribe this with his name! and he added, "*in this*
"*case what risk did he not run?*"—I will complete the
meaning of this sentence which he was unwilling to
finish. *Had he not found a protector and accomplice in
the head of the Government?* Pétion after speaking of
prudence and moderation, concluded this assemblage of
baseness, villainy and falsehood, by saying that the spy
"*has returned to France, after having received every*
"*testimony of the most sacred hospitality,*" as if the
laws of hospitality extended to a spy.

These last avowals of Pétion, complete the proofs
of the crime of high treason with which he is charged:
these it is which fix an indelible blot upon his life, and
cover his memory with eternal disgrace!

At length, to put the seal to all his absurdities, his
crimes and his attempts, he ends his letter to the
Vicount de Fontanges thus. "*The Commissioners*
"*whom it has pleased his Majesty to send to this Repub-*
"*lic will find, as soon as they land, how sacred the laws*
"*of nations are held by this government; and that the*
"*whole world without exception of colour or of nation,*
"*enjoys here under the protection of the laws, the most*
"*perfect equality.*"* The conclusion crowns the work.
Finius coronat opus.

Thus Pétion, to deceive and mislead the people,
confounded all ideas of justice and injustice; that by a
general inversion of the order of nature, all notions of
morality of justice and of humanity might become

---

* Appendix E, No. 2, p. ix.

perverted, or overturned. In the midst of this confusion is to be seen a total ignorance of the laws and rights of nations, a violation of their principles and rules and a profound contempt for the fundamental laws of his country.

Here the principles of public honesty and morality had been violated by the French cabinet : a shameful *espionnage*, accompanied by the most atrocious circumstances was in contemplation. Instead of seeing the chief of the Republic enraged at this infamy, indignant, and speaking only of punishments and scaffolds, you hear him say that the spy has returned to France after having received testimonies of the *most sacred hospitality*; as though the sacred rights and duties of hospitality extended to a criminal, to a base spy! There the French cabinet trampled under foot every regulation of the laws of nations, by the dispatch of commissioners, all *ex-colonists*, to notify its *orders* to the Republic : the people is insulted in its rights ; the constitution is violated, despised, and abused ; in place of repelling these insults and outrages with dignity, the President replies, that, " the commissioners whom *it has* " *pleased* his Majesty to send to this Republic, will " find, as soon as they land, how *sacred the law of* " *nations are held by this Government.*"

The Act of Independence excludes the French from the country, the 38th article of the constitution extends this exclusion to whites of whatever nation they may be : the 44th article admits into the Republic only Africans, Indians or their descendants, and Pétion had impudence enough to write to the commissioners, ex-colonists, that all the world *without exception of colour or nation*, lived there *under the protection of the laws in the most perfect equality.* What nonsense ! of what laws, of what equality does he speak ; this it is that Pétion violates the constitution, and turns it into ridicule by the bitterest irony.

While writing these lines, I feel ashamed of myself. To what then ought we to ascribe such inconsistencies and absurdities? Is it to the effect of ignorance or treason?—To both;—to treason on the part of the Governors, and ignorance on that of the governed. Had the governors been patriots and honest men, they would have had knowledge enough to guide them, to teach them to respect themselves, and cause the laws of the Republic to be respected; and if the governed, or in other words, the mass of the people, had possessed sufficient learning, they would have been able to read, and detect in the acts of their government and its proceedings incontestible proofs of its infamous treason; and they would have had sufficient firmness and energy to drive from their stations and bring to trial the traitors who last dishonoured and sold them to the French.

But that which in all this is truly painful and afflicting to the hearts of all true Haytians, and which we cannot dissemble from ourselves, is that the treason, dastardliness, ignorance, and versatility of the government of the South-west, joined to the want of energy and blindness of the Haytians of that part, who have shewn a shameful neglect of their dearest interests, have been singularly injurious to the cause, the liberty, and the independence of the Haytian people! This culpable forgetfulness of their duties has served only to confirm the ex-colonists in their system of fraud and duplicity! Meanwhile the government of the South-west is composed of *a senate* and a chamber of *representatives*, in which sit doubtless enlightened men, vigilant guardians of the interests of the people!

What were ye doing then ye conscript fathers, seated in your curule chairs, when the president of the Republic plotted before your eyes, and in writing, the slavery of the blacks, the ruin of your country, and the destruction of your fellow citizens? You were buried, alas! no doubt in a profound sleep! For all the cries of the barbarous savages, of the maroon negroes, of the isle of Ratau, which re-echoed in your ears, were unable to awaken you out of your deep lethargy. You were then wholly lost, and perfectly forgetful of the affairs of the world! for you would otherwise have been alive to the fate of your country and your unfortunate fellow citizens; you would have been able to read in the writings and acts of Pétion, how shamefully he had deceived, betrayed, and disgraced you; and in place of yoking yourselves as you have done to his funeral car like base republicans, you would have thrown the dead body of this traitor into the charnel house! But, conscript fathers, you slumbered then: you had lost all consciousness of your own existence, and were totally lost to the affairs of the world! Nevertheless you have erred; but it was without knowledge of the cause, without premeditation, you were therefore excusable, and I excuse you.

On the 6th of October, the Viscount de Fontanges communicated to Pétion the ordinance of Louis xviii, which named the commissioners to St. Domingo. "*This ordinance*," says Fontanges, "*ought to calm every uneasiness, and fill all hearts with hope. It will acquaint you likewise, general, with the extent of our powers.*"*

By the ordinance in question, the commissioners were to confer with the existing authorities on every thing which related to the legislation of the colony, the internal administration, and public order, the civil

---

* Appendix E, No. 3, p. lx.

and military functionaries, the state of persons, and the commercial intercourse with the mother country, &c.*

Now what more did Pétion require to know? Had he not before his eyes the whole extent of the powers of the commissioners? Did not all the most favourable propositions which could be made to him resolve themselves into a recognition of the sovereignty of France? Could he do this?—did he possess either the right or the power? He could not then commence overtures upon bases which were inadmissible; yet this, nevertheless, is the very thing which he did.

It appears from the correspondence now before me, that Pétion had secret conferences with the old Viscount de Fontanges, before he had public ones, at which he doubtless communicated to him all the difficulties of his situation: it was not till after he had these private interviews, that Pétion gave these ex-colonist commissioners an audience, at seven o'clock in the evening, in the presence of the chief authorities of the Republic.

This nocturnal audience by torch light must have presented a curious and even ludicrous scene. The *masters* on the one side making good their ancient pretensions, and the subjects on the other who were base enough to listen to them. A question arose respecting the espionnage of Dauxion Lavaysse. At length it was doubtless agreed between Pétion and the ex-colonists, that it was necessary to sound the disposition of the North-west, before any thing could be entered upon.

Under these circumstances, had misfortune so willed it, that the reins of government in the North-west had likewise been entrusted to a chief as unprincipled as the one in the South-west. These two governments

* App. E. No. 4, page lxi.

would have been seen, to the disgrace of the human species, vying with each other in the baseness of returning beneath the yoke of these haughty masters: and the people, shamefully sacrificed, would have been obliged to reclaim their rights anew by force of arms.

Happily for the Haytain people, for their honour and glory, Henry held the reins of government in the North-west with a firm and prudent hand. His energy, his patriotism, his unvarying principles of honour and probity, have been the guides which have conducted them back to the cause of liberty and independence.

The ex-colonist commissioners then took their departure for the North, with the design of returning to Port-au-Prince, to confer again with Pétion, after having sounded the disposition of the King of Hayti.

Here is the manner in which the Royal Gazette of Hayti for the 27th of October gives an account of this event. I cannot do it more exactly and faithfully.

"For the first time," says the Royal Gazette, "during twenty-seven years, the white flag has exhi-
"bited itself upon our shores in a manner as disgraceful
"as it was ridiculous for the French government: the
"sight of this contemptible flag, the symbol of the
"slavery under which we groaned for ages, excited the
"deepest indignation in all hearts.

"The cause of a just, brave, and generous people
"which resisted persecution and the most monstrous
"of all tyrannies of which an instance can be found
"among the records of nations; this cause, I say, can-
"not be indifferent to the great mass of mankind: we
"should then never cease to make our voice heard, to
"discuss our rights, and plead before the tribunal of
"the whole world the most just of all causes. Should
"the passions, injustice, and avarice succeed in stifling
"our voice and paralyzing our efforts; should our

" contemporaries be deaf and insensible to the voices of
" humanity and of justice, posterity at least, more just,
" will collect the materials which we transmit to them;
" they will sit in judgment upon the men, and the
" learning of the age in which we live; they will re-
" cognize the rights of oppressed innocence, and turn
" the shaft of ignominy against the oppressors."

After this energetic exordium, the editor gives an account of the event which was the subject of his remarks as follows:

" On the morning of the 17th of October 1816, the
" signal station of Cape Henry made a signal for two
" vessels, a frigate and a brig, beating to windward,
" known to be ships of war; from their manœuvres they
" were suspected to be enemies ships cruising off the
" harbour without daring to approach too near.

" Next morning they approached the port, and hove
" to at a distance of about four leagues.

" The Duke de la Marmelade, governor of the capital,
" repaired to Fort Picolet to observe the manœuvres of
" these vessels. They were recognised as French by
" their flags.

" About two in the afternoon, the frigate made a
" signal to the brig, which was at a distance, to come
" near her; a boat from the brig was sent on board
" the frigate, apparently to receive orders, and in half
" an hour returned to the brig: the frigate and brig
" then hoisted the Haytian flag at the mizen, and the
" white flag at the main and foremasts, and made full
" sail for Fort Picolet.

" Then the governor, presuming that they were
" vessels of truce, ordered the pilot's boat to approach
" under the protection of the fort, to be ready to con-
" duct them into the harbour in case they required it.

" On this manœuvre every one supposed they were

" about to come into the port. The pilot remained
" abreast of the fort with the Haytian flag displayed,
" waiting for them.

" The brig came within about two leagues of the
" fort, backed her topsails, came about, and fired a gun.

" We momently expected that she would lower
" her boat with a flag of truce to come and speak
" with the commandant of the fort, and communicate
" to him the purport of her mission, or ask for a pilot,
" if she wanted to come into the harbour, as is the
" practice of all nations: not so however, the brig
" continued to manœuvre, and fired a number of guns.

" The frigate and brig, tired of waiting in vain for
" us to send on board them, made sail, and took the
" direction of the channel of la Tortue. The same
" day the signal station announced a brigantine steering
" west; the French brig bore down upon her, boarded
" her, spoke her for a long time, and thus left her.
" The brigantine, which was discovered to be an Ame-
" rican, altered her course, and kept cruising off the
" harbour for several days; she appeared desirous of
" coming in: one evening she approached so close,
" that she was supposed to be entering: the pilot
" approached, when, to the great surprise of all, she
" stood out to sea again: at length after having cruized
" six days off the port, she determined on coming in.

" The interpreter of Cape Henry immediately re-
" paired on board to fulfil his accustomed duties: he
" learned that the brigantine was the Sidney Crispin
" of New York, Captain Elisha Kenn, with Mr. Jacob
" M. King as supercargo. These two gentlemen de-
" clared themselves bearers of two letters for his Ma-
" jesty the King of Hayti, which had been delivered
" to them by the Captain of the French brig *le Railleur*.

" The interpreter hastened to make his report to

" the governor, who immediately repaired to the King's
" wharf, to question the captain and supercargo, and
" learn what these letters were: but what was his
" astonishment and indignation when the American
" captain and supercargo presented him with two let-
" ters, the direction of which was insulting to the
" Haytian government, being in the unusual form of
" *To Monsieur General Christophe, at Cape Français.*
" The governor expressed his extreme surprise and
" indignation; and told the captain and supercargo
" that he was astonished that Americans, who had
" traded for so many years with Hayti, who enjoyed
" the protection of the laws, and who had, like our-
" selves, attained their freedom and independence,
" should have undertaken a commission which was
" no less dishonourable than misplaced, for the subjects
" of a nation at amity with the Haytians; the governor
" instantly returned the letters without breaking the
" seal, ordered them to take them back to those from
" whom they had received them, and quit the harbour
" forthwith; which was done. All the boats in the
" port towed the brigantine, which was quickly out of
" harbour.

" The brig *Speculant*, bound from Cape Henry to
" Gonaïves, fell in with the French frigate and brig off
" Cap-à-Foux.

" The commissioners, naturally concluding that
" their letters would not be received unless directed in
" the usual form, embraced the opportunity presented
" by this brig, to transmit a packet under cover to the
" commandant of the port of Gonaïves, containing the
" letter and ordinance.*

" It is worth while to observe that by the letter of

---

* Appendix E. No. 8, p. lxv. and No. 4, p. lxi.

"the commissioners dated off Cap-à-Foux on the 12th "of October,* they acquaint us that they were bound "to Port-au-Prince, as a central point of communica-"tion with the south and the north, whilst we are "well informed that the frigate Flora and brig Rail-"leur, with these commissioners on board, had touched "at Port-au-Prince, on the evening of the 5th October.† "The traitors! even before they had opened a com-"munication with us, they had already employed "fraud and treachery to deceive us."

Pétion impatiently awaited the return of the ex-colonist commissioners, prepared to yield or resist according to the reception they had experienced from the King of Hayti. The arrival of these ex-colonist commissioners so long announced and expected, had given great uneasiness to Pétion, and such was his anxiety that, on their return to Port-au-Prince, they found him sick.

I will give an account of what passed at Port-au-Prince until the departure of the commissioners: after which I will return to the north-west, for the purpose of explaining the measures adopted by the King of Hayti, in consequence of their appearance on our coasts.

Immediately on his return to the roadstead of Port-au-Prince, the Viscount de Fontanges wrote‡ to General Pétion, to acquaint him that he had been unable to communicate with the north, having been refused admittance into the ports. He sent Pétion a copy of the letter§ he had written to General Christóphe under

---

* See notes p. 231.

† The truth of this statement is established by the correspondence of the commissioners with Petion, especially the Viscount's letter of the 8th October. See App. E. No. 5, p. lxii.

‡ App. E. No. 7, p. lxiii.   § App. E. No. 8, p. lxv.

cover to the commandant of Gonaïves; and having returned he hastened to resume the communications which were the object of his mission. In the course of his letter he acquainted Pétion that Louis xviii. had disavowed the mission of Dauxion Lavaysse, together with his proceedings; and he desired Pétion, in a postscript, to acknowledge the receipt of the ordinance of the King, naming the commissioners to St. Domingo.

The news from the north-west had entirely reassured Pétion, he was no longer the same man; after acknowledging the receipt of the Viscount de Fontanges' letter with the copy of that addressed to General Christóphe, and the ordinance of the King, here is the manner in which he entered upon the subject with the ex-colonist.

" After the horrible crimes perpetrated by the
" French, crimes which shame the page of history, the
" independence of Hayti has been solemnly sworn,
" over the yet smoking remains of our unfortunate
" compatriots, by the intrepid warriors who achieved
" its conquest. This sacred oath, pronounced for the
" first time by an enraged people, has never ceased to
" echo from every heart; it is annually renewed with fresh
" enthusiasm; it is the palladium of public liberty; to
" retract it, or to entertain a thought hostile to it, would
" be to bring down upon ourselves merited calamities;
" our laws imperatively forbid it; and as first magis-
" trate of the Republic, it is my most sacred duty to
" cause it to be respected. I have sworn this in the
" face of heaven and of men, and *I have never sworn in*
" *vain*. To make us swerve from this holy resolution
" is beyond the utmost stretch of human power. We
" possess, and deem ourselves worthy of preserving
" our independence: to wrest it from us we must first
" be exterminated. Well! should this even be possi-

"ble, we would determine to endure it, rather than "retract."*

It is needless to go farther: my readers will easily perceive by the fierce, vigorous, and imposing style, that it was no longer Pétion the *Frenchman* who spake, but Pétion, the *Haytian* in despite of himself, who held this language! What a man! What a Proteus! Into how many forms has not he metamorphosed himself in the course of his life.

Meanwhile the *espionnage* of Dauxion Lavaysse perpetually recurred to Pétion's recollection, and occupied his thoughts in a disagreeable manner: to put an end to it, and to have nothing more to say to it, he addressed himself to the Viscount de Fontanges on the subject in his letter, in which he said to him " you do me the " honour to repeat to me that this mission has been " disavowed by his Majesty. I assent to this, and in " consequence to the nullity of all the proceedings " arising out of it, I will therefore speak of it no " more."* Pétion who, as I beg my readers to recollect, had consented to all the proceedings in question, namely to pay *an indemnity*, or in other words *a tribute* to France; to grant her an exclusive commerce as in 1789; and to recognize the sovereignty of France, provided that she should acknowledge the *independence of the rights* of the Haytians, or, in other words the civil and political rights of French subjects and citizens. Pétion was glad to seize upon the opportunity of retracting his promises; promises which were far beyond his ability to fulfil; and notwithstanding that even in private individuals any retraction implies some error, mistake, or breach of faith, and bears an appearance of disgrace, Pétion, I say, was not the less pleased to

---

* Appendix E. No. 9, p. lxviii.

assent to the nullity of the proceedings of his government, and to speak of them no more.

It is a thing well worthy of remark and attention to see how the French Cabinet lowered its pretensions, making to General Pétion, through its commissioners, the very offers which Dauxion Lavaysse in the first place had not the power to propose; and how General Pétion's pretensions increased with time, insomuch that he rejected in the second place the very proposals which he had before so anxiously solicited, and to obtain which he had made the greatest efforts.

The explanation of this forced change in General Pétion is this; that what he deemed practicable in 1814, he found impracticable in 1816; he therefore made a shew of despising the very favours which he had before sought and solicited with so much ardour.

We should not however be deceived by this apparent change, resulting from the force of circumstances; Pétion continued no less to pursue the execution of his projects: he was merely obliged to pursue a different course, longer and more circuitous, to the attainment of his object.

Woe to those blind sceptics who should think otherwise. I am convinced that in the conferences which Fontanges and Esmangart had with the traitor Pétion, they arranged a new scheme to be executed by the French cabinet in concert with Pétion for the overthrow of the kingdom of Hayti, and the reduction of the Blacks to slavery.

Pétion is dead, but his plan and his projects survive him; I need only cast my eyes to the intrigues of the *ex-colonists* in France, and the transactions which are taking place at this moment in the south-west, in order to be convinced of the existence of this plan. All the *process verbals* of the fêtes of independence, of oaths purposely administered in all the parishes, far from blinding me, serve only as incontestible proofs of its existence. The war carried on against *Gomand* in the south, in order to free his rear from a dangerous enemy, sufficiently unmasks the ulterior views of Pétion's successor, who treads in the same steps, and assumes the same air of preaching up liberty and independence, which in his hands are only the means which he employs for the subjection of the country, and the re-enslaving of the Haytians.

Independence, say the ex-colonists, is the *hobby* of this people; by means of a *nominal* independence, they might be led to any thing. Well, let us grant them what they ask, and we shall immediately succeed in leading them wherever we wish! As we see that the lessons of the ex-colonists have budded, and are put in practice in the Republic, this plan is nothing more than the *ne plus ultra* of the perfidy of the ex-colonists and their partizans in the south-west.

I have said enough to let it be understood that we have detected their treacherous plans, and know how to counteract them.*

(*Paris, 7th September.*)—It is reported that General Boyer, president of the Republic of Hayti, has sent an agent to the French Government with an offer of paying an annual sum to France, and placing this power on the most favourable footing for commerce, provided the Court of the Tuileries will recognise the independence of that part of St. Domingo which is under his dominion. "This word *Independence* is the *hobby* of the people," says the agent in question,† "no authority can outweigh this sentiment, and there are hardly any conditions to which they would not consent, were this *nominal* concession only made to them." *Extract from l'Ambigu*, No. 520, page 537.

† This agent can be no other than Mr. Colombel.

Pétion being unable to act differently, required the Viscount de Fontanges, to consider his government as *free* and *independent*. After having received the ordinance of Louis xviii. which contained the extent of the commissioners powers, this was making a demand as inconvenient as inadmissible; on the supposition that these ex-colonist commissioners had been sent cloathed with the character of public ministers, previous to communicating with them; this was a *sine qua non* proposition which he ought to have made them, *to recognize the independence of Hayti* as a preliminary basis, before proceeding further. But Pétion had commenced so well he could not do otherwise than go on from absurdity to absurdity.

Meanwhile the people and the troops at Port-au-Prince, murmured greatly at seeing these ex-colonists lengthen out their communications; discontents manifested themselves in the town; the most trifling dispute which might arise between a French sailor and a Haytian at this moment might have produced a general insurrection.

The ex-colonist commissioners expressed their fears, and under pretence that their sailors were seduced by the Mexicans and Carthagenians whom they met at Port-au-Prince, they wrote to claim the rights of nations and the protection of Pétion.*

At length after a multitude of conferences, correspondences and interviews, which were not without their object; it was necessary to come to a definitive explanation, and to put an end to the negociation.

Pétion, whether designedly, or through ignorance, had furnished the ex-colonists with victorious arms to combat him, which they will not fail to profit by.

* App. E. No. 10, p. lxx.

On the 30th of October, Fontanges wrote to him; "on a cool and dispassionate perusal of the first pages of this act which forms the groundwork of your institutions, it is immediately manifest that it carries with it the germ of your own destruction."*

And to demonstrate this truth to Pétion, he referred him to the 38th, 39th and 44th articles of the *soi-disant* revised Constitution.

I will refrain from mentioning the observations made by this ex-colonist, and which may be seen in his letter : * I have elsewhere explained the contents of these articles, † I shall therefore only observe by the way that Pétion deserved to have the enemies of his country come and insult him in his own government, by comparing the Republic with the Barbary powers ; ‡ he deserved this well I say, for having had the baseness to violate his duties by welcoming these ex-colonist commissioners, in contempt of that very constitution which furnished them with arms to combat him, and in contempt of the laws of nations which banished them from the Republic.

And in what manner did he reply to these insults ? By falsehoods and absurdities. These articles, says he, "have never ceased to be in force, and have no other object than our security,"§ and to prove how well they are executed he proceeds to say "You may see multitudes of Europeans in this town trading with us unimpeded by the prescription of colour :"§ and the presence alone of these ex-colonists, these enemies of their country, prove still more forcibly than any thing he could say how well these articles were enforced, and how well the Constitution was executed in the Republic !

* App. E. No. 12. p. lxxii. † Pages 207 et seq.
‡ App. E. No. 12, p. lxxiii. § App. E. No. 13, p. lxxv.

Haytians of the south-west, make your choice; execute your Constitution, if you think it necessary to your security ; or if it is absurd and even incapable of being executed, abolish it, and you will do well! abolish this phantom of a Constitution which neither secures to you any right, or offers to you any security, either foreign or domestic. Annihilate this democracy which tends only to disgrace and debase you in the eyes of nations. Annihilate it I say! At home it serves only to produce disunion among yourselves, to plunge you into the most complete anarchy, and bring down upon you a certain and inevitable destruction; abroad it makes you the sport, the laughing stock, and the victims of the enemies of Hayti.—What do I say? it even converts those who were your friends into formidable enemies.

Believe me, my friends and beloved countrymen! listen to the voice of nature and of reason which addresses you, and recommends your uniting yourselves to us, rather than the voice of passion which leads you to separate from us.

Believe me we form but one and the same body of the nation! Are we too numerous? Is our territory too extensive? Have we not the same interests, and the same cause to defend? Wherefore then should we continue divided? Why for ever this cruel separation which is at once so impolitic, and so contrary to our true interests? Have we not committed blunders enough in politics? Let then good sense and reason become our guides, let us form a consolidation of all our rights and interests ;—let us commence by coming to an understanding ; this is the first point—all the rest will follow after.

Pétion, forced by the people to demand a recognition of the independence of Hayti, could not come to an agreement with the ex-colonist commissioners, who possessed neither the power nor the inclination to negociate on this basis; they parted then without having come to any conclusion, at least *publicly*; but I feel a strong presumption that they had adjusted the conditions of a *sceret treaty*.

Let us now transport ourselves to the north-west.

We have seen that the letter of the commissioners and the ordinance of Louis xviii. had been transmitted to government under the cover of the commandant at Gonaïves.

In order to put an end to the audacious insults perpetually offered to the Haytians by the French cabinet, enraged at the obstinacy with which he saw this cabinet persevere in its unjust and barbarous designs against Hayti, and the treacherous and crooked methods which it employed for the attainment of its end, Henry issued his declaration of the 20th of November 1816.

" The Sovereign of France," said the King of Hayti in this declaration*—" The Sovereign of France
" has declared, that in negociation with us, nothing
" should be done which could detract from *what he
" owes to the dignity of his crown, to justice, and the
" interests of his people!* And we—we also declare
" that we shall not be found wanting in what we owe
" to the interests of our people, and the dignity of
" our crown."

" The high interests of the Haytian people, toge-
" ther with our duties, oblige us to make known to
" the world the powerful motives which have led to
" the adoption of this determination, in order to put a
" final period to all the aggressions and insults of which
" the French Government is perpetually guilty with

---

* App. F. No. 1. page xciv.

" regard to the Haytian people; as well as to destroy all
" those unjust and illusory pretensions to sovereignty which
" the cabinet of France may yet entertain respecting the free
" and independent kingdom of Hayti.

" For these causes we have declared, and do solemnly
" declare, that we will not negociate with the French govern-
" ment on any other footing than that of power with power,
" and sovereign with sovereign. That no negociation will be
" entered upon by us with this government, which has not for
" its preliminary basis the independence of the kingdom of
" Hayti, as well in affairs of Government as commerce; and
" that no definitive treaty shall be concluded with this govern-
" ment without having previously obtained the good offices
" and mediation of a great maritime power which will guaran-
" tee the faith of the treaty from being ever broken by the
" French:

" Whenever we negociate we will withhold our consent
" from any treaty which does not comprehend the liberty and
" independence of the whole of the Haytians who inhabit the
" three provinces of the kingdom, known by the names of the
" North, the West, and the South, our territory; the cause of
" the Haytian people being one and indivisible:

" No overture or communication from the French to the
" Haytian government, whether oral or written, shall be re-
" ceived, unless made in the form, and according to the
" usages established in the kingdom for diplomatic commu-
" nications:

" Neither the French flag nor individuals of that nation
" shall be admitted within any of the ports of the kingdom,
" until the independence of Hayti has been definitively recog-
" nised by the French government.

" We declare anew, that *our invariable determination is,*
" *never to interfere directly or indirectly in matters foreign to*
" *our kingdom:*

"That it shall be our unceasing endeavour to live in good understanding and harmony with the friendly powers and their colonies in our neighbourhood, to maintain the strictest neutrality, and prove to them by the prudence of our conduct, our laws, and our labours, that we are worthy of Liberty and Independence."

This wise and prudent Declaration of the King of Hayti, has put an end to the aggressions and insults of the French Cabinet, and opposes an insurmountable obstacle to the accomplishment of their ulterior designs upon the Liberty and Independence of the Haytian people.

This declaration, which overthrows and annihilates all the hopes of the Ex-colonists, has been the subject of their remarks and criticisms.

The express and indispensable condition of recognizing the Independence of Hayti, both in respect of Government and Commerce, previous to entering upon any negociations, annoys them so much, that they have recourse to a multitude of sophistical arguments, equally destitute of reason and solidity, in order to induce us to abandon it. From this time forward say they, all overtures between the two Governments are rendered impossible, since one side is required to make every concession before any thing can be obtained from the other; and then follow a succession of idle common place remarks, as though the French Government had any great concession or sacrifice to make in recognizing that *Independence* of which we have been in full possession both in *fact* and *right*, for more than sixteen years; as though all these pretended concessions and sacrifices were not already accomplished by the conquest we have made of them, and by the force of events.

As the politics of our Government are frank and upright, and it is far from my intention to mislead or deceive, I shall, I think, give the ex-colonists full satisfaction by commenting on the principles, which form the basis of this declaration of the King, now the source of all their terrors and complaint.

In this commentary I will not deviate from those maxims and principles of the Laws of Nations, which the government of Hayti is far from wishing to violate, and the French Government doubtless as little. I will endeavour to express myself with all possible precision and perspicuity, and will even enter into the most minute details, in order to leave nothing for the ex-colonists to desire. I will proceed article by article, and paragraph by paragraph, commencing with the first paragraph of the first article.

"*We will not negociate* (it is the King of Hayti who speaks) "*with the French Government on any other footing, than that* "*of power with power, and Sovereign with Sovereign*"

This first paragraph contains nothing contrary to the Laws of nations; for, according to both natural and political right, all People, Nations, and Sovereigns, whether great or small, are equal in point of Right; now the political justice which governs the civilized world and is founded upon natural justice, teaches us in the plainest manner that the king of Hayti is equal, and the brother, with your leave Gentlemen Ex-colonists, of the King of France; and that his Haytian Majesty, neither *can* nor *ought* to treat with his most Christian Majesty, upon any other footing than that of *Equal* with *Equal*, *Sovereign* with *Sovereign!!* And it is equally clear and sufficiently intelligible, that the King of a *Free* and *Independent* people, neither *can*, nor *ought*, to be the *tributary* or *vassal*, much less the subject of a Monarch, who is his brother and equal; such are the laws and maxims which govern the polished and civilized nations of Europe. I am aware that these sacred, and eternal maxims, of the natural and political rights of nations, are repugnant and offensive to the pride and prejudices of the ex-colonists; but these sacred and eternal laws, have not been created by us; they trace their origin from an higher and more ancient source; in vain then do the enemies of humanity, strive to pervert and overthrow them; they continue to exist, they are universal and indestructible, they are graven in characters which cannot be effaced in the hearts of all men, *blacks* no less than *whites;* they exist, and we are in the daily habit of appealing to them! we have made them the invariable guide of our conduct, from which we are resolved never to deviate! The Laws of nations and Political Justice, are founded upon reciprocity, hence the King of Hayti, is no more under an obligation to the King of France, than the King of France is to him.

Let us proceed to the second paragraph of the same article, " *That no negociation will be entered upon by us with this power* [France] *which has not for its preliminary basis the independence of the kingdom of Hayti.*"

This is the *Sine qua Non* which cuts short the ex-colonists in their diabolical attempts upon Hayti; nevertheless it is in strict conformity with the first principles of the Laws of Nations. The Haytians have been for *sixteen years* independent, both in *fact* and *right*: never was there a cause more just, or better founded than theirs; now since the Laws of Nations do not permit one nation to propose to another, to renounce its rights of Sovereignty, for the purpose of submitting to its dominion, we have done perfectly right, before we commence negociations, to require as a preliminary condition the *Sine qua Non* of a recognition of the Independence of Hayti. The States General of Holland, and the United States of America have done so before us, and no one has found fault with their conduct.

If the Government of France means to recognize the Independence of Hayti, it ought not to hesitate in admitting this preliminary and indispensible basis; every other condition should be the subject of a subsequent treaty. If, on the contrary it regards us as insurgents, we ought to have no communication of any description or under any pretext with it. To deviate from these principles would be to deceive and disgrace ourselves without receiving the smallest advantage. Every secret mission, every *clandestine treaty*, serves only to do us the most incalculable injury.

3rd. Paragraph of the same article, "*as well in affairs of* "*Government as Commerce.*"

In other words, that we do not wish for a *merely nominal* and *fictitious* Independence, but desire to be *free* and *Independent*, in the fullest extent and signification of the words, *clearly* and *unequovically* expressed in a solemn treaty: that we do not mean to submit to any degree of supremacy; to become in any manner tributaries or vassals ; that we equally design to have our trade free from all restrictions ; that is to say, we will not grant an *exclusive* commerce to any nation whatsoever. All this is so clearly expressed in the Royal Declaration, as to render further explanation superfluous.

Proceed we next to the 2nd. Article. "*Whenever we nego-* "*ciate we will with-hold our consent &c.*" (See Article 2nd.

This is the basis of the Act of Independence and the Constitution of Hayti. The cause and territory of the Haytians is one and indivisible. The temporary separation of the Country into two governments, is merely the result of a civil war, with which no foreign Government has any concern.

The government of Hayti, being unable to deviate from the constitutional basis on which the kingdom is founded, I presume that all questions or propositions, which tend to interfere with matters connected with our civil dissentions, will be carefully rejected as inadmissible, the cause and territory of the Haytians being one and indivisible.

Let us examine the 3rd. Article, "*No overture &c.*"

The forms and usages established throughout the kingdom of Hayti, for diplomatic communications, are the same with those observed in all the Courts of Europe. This is as clear as day, and needs no commentary ; it is unnecessary to say to

French Diplomatists, that they are not to send us *terrorists, smugglers, imposters, ex-colonists* &c. &c. It is not our business to instruct them in the laws of Diplomacy: if they wish to negociate with us according to the received practice of Governments, they are sufficiently acquainted with the method in which they ought to proceed.

Pass we to the 4th. Article, " *Neither the French Flag nor " individuals of that nation shall be admitted &c.*"

This exclusion is limited to the French Flag, and to individuals of that nation for a *specific time* only; namely, till the Independence of Hayti has been definitively recognized by the French Government: this limitation alone points out that, once this Independence has been recognized, the French Flag and individuals of that nation, will be admitted. This exclusion differs widely from that of the 38th. Article of the constitution of the South West, which excludes *all whites* in general;* we exclude the French only, *because we are at war with them*, a measure at once wise, just, and politic.

The principles contained in the 5th. and 6th. Articles, are in conformity with our fundamental laws, which forbid our interfering, directly or indirectly, in the affairs of our neighbours. It was in conformity with these principles and the laws of good neighbourhood, that the king of Hayti, issued his Proclamation of the 23rd of May 1819†, whereby he ordered that every British Subject, discovered to be a fugitive from the neighbouring islands, seeking an asylum within this kingdom, should be arrested, for the purpose of being sent back in the first vessel to the place from whence he fled. His Haytian

* See p. 207 and App E. No 12 page lxxii.

†The translator having returned to England before this Proclamation was issued and the Author not having given it a place in his Appendix, the translator cannot but regret his inability to lay it before his readers, he can however vouch for the King's adherence to the principle of the Proclamation, in an instance which occured early in the year 1818. Compare this with the 44th. Article of the Constitution of the South West of which a copy will be found in Appendix E. No 12 p. lxxii.

Majesty being firmly resolved never to deviate from the system of neutrality and good neighbourhood which he has uniformly observed; which differs widely from the 44th. article of the Constitution of the South West.

I have sufficiently explained myself in the course of this work to be fully understood by the ex-colonists. Let them then know that they have nothing to expect, or ask, and no business to interfere with us. Let them judge from what has been said, whether we can *renew connexions with France, which could only have the character of an Independence which was not contested, at a period too, when the singular political situation of France will not yet allow her publicly to acknowledge the word in the full extent of its signification.*

What sophistry, what equivocations! to avoid saying a *nominal Independence!* a *kind of Independence!* What is the singular political situation of France to us? What have we in common with her family connexions and the interests of her colonies in the windward islands? We wish for no deviations from the straight road, no secret missions, no *clandestine* treaties. We desire to be *free* and *independent,* in the face of the Universe, and in the fullest extent and signification of the words, this then is our *Sine qua non.*

Forced to stop in the middle of my course, in order not to lose the opportunity, I feel the greatest regret at being obliged to pass over the years 1817, 1818, and 1819, for although no event of importance took place during that period, I could nevertheless interest my readers by details of the great improvements which have been made in the kingdom. As, for example, the sale of the national domains; of the *ci-devant* properties of the *ci-devant* colonists; the distribution of lands to the whole of the military; the augmentation of the number of proprietors; the rights of property respected; the encouragement and protection of industry; the increase of marriages,; the improvement of morals; the diffusion of knowledge; the establishment of a Royal Chamber of Public Education; the progress of our national schools and Academies. I could moreover follow Henry in one of his progresses through his kingdom ; exhibit him in the midst of his people, dispensing his bounty and chatting familiarly with the peasants. I could introduce my readers into the cottage of the industrious cultivator, heretofore so wretched and miserable; we should unite in rejoicing to see him surrounded by his wife and children, living in comfortable independence, with good furniture in place of decayed benches and old calabashes, a handsome bedstead in place of an old truckle bed, and enjoying besides that most precious of all earthly blessings, Liberty ! O! what have I lost! why has the shortness of my time robbed me of this sweet enjoyment, the only one capable of sustaining my courage, and rewarding my labours, the contemplation of the happiness of my fellow citizens.

I should have been happy to have concluded here ; but it yet remains to give an account of an important event which has taken place in the South West.

In the course of April 1818 the traitor Pétion died, a prey to remorse and grief : weary of a hateful life he died of famine from a reluctance to take either food or medicine to his last moment. The public prints of *Port-au-Prince* have detailed the circumstances of his death and the ceremonials of his funeral, the honours and the vile and fulsome flatteries which took place on this occasion never could wash out the indelible blot of High Treason from his memory ; General Boyer, who had been his Secretary, caused himself to be named to the office of **President** *of the republic* : a few days after *Pétion's* death, he was elected nearly in the same manner, as the Roman Emperors were by the Pretorian guards.

It is not known how they came not to find in the important casket, secured with two locks, the precious deposit which it should have contained, and which pointed out *Pétion's* successor. It is not known, I say, how the autograph Letter sealed and addressed to the Senate, was conjured away, this however is well known that *Petion* had named a Successor and that Successor was not *Boyer*!

In the Months of May and June 1818 the King, accompanied by his Family and Court, made a progress through the Kingdom, he was at *Port-de-Paix* when he learned the death of *Pétion*. On his arrival at St. Marc, Henry issued his Proclamation of the 9th. of June, § addressed to the Haytians of the South West, for the purpose of promoting an accommodation upon principles at once just and honourable, and conducive to the common interest of the Haytians. The King dispatched three persons of rank, *M. M. the Barons de Dessalines* and *de Bottex*, and *Commissioner Amant*, to *Port-au-Prince*, who were commissioned to deliver his Majesty's Proclamation, † together with a Letter announcing his pacific intentions, to the Generals and Magistrates assembled there.

My readers will find this Proclamation and Letter, as well as the absurd and extravagant reply made to them, among the documents inserted in the Appendix. *

This conciliatory overture, these words of *peace*, of *union*, and of *common interest*, have brought down upon us hosts of pamphlets, filled with the vapid jests and unfounded calumnies of the *Colombels* and the *Milcents*, the mere tools of the ex-colonists. I have answered their infamous falsehoods, whose only object was to defame the Haytian Monarchy, and the Sovereign who sways it with equal wisdom and justice.

§ See App. G. No. 1. p cvi.

† See App. G. No. 2. p cviii.

* See App. G. Nos. 1, 2 and 3. p. cvi. cviii. and cx.

FINIS.

ERRATA.

Page 16. Note. For *Malonet* read *Malouet*.
     ibid. —— For *of Ex-colonists* read *of the Ex-colonists*.
     18. last line but one. for *Year* read *ear*.
     21. last line, for *Touissaint*, read *Toussaint*.
     27. line 7. for *nonconformatists* read *nonconformatist*.
     34. line 9. note, for *alreado* read *already*.
     38. note for Page 22 read Page 23.
     41. note for 6000 read 60,000.
     64. line 27 for *election or the* read *election of the*.
     90. last line for *as*, read *so*.
    144. line 5 for *refletion*. read, *reflection*.
    147. line 30. for *the French*, read, *Ye French*,

APPENDIX.

The duplicate pages cxi and cxii to be cancelled by the binder.
cxii. line 22. for *throne of the grace*. read *throne of Grace*.
cxiii. line 2 for, *iberty* read *liberty*
ibid. line 4. for, *ionour*, read, *honour*
ibid. line 1, for, *combatting*. read *combating*.
ibid. line 13, after the word *glory*, erase the Comma.

(W. GRAY, Printer &c. Stonehouse.)

APPENDIX.

A

A Reply to a Publication of M. H. HENRY, *entitled "Sugges-"tions offered to the inhabitants of Hayti respecting their "present situation, and the probable fate which awaits "them"*—*by* Columbus.

I AM a stranger in Hayti. I write as a traveller actuated solely by the regard I feel for a people with whose customs and manners I wished to be acquainted. Greater knowledge, and a more skilful pen than mine, is necessary to describe them. The impartial reader will find in them marks of greatness, generosity, and integrity, which reflect honour on those who call themselves Haytians; and he will see that they merit the praises bestowed on them by those who have had dealings with them, *without distinction of nation*. Never having visited the North of the island, I shall speak more particularly of the Government called *The Republic of Hayti*. The private character of the head of this Government, his peaceable virtues, his feeling of justice towards all the world, his distinguished talents, and the confidence he inspires, present the picture of a parent surrounded by his children, rather than that of any other Government. Those who constitute that of this Republic, have all a more or less active share, and really participate in the maintenance of their rights, of which they appear extremely jealous, under the administration of an adored chief of their own choice.

There is no doubt that, though they write little, they have observed attentively the spirit and progress of all that has taken place in Europe since their separation from France, in consequence of the conduct of the chiefs who figured at the head of the last expedition against this island: conduct which finds no apology in the page of history, and which will be an eternal opprobrium to them. I do not design to retrace this conduct, with the details of which I am not sufficiently acquainted, to enter into a serious discussion of it: I am far from having such an object in view, or desiring to irritate their minds; but the conclusion I have drawn from it is, that it justifies the Haytians, and in the choice of principles which they should permanently adopt, the idea of forming themselves into a regular government like other nations, the manner in which they have reduced it to practice, and their astonishing progress in civilization, reflect the highest honour upon them, especially in the eyes of all impartial observers.

They have followed, since their emancipation, all the operations of the European powers, as it may be said, with the map in their hands. Their interest has fitted them for discerning every thing which is connected with it; they have viewed with admiration the mighty efforts which have been made, and have prepared themselves insensibly for the events which have taken place. In their individual conduct they have acted, as it were, in concert with the plans of the allied powers. The elevation of the house of Bourbon to the throne has not surprised them: their revolution had no connection with its Government, and never having offended it, they did not seem to apprehend any recrimination on its part. *Many of them have told me, they hoped that, on a return of general order, their situation would be attentively discussed; that they would necessarily be consulted; that every hostile and premature measure would be rejected; that all animosities, prejudices, and above all, every idea of the colonial system would be carefully avoided, in bringing about a reconciliation founded upon the relations of commerce and industry; for it is difficult to have, at a distance of two thousand leagues from the country, and after a long interruption of communication, an omniscience of the real state of passing events, and applying remedies often worse than bad, as has been uniformly the case with the French Government through the whole course of the revolution of the colonies. They have said to themselves, we have reached the moment of a great political crisis: let us be prudent and strictly united: let us have confidence in ourselves, in the justice of our cause, and let us prepare for a decision, the result of which cannot but be favourable to us when we shall be better known: for there are certain retrograde steps which we can no longer take, and which it belongs to the justice of the Sovereigns not to forget.*

It is thus that I formed my judgment of the public feeling in Hayti, when the arrival of a delegation at Jamaica, sent by his Majesty Louis xviii. to treat with this Government, was announced. This news created no unfavourable impression among the Haytians: their eyes have been often turned to the shore to see the arrival of the deputies: honourable preparations have been made for their reception, and an electric feeling of sensi-

APPENDIX.—A.

bility, of regard, of prepossession, and of every thing which the laws of nations hold most sacred, shot through every heart.— This expectation has been, for the present, disappointed; and I regret it, after the sensation produced by a publication, entitled " Suggestions, offered to the inhabitants of Hayti, respecting " their present situation, and the probable fate which awaits " them."

In it I have seen an act little calculated to conciliate their minds, especially under existing circumstances; and its consequences would have alarmed me for the public tranquillity, had I not observed a prudent caution among the people, and a fixed determination not to quarrel among themselves. This idea encouraged me, since the utmost latitude in expressing one's sentiments prevails under this Government, and is unattended with any danger; and I propose to hazard, with all the caution due to the country, and the delicacy of the subject, some remarks, which I proceed to explain with confidence.

The author, M. H. Henry, after some general observations arising from the interest created by the misfortunes of this country, to which he is nevertheless a stranger, enters upon his subject, and considers the population as divided into six classes.

" The first is composed," says he, " of those who have " been called, for their talents or their courage, to the first civil " or military employments under the existing Government."

" The second, of those who legally possess property, in " moveables or immoveables.

" The third, of individuals who were free before the revo-" lution, and who follow some industrious calling.

" The fourth, of soldiers, who form what are called the " regular troops of Hayti.

" The fifth, of those employed in agriculture and other " labours, heretofore denominated *plantation negroes.*

" The sixth, it must be said, of those wicked and sangui-" nary wretches, enemies to order and industry, who are to be " met with in all classes and all countries, during revolutions, " and incessantly labour to turn the calamities of the public " to their own private gain. This last (which I am disposed " to believe far from numerous among you) does not, from " the small interest it excites, at present deserve our consi-" deration. Let us then be content to examine impartially, " whether it be more advantageous for the first five classes to " continue as at present, or to return to the laws of order and " of duty."

I have repeated M. H. Henry's words verbatim, because I conceived his pamphlet might not perhaps be read by every body, and that this, printed in the country, would be more generally known. I wished also to pay public homage to truth, and to the character of the Haytians, who will be themselves able to judge how far I have succeeded in describing their situation with justice and accuracy, because I cannot relate with equal exactness the developements of the author, which I shall consider in a general point of view, without deviating from their real meaning, referring for this purpose to the writing itself, and to the fine feelings of the indigénes, who have a most just view of the subject, and who, as sincerely disposed to peace as I believe them, will perhaps be pleased with my reserve in this discussion.

Properly speaking there is in Hayti but one class of men, who are actuated by the same principles, the same connexions among themselves, and the same skin, with some slight shades lost in the general whole of the population with which they concur, by the ties of blood and family, to form the Government. It is in vain to attempt dividing them into separate classes, they have always been found united whenever it was in agitation to crush them. Never distinguished in punishments and proscriptions, they have always resisted courageously together, and no attempt which has been made to effect the contrary, has been able to weaken this first want; that of the necessity of mutually contributing to their own preservation. It was in this spirit that they acted simultaneously on last taking arms against the French, and cementing for ever that bond of union, from which they have never swerved, at least in the republic of Hayti, where I write. The elements of the Government of the Republic are derived from the mass of the people without distinction of shade or privilege, for none exists; and never was equality more perfect. even to the exercise of the supreme power, since it is elective.

The civil and military chiefs are undoubtedly those named by M. H Henry " who have been admitted to fill the first
" offices in consequence of their talents or their courage."—
" Their existence is incessantly embittered by trouble, sur-
" rounded by hatreds and jealousies of every sort. This anxi-
" ety, these vexations of the chiefs are lessened for the moment
" by the appearance of respect which fear forces from their
" inferiors; by the erjoyments which their residence in the
" towns allows; by the comforts which the revenue of the
" customs and that of the plantations, which they provision-
" ally enjoy, affords.—What will they not have to expect, if
" they first set the example of submission to the laws of the
" mother country ? Offices or employments (less brilliant
" perhaps, but more solid and honourable). Can they hesi-

" tate an instant between honour and dishonour, rewards and
" punishments?" &c. &c. &c.

We may, without fear of asserting too much, call the Chiefs of Hayti, the first among equals. They have a just claim to command in every thing which relates to the government of the community, regulated upon the basis which it has assumed for itself, but they have no power of entering into engagements for it without its consent: it follows of necessity that they must act in the manner most suitable to its interests, and that it must adhere to every alteration made in its existing situation. The resources of the country arising from the culture of the land, of which the produce is exported, supply, it is true, the public expences, and the maintenance of the functionaries. It was necessary that the plantations should be cultivated for the benefit of those who had obtained and possessed them by right of conquest, in order that the republic might maintain itself to the present time so advantageously. The use which the chiefs make of these advantages is so moderate, and the principles of the President are so well known, that it cannot be supposed they would cling to power from such motives. Besides, nothing has been proposed to them, and I am far from imagining it to be their intention to refuse to confirm by their efforts the happiness of their fellow citizens, should they foresee their being able to fix it in a secure and permanent manner with a sufficient guarantee.

As to the second class, that of proprietors, their property, of whatever description, " will be lost to all who shall side " with the rebels, should any such exist on the arrival of the " French forces." Here M. H. Henry draws a picture of the condition of these last, should they take shelter in the woods. He labours to describe the dangers which await them; the loss of whatever money they may have saved and carried with them; the constant risk to which their lives will be exposed, &c. &c. Those whom the author has thus classed, form an integral part of the common family of Haytians. Twenty-two years of revolution have so blended and combined the inhabitants of this country into one class, that hardly any can be found to whom this reasoning applies: past experience sufficiently shews the opinion which should be entertained on this subject. All the citizens are soldiers: all have their families to protect: and the protection of property is a common interest. The reasons which would compel them to have recourse to the violent measure of retiring to the woods should be so forcible that each would be convinced of the necessity of doing so: this was the case in the last expedition from France: and it was on this occasion that the true character of the Haytians was displayed. Never were they more firmly united; and, notwithstanding its privations, this situation afforded some moments of gratification; for many Haytians have repeatedly said, in my hearing, *we were much more closely united when we were in the woods: united by a community of danger, we lived together truly like brethren: a residence in towns, and the enjoyments resulting from it, have spoiled and taken from us that frankness, and that natural equality which cheered us, in the hour of calamity, with transitory gleams of consolation.*— Hence it is evident that, if pushed to the last extremity (which God forbid) they would mutually aid each other, and that the Government would adopt proper and secure measures for the welfare of the family. This, I trust, will never come to pass, if truth can obtain a hearing divested of passion and selfish interests.

What has been said, applies equally to those who exercise any industrious calling, for their situation is the same, and a similar fate awaits them. The importance, not of destroying but, of re-edifying every thing, convinced the Haytians, who were soldiers and for the most part the sons of cultivators, of the necessity of acquiring a knowledge of mechanics : numerous manufactories have been established, chiefly in the arsenals of the republic, and the young pupils have become artificers during the revolution. It will be a great error to imagine that they can have any interest or prosperity distinct from that of their brethren, or can enjoy any advantage in which the others do not participate: the offer would also be unpardonable in those who could propose a measure so little acceptable to them.

The military are next considered by the author as forming the fourth class of the population of Hayti. " *Should they* " *prefer the dangerous trade of arms to the peaceful occupa-* " *tion of cultivators, the French Government will possibly grant* " *their desire; but then what a happy change will take place* " *in their favour: in place of being naked, or covered with rags* " *—in place of being ill paid, and worse fed—instead of passing* " *their days in doing mischief to all around them, they will be* " *maintained, cloathed, fed, and paid like other French troops.*"

The military force of Hayti is composed of the *whole* of the citizens; all are born, and are of necessity, soldiers: it is a patriotic virtue which in this country leads them to arms, and a service almost voluntary; all do this with eagerness and delight when necessity demands it: the troops are never kept in barracks, or ever subjected to the minute details of European discipline, to which, as M. Moreau de St. Méry observes, it is almost impossible to habituate them.* The soldier repairs to his alarm post with a singular promptitude, on an alarm being fired, or on the appearance of danger. In ordinary times he commonly remains at his home, and only appears in arms at the inspections which take place every Sunday, or when a certain proportion of men are required for the service of the military stations: the rest, are during this time, with their families on the plantations, where they have gardens abundantly furnished with provisions: and those who prefer a town residence, exercise there every species of industry, from whence they derive substantial advantages. They receive pay *whenever the state of the treasury allows of it*; but they are too just to insist upon regularity in this respect, since they form such a part of the state, that they are convinced they only serve their own cause, and because they are in no absolute want of this pay for their cloathing and support, with the exception of their uniform. All the soldiers take their turn for promotion, which is sufficiently rapid, and they have nothing to fear from injustice, intrigues, or partiality: those who demand their discharge on the plea of wounds or infirmities, form the corps of invalids; and this body receives regular pay, together with grants of land according to the nature of their services: or else, more frequently, they retire to their families and pass their days happy and tranquil. I have not, I believe, exaggerated any thing in my account of the Haytian soldiers: I will add that, thus organized, they have performed prodigies of valour, and it is certain that the situation so vaguely offered, will not appear to them preferable to that which they at present enjoy.

Let us come to M. H. Henry's fifth class, consisting of those " heretofore called *Plantation Negroes*. This class is
" altogether the most numerous, useful and unfortunate of all
" the inhabitants of Hayti, and has under this threefold point
" of view a special claim to our attention, and to give it the
" whole of this, we must go somewhat back.

" Uniformly victims throughout the whole course of the revo-
" lution, plunged into an abyss of misery, the numbers of this
" class sustained a reduction of ninety-nine hundredths during
" the struggle to shake off the salutary and paternal yoke of
" those masters, of whose tender solicitude they are yet the un-
" fortunate objects; their lot was regulated by the principles of
" justice: the hours of labour and rest were fixed: they enjoyed
" wholesome and abundant food: each had a small property

* The black troops in the British service, as well as those in the service of King Henry, prove the fallacy of this observation; being most of them little, if at all, inferior in discipline to the steadiest white troops. – *Translator.*

"allotted to him, which yielded him more or less profit: the
"infirmaries established on the large plantations secured them
"against the evils and infirmities of age: on the smaller ones
"their masters themselves took care of them: nor did the white
"ladies disdain to bring up the negro children in the same
"apartments with themselves, while they lavished attentions
"on them little inferior to those bestowed on their own chil-
"dren. In a word, slavery had insensibly passed into a state of
"servitude, which, in many respects, afforded the negroes ad-
"vantages unknown to the white domestics in Europe. As for
"all the inflammatory declamations uttered by perfidious men,
"athirst for disorder and novelty, the foes of humanity and
"philosophy, whose sacred names they incessantly profane by
"invoking their support to the horrible cause of which they
"are the avowed apostles, they will be instantly overturned.
"This act which, but for the horrors it produced, would have
"been merely ridiculous; this climax of folly and madness
"which was, say they, commanded by humanity, dictated by
"wisdom, proclaimed by philosophy, and the effect of which
"was to render all the negroes instantly happy by conferring
"on them what they called the most lovely, as it is the most
"sacred privilege of every human being, *liberty*, what has it
"produced? The destruction of four thousand of your breth-
"ren, and eventually the loss of all those comforts to which the
"compassionate bounty of your masters had habituated you.
"Inhabitants of Hayti! open your eyes, you have suffered your-
"selves to be once deceived, the annihilation of what yet
"remains of your original population will be the inevitable
"consequence of a second error."

I have copied the author's expressions word for word. I endeavour to depict the condition of Hayti and its inhabitants, not as it was formerly, but as it is at present, and as I have myself beheld it. It is the condition of the cultivator in society which has chiefly attracted my attention in my travels, and is so interesting in itself. It is besides an easy thing for a stranger who lives in the greatest familiarity with the indigénes, and is invited to all their parties of pleasure in the country! and however indisposed he may feel to grant them all the interest which they inspire, it will be extorted from him by their honest simplicity, and their gentleness. I believe myself then thoroughly acquainted with their habits, and I shall endeavour to pourtray them as faithfully as possible. I shall go back first to the formation of the republic, and I find that agriculture is respected there as the first and noblest art; that fêtes are established in honour of it, at which the meritorious cultivator receives marks of distinction, and I have been present at an entertainment at which I saw a venerable agriculturist seated on the right hand of the first magistrate of the state. On the plantations the planters and cultivators are in effect joint proprietors—their duties are reciprocal. The rights which the cultivator has in the estate are, the portion of its profits to which he is entitled, and the advantages which he draws from it by the privilege of cultivating upon it as much provision grounds as he is able to manage. His hours of labour are fixed by the ordinary course of the sun, and he is driven to it by no other compulsion than that of custom and reason. When a woman is pregnant, she withdraws from the common labour of the plantation, for the preservation of her offspring; after delivery she gives her child all the necessary time to acquire strength. If a cultivator is sick, his indisposition has only to be made known for him to receive every attention humanity can suggest. When old and infirm, without losing his advantages upon the plantation, he is considered as an invalid. The soldier, officer, or artisan, born upon a plantation, retains all his right of residence upon it, provided he conducts himself well, and continues to form part of the family. The majority of the cultivators have cattle that pasture in common with those of the proprietors. Persuasion, justice and kind treatment are the means which the laws afford the proprietors for maintaining and preserving the cultivators, and imprisonment, a most rare punishment, is the heaviest penalty inflicted upon the idle and insubordinate. The situation of the cultivators in the mountains is precisely the same, except that their advantages are still more abundant, and that they receive a moiety of the coffee along with the proprietor. The extraordinary exportation of these berries, especially since the war between England and America, arising wholly from the industry of the cultivators, the immense cargoes of English manufactures annually sold in Hayti, and of which they are the chief consumers, prove the extent of their comforts in their present situation; so that the class of cultivators and of these new proprietors is indisputably the most happy, and this is a reflection which must occur to every reader of M. H. Henry's work. It is only necessary to see them upon their plantations, to share in their rural enjoyments, to behold their elegant simplicity when they visit the towns with the surplus produce of their labours, the spirits which animate them, and that happy fecundity which is the true source of prosperity, to be satisfied they have nothing to desire in their present state; and admitting M. H. Henry's calculation that the population of Hayti has been reduced ninety-nine hundredths by the tempests of the revolution, to be correct it follows hence that it has almost entirely recovered itself, for I take it for granted that there is above half a million of souls in Hayti who have consequently been born in the principles or during the progress of the revolution, and since the declaration of general liberty, and who are perfect strangers to the antient *regime*. When we look to the vigorous youths to be met with in the streets, or cast an eye over the ranks of the troops, we must feel the truth of what I advance, and be convinced that the reasonings of the author apply to times widely different from the present, and that he addresses the cultivators in a language which they cannot possibly comprehend. It is evident that, with all their mildness, there is nothing dearer to the Haytians than liberty: they carry this idea to the last degree of enthusiasm, and it is so deeply graven on their hearts, that were the alternative of death or a renunciation of their freedom offered to them, they would not, I am convinced, hesitate to accept the former.

As to the 6th class, composed of troublesome individuals, (says the author, who points it out to the others only to guard them against the mischief it may do them) I think with him it is but small; and I am far from attributing to him another design which might recall to the readers recollection the fable of the dogs who guarded the sheep, and whom the wolves demanded as hostages.

I have now shewn how experience has taught me to view the inhabitants of Hayti in a state of society, it is for them to decide upon my performance, and if they determine favorably what will they say then to M. H. Henry's production? They will conclude that he has collected his information from men who are prejudiced or deceived either by false principles or disappointed hopes, and who unfortunately suffer their passions to stifle the suggestions of reason. Happily these are the remarks of an individual who, possibly with honest intentions, reasons from suppositions which have been represented to him as truths, and which can have no influence upon the existing state of affairs. It might be supposed that, after all that has taken place in France, where we have seen so much contrivance, and witnessed so many sacrifices made in order to avoid interfering with what long habit and the course of the revolution had sanctioned, they would have acted in the same manner towards the inhabitants of Hayti, who cannot be guilty of any offence against the Government of France as at present established, since they did not separate from France till after its suspension. What strong claims have they on its equitable consideration? What reproaches can they reasonably fear from the monarch now restored to the throne? They have been fellow-sufferers with him. Whilst then conciliations, towards which he has laudably made the first advances, give peace and happiness to one portion of mankind, how can it be that the inhabitants of Hayti should be treated, not in the same conciliatory spirit, but according to the suggestions of a cruel and illiberal prejudice excited by the colour of their skins? He must resolve then to see them attacked and pursued like wild beasts, merely because they were unwilling to be slaves!!!—" Not only," says the author, " will they be menaced by the whole disposable force " of France, which will be continually reinforced to harrass " them, but these will be aided, if necessary, by the other colo-" nial powers, who must dread the influence of the dangerous " example of the independence of Hayti, upon their own pos-" sessions, and aided even by England, which would not, in " such a case, refuse France all the assistance she required.— " Menaced also by a maritime force to blockade all the ports " of the island, to provision and recruit the army employed in " fighting, to furnish it with the necessary supplies to enable it " to withstand the malignant influence of the climate, and " afford a shelter from maladies which are frequently so de-" structive only from neglecting to employ those preservatives " of which art and experience have taught the use: but weak-" ened also by the number of deserters who will hasten to join " the French army as soon as want, misery and disappointment " begin to be felt."

In answer to all this I will observe, that these threats and preparations, so frightful if executed, far from disposing their minds to submission, would only irritate them the more, from their seeing nothing but projects of vengeance and re-enslaving marshalled against them. They will even deem resistence the more necessary. They seem to understand with whom they have to deal, and that the fruit of their submission, in the manner proposed by the author, would, as far as regarded them, be nearly the same, except that it would cost less pains.

It is a question, whether, supposing such measures just and reasonable on the part of France, she would derive any beneficial result from them, since destruction would march in the van of her armies, and the evils they would inflict on the Haytians would not secure themselves from a participation in them, without gaining any advantage for the future beyond the inhuman gratification of exterminating the present race of these islanders, and causing the death of so many thousands of Frenchmen, who, after having drenched all Europe with their blood, would have to shed it anew here beneath the Torrid Zone to establish, what—? Systems dictated by avarice and prejudice.

It is very improbable that the British Government would lend itself to such projects, its liberality and sentimens are too well known. It acts upon principles diametrically opposite; it was the first to proscribe the slave trade, and perseveres unremittingly in its endeavours to accomplish its total abolition: for the good of humanity it will doubtless succeed in effecting this. Let us read the noble Lord Castlereagh's speech in the House of Commons, and we shall see the abhorrence with which England regards all sanguinary measures, and how earnestly the noble lord recommends to France never to employ them. Would he not be the first to say to them, " What " would you gain by destroying the population of Hayti, since " you cannot replace it? *Grant them the sacrifice of your co-* " *lonial system; make such overtures as they can accept, then* " *you will gain not only the expences of your expedition, but* " *those resources which the commerce of a country, already cul-* " *tivated, offers to you.*"

The means of defence in Hayti are a secret known only to the chiefs; I shall merely observe that I am unacquainted with any preservative against the influence of the ardent rays of the sun upon the rich blood of Europeans, against the inclemency of a burning climate, against the natural fortifications of the country, and its mountainous positions. I will remind the author that the experience of many nations has led them to regard the conquest of this country, without the consent of its inhabitants, as nearly an impossibility.

I will say nothing respecting the guarantee which the author of the work in question offers to the indigénes, since I admit that his propositions are not calculated for them, and that they will perhaps see, in the men of whom he speaks, the same who accompanied Gen. Leclerc, and who, however changed the French Government may be, are not changed with it. Frequently the measures of government are only the effects of a wise precaution, and I can confidently say, that under these circumstances they will be useless. Every one in Hayti has a right to reason as he pleases: in this respect government has never restricted any person in the expression of his opinions, without being on this account the less wise or prudent in its proceedings. Wishing to follow the author as accurately as possibly, I have sought in vain for the emblem of blood of which he speaks. Can it be that of the flag? The French flag was hitherto *blue, white,* and *red*, when the Haytians proclaimed their independence, they left out the second colour, without, however, any reference to the human complexion, as far as I can judge: and in this respect the multitude of strangers resident in Hayti, where they carry on an advantageous commerce, and are specially protected by the Government of the republic, have never discovered the existence of any marks of proscription against their colour.

I entertain the most ardent wishes for the prosperity of this country; I am anxious that the Haytians may be able, by coming to an happy understanding, to escape all the calamities which threaten them: humanity desires it: it was with these sentiments that I took up my pen, and have proceeded so far. Should it turn out otherwise, I would raise my heart in their favour towards that Supreme Being, that avenging Deity, who has said to all men, *love one another! you are all equal in my sight! you will be judged by your actions, and not by the colour of your skin.*

Port-au-Prince:—Printed at the Government press. 1814.

B

DOCUMENTS PRINTED AT THE GOVERNMENT PRESS AT PORT-AU-PRINCE.

Documents relative to the Communications made in the name of the French Government to the President of Hayti, by General Dauxion Lavaysse, deputed by his Majesty Louis xviii. King of France and Navarre.

No. 1.

Letter from Gen. Dauxion Lavaysse to the President of Hayti.

Kingston, Jamaica, 6th Sept. 1814.

General,

ONE of the persons who is in your Excellency's confidence, and with whom I had an interview at Curaçao through the kindness of General Hodgson, has doubtless communicated to you the nature of my mission, and the paternal and liberal intentions of our King, the well-beloved Louis xviii.

You are too enlightened, General, and doubtless too prudent, not to perceive the wide difference which exists between the order of things established on the restoration of Louis xviii, and that which was known by the name of the *ancient regime*, as well as the arbitrary and despotic government which Bonaparte endeavoured to establish in France.

To deceive for the purpose of enslaving was, for ten years, the grand secret, the *primum mobile*, of the policy of that treacherous, and malicious usurper. Execrated by the whole world, abandoned by the companions of his military glory, the fate of this demoniac, will, it is to be hoped, furnish a lesson to those who, while exercising an illegitimate and precarious power, retain their senses. No great knowledge of public law is necessary to enable us to perceive the difference which exists between the present constitutional form of the Government of France, and that which prevailed before the year 1789.

This, which has re-seated the Bourbons on the throne of France, is not what was some years ago called a counter-revolution, by the emigrants and republicans. The generous Alexander and his allies entered France in order to avenge themselves of an insane tyrant, and furnished a rallying point to the French long worn out by the most grievous and sanguinary despotism.

It was around Alexander that those distinguished men who had been so conspicuous in our revolution rallied themselves: namely the *Tallyrands*, the *Dessoles*, the *Duponts*, the *Marmonts*, the *Bournonvilles*, &c. who, after having for more than twenty years laboured, through all the vicissitudes of our revolution, to accomplish the work of liberty and independence in France, have succeeded in re-erecting the French Monarchy upon the basis of a free and representative Constitution; and of this constitution Louis xviii. was himself one of the principal framers.

How dear ought not this consideration, General, to render his name in the eyes of all true friends of liberty! What an auspicious omen does it not afford to our Haytian brethren!

Yes, General, it is a royal philosopher, a new Marcus Aurelius, another Henry the fourth, who is seated upon the throne of France.

This, believe me, is not the language of flattery, but of truth, and that of all my compatriots.

To satisfy yourself of the spirit which prevails at this day in France, cast your eyes over the list of the Chamber of Peers, and the principal authorities of the State. There you may see the ancient Corinthian pillars of the French monarchy, the *Montmorencies*, the *Rohans*, the *Larochefoucaults*, &c. &c. intermingled with the heroic pillars of the modern order, the *Neys*, the *Suchets*, the *Marmonts*, the *Bournonvilles*, the *Dessoles*, the *Duponts*, &c., those defenders of the independence and the glory of our dear France.

You will see all these men, who by their talents, their genius, their valour and their virtues have ennobled themselves during the tempests and agitations of our revolutions, you will see these, I say, worthily placed between the King and the people, equally the supporters of majesty and the power of the crown, the rights of the nation and public liberty.

Read the Constitutional Charter, and the acts of the present government, and you will see that, in despite of all the clamour and absurdity of the blind or insane partizans of the ancient *regime*, that all which revolution has produced of good and liberal principles, compatible with our monarchical habits, has been religiously preserved.

Reflect well upon these things, General, and reason thus, I pray you, with yourself. " *Louis* xviii. *is a philosophic King, who, before the commencement of the revolution* was one of the most zealous defenders of public freedom. The great officers and generals, who surround him, are almost all the children of the revolution, consequently foes to the ancient abuses and prejudices. These men have raised themselves by the revolution to a level with the first families of France, and we, raised, like them, by the tempests of the same revolution, and by the same causes, should we remain in abasement? Impossible!*

Say likewise to yourself " *Bonaparte was a perfidious and cruel despot, who in politics hardly employed any agents who were not as immoral and perfidious as himself. Better would it have been for us to fight him in our last entrenchments, than conclude any treaty with this Corsican who never respected his promises. But Louis* xviii. *is a legitimate monarch, the descendent of St. Louis and Henry* iv. *who will, in treating with us, only employ honourable means and unprejudiced men, men possibly who, under another Government, have, in their writings or their speeches, advocated our cause"—who does not listen to men blinded by their prejudices, and soured by their misfortunes. Let us repose our confidence in this enlightened, generous and loyal King.* HE WILL EXTEND TO US THE RIGHTS OF FRENCH SUBJECTS AND CITIZENS, WHICH IS UNDOUBTEDLY BETTER THAN TO BE TREATED AS BARBAROUS SAVAGES, OR HUNTED AS MAROON NEGROES."

Make these reflections, this soliloquy, General; instill them into the minds of reasonable men who merit your confidence, and you will deserve the most honourable testimony of your Sovereign's satisfaction, and the gratitude both of your country

---

* Every one is acquainted with the liberal opinions expressed by Louis xviii. (Monsieur) in the Assembly of Notables, and which his long misfortunes have not made him abjure.

and the inhabitants of Hayti, whom we must ever regard as French.

You have too much good sense and discrimination, and are too well acquainted with France, General, to mistake this for the language of weakness. Weakness menaces, but the strong and the powerful crush those who spurn their generosity.

Accept, General, my highest respect,
(Signed) DAUXION LAVAYSSE.

Liberty.   No. 2.   *Equality.*

REPUBLIC OF HAYTI.

Alexander Pétion, President of Hayti, to his Excellency Monsieur Dauxion Lavaysse.

Sir,

By the arrival of his Britannic Majesty's brig *Moselle*, I have been favoured with the letter you did me the honour of addressing to me on the 6th inst. announcing the mission with which you are charged by his most Christian Majesty.

Europe has, for upwards of twenty years, been convulsed with tempests, whose violence has been felt to the extremities of the globe, and of which Hayti has experienced the cruel and painful effects. From the chaos produced by the conflict of so many contending passions and interests, events have arisen which, however extraordinary, resulted from causes perfectly natural, and occasioned a total change in the aspect of affairs.

By a revolution no less surprising than admirable, and by the aid of the allied sovereigns, peace has been restored to the world, and his Majesty Louis xviii. has remounted the throne of his ancestors. All the events which have led to this glorious result bear strongly imprinted on them the stamp of grandeur, generosity, and every thing great and magnanimous which philosophy and virtue can boast; a noble rivalry of justice and disinterestedness on the part of the sovereigns; the security of rights and privileges to all and each individually; the French consulted on the choice of their laws and constitution; the glorious and honourable conduct of Great Britain in abolishing for ever the shameful and inhuman traffic in slaves, fill our hearts with hope, and inspire innocent men, who rely upon the purity of their conscience, the justice of their cause, and the sincerity of their sentiments, with the most perfect confidence guaranteed by such honourable traits.

Entrusted, by their free consent, with the precious deposit of the guardianship of the rights of my fellow citizens whom I represent, I regretted, after reading your Excellency's dispatches, that you have not undertaken a voyage in person to Port-au-Prince, where I should be better able to communicate with you on the nature and extent of your mission. Such a step I take the liberty of recommending. The frankness and loyalty which have been the uniform principles of my conduct assure your Excellency that you will experience among us that politeness, attention and respect, which is due to your person, to the distinguished character you bear, and the sovereign whose orders you convey.

I beg your Excellency to believe the sentiments of high consideration with which I have the honour to remain

your Excellency's most obedient and humble servant,
(Signed) PETION.

Port-au-Prince, 24th Sept. 1814 : 11th year of Independence.

No. 3.

The undersigned principal agent of his Excellency the Minister of Marine and the Colonies of his most Christian Majesty, for the restoration of the French colony in the island of Hayti, has the honour to propose the undermentioned considerations and measures to Mr. President Pétion, and the provisional authorities of that colony.

After twenty-four years of troubles and wars carried on with an animosity and perfidiousness long unusual amongst the civilized nations of Europe, these nations once more repose beneath the shade of peace. This blessing they owe to the downfal of the revolutionary government which desolated France; to the overthrow of that treacherous and sanguinary usurper, *that scourge of God, that modern Attila*, who had been suffered to tyrannize over the French and other nations for the purpose of curing and punishing them for their revolutionary follies and crimes; above all they are indebted for this blessing of peace to the restoration of the august and benevolent house of Bourbon.

While cries of joy ascending to Heaven from every part, not only of the French empire, but of Europe, hail this glorious event, shall discordant voices be heard from the queen of the French colonies?

The nations so long in arms against revolutionary France, or rather against her revolutionary government, having made a sincere peace with our legitimate government; will the existing government of Hayti display less respect, esteem and confidence towards the ancient and venerable government of the Bourbons, than those of civilized Europe?

The Haytians have been so often and so cruelly deceived, that an almost invincible spirit of mistrust has arisen among them. But by whom have they been deceived, betrayed, butchered and drowned?

By the same profligate and blood-thirsty wretches, the refuse and disgrace of the French nation, the enemies and persecutors of the house of Bourbon, and of all virtuous people: the disciples of the Robespierres, the Marats, and the Carriers: the worthy satellites of their successor the Corsican tyrant.

Yes! the butchers and foes of the Haytians are no others than the guilty enemies of our dear and venerable Bourbons.

Inhabitants of Hayti! reflect well on this circumstance; above all reflect upon it well you who are the supreme head of the government, and all ye generals and magistrates to whom Providence has entrusted the care of this people, the care of instructing them in their true interests: doubt not that this people will one day or other demand from you a rigorous account of your administration.

After these preliminary observations I shall have the honour of proposing to the President of Hayti to recognise and proclaim the sovereignty of the French monarch, as soon as he shall judge in his wisdom, that the people of this country are sufficiently prepared for this great and happy event.

Why, like the wise and energetic men who, in the interval between the downfal of Bonaparte and the restoration of the Bourbons in France—why should not the President of Hayti in conjunction with some of the principal inhabitants form themselves into the President and Members of a Provisional Government for Hayti, in the name of his Majesty Louis xviii.

Should they have the energy and prudence to adopt this benevolent measure, what splendid rewards will they not deserve at the hands of the worthy descendant of the virtuous Henry iv.; what gratitude from France, their country, and their countrymen of Hayti.

Let the supreme head of the government and his subordinate officers convince their countrymen that the progress of knowledge has overthrown in France the tyranny of those colonial prejudices so injurious to humanity: that, like those volcanoes which, though at the time they desolate their vicinity by their eruptions, fertilize them afterwards by their ashes, the French revolution has left behind some important truths and principles which have given birth to the free and wise constitution we have received from our benevolent legislator Louis xviii.; that, like the Deity, whose image and representative he is, this monarch, the father of all the French, whether born beneath the climate of Europe, or that of the torrid zone, whatever be the colour nature has imprinted on their visage; this monarch I say, equally enlightened and good, like the Deity, cherishes all alike, wishes them all to share the new order of affairs which has regenerated France, and to establish no distinctions save those of virtue, learning, and talent.

Let them be assured that those violent and incorrigible men, whose prejudices would have been incompatible with the peace of the colony, have been banished from her bosom.

Let them bear in mind that it is a Malouet who is now Minister of Marine and the Colonies; that Malouet was the friend of the Abbé Raynal who pleaded their cause before the constituent assembly. Let them know that the names of *Nestor* among the Greeks, *Cato* among the Romans, or *Sully* in the days of Henry iv. do not awaken more lively recollections of virtue than that of the *Malouet* of our own days, and consequently that whatever shall be promised by such a minister in the name of the best of kings, will be as religiously fulfilled as if promised by the Divinity himself.

Let them consider that a government so widely different from that of the Corsican* will send them none but chiefs as distinguished for their probity, their disinterestedness and their humanity, as the *Bachas, Leclercs* and other brigands, sent some years ago by the usurper, were horribly conspicuous for rapacity, perfidy and cruelty.

* If I speak with such indignation of this usurper whose name is so united to military glory, it is because in the eye of every virtuous man all his glory is tarnished by his robberies, his cruelties, and his treachery. Possessing the greatest talents, united to the most unprincipled and unbounded ambition, Bonaparte fully answered the celebrated description of the Corsicans given by Seneca, in these lines.

" Prima lex est mentiri,
" Secunda ulcisci,
" Tertia vivere rapto,
" Quarta non agnoscere Deum."

Which may be thus rendered—

First 'midst their laws unblushing falsehood stands,
Next dark revenge displays her bloodstained hands;
Third on the list fell plunder shames the day,
While trembling victims own her fearful sway;
Creation's Lord, these wretches next disown,
And drag religion from her sacred throne.

What a portrait!—what a people! Such was the contempt in which they were held by the Romans that they would not have them even as slaves, as the Senator Lanjuinais had the courage to remark to his colleagues when they proposed to elect Bonaparte Emperor.

How rejoiced should I be if these observations and propositions which merely express the paternal views of our excellent sovereign and his virtuous minister should make any impression on the hearts of the chiefs and inhabitants of Hayti. Ah! should they induce them voluntarily to hoist the royal standard, that emblem of French fidelity and honour, with what extatic joy would I not hasten to place myself under the command of the present head of the Haytian government, offer to range myself amidst his military staff, and embrace them as my comrades and brethren in arms.

Then would the Haytians see their agriculture, their trade and their industry, revive. Ease, riches, and happiness would be diffused amongst them, and the reign of confidence would supersede that of anxiety and mistrust, so painful to all generous souls. (Signed)

DAUXION LAVAYSSE.

To his Excellency the President of Hayti.
Port-au-Prince, 9th Nov. 1814.

Liberty.   No. 4.   *Equality.*

REPUBLIC OF HAYTI.

Alexander Pétion, President of Hayti, has the honour to acknowledge the receipt of the note addressed to him on the 9th of the present month by his Excellency General Dauxion Lavaysse, in his capacity of principal agent of his Excellency the minister of Marine and the Colonies to his Most Christian Majesty, for the restoration of the French colony in St. Domingo.

A revolution, as long as it was surprising, which had nearly overturned the whole world, whose character and progress is unexampled in the annals of history, has terminated in a manner no less wonderful than unexpected, and the nations of the earth once more retrace the obliterated or forgotten vestiges of their ancient institutions. The island of Hayti, roused by the shouts of liberty which re-echoed in France on the first dawning of the revolution, was naturally disposed to take an active share in these commotions, and was likewise made to feel them in their full force, and the events, by which they were accompanied, prepared her for her present situation.

It is with pain that the President of Hayti reminds his Excellency General Lavaysse, that all the calamities of this country originated in revolutionary France, and that she has never ceased to provoke them by a conduct so uniformly cruel as to drive the inhabitants of Hayti to despair. Never did a people display more devotion to the mother country than the Haytians. Abandoned by her to the sanguinary caprice and fury of those savage and corrupt agents, who have in turn successively persecuted them more and more, the Haytians, ever faithful to France, fought for her beneath her flag, made her arms victorious at a distance of two thousand leagues, and never ceased to give proofs of the most unexampled attachment; when, at the peace of Amiens she sent an expedition which ought to have established permanently the prosperity of this beautiful island, and rewarded the services rendered to the mother country by a number of men who alone and left to themselves had for fourteen years sustained the lustre of the French arms. An expedition of cannibals! in which the planters and the French vied with each other in their insatiable thirst for Haytian blood. The arms which they had used to assist the French army in taking possession of the country were torn from their hands, while they themselves were dragged on board floating prisons called *etouffoirs*, smothered, drowned, hung, bayonetted, burned, torn in pieces by blood hounds, trained to this horrible sport and brought from the Spanish main at a heavy expence.

The shades of each succeeding night came but to veil the horror of these dreadful executions, and the day was occupied in collecting the victims without distinction! It was enough to have borne arms either as an officer or a private; to have appeared in any capacity upon the revolutionary stage, to be put to death. Neither *women,* nor *infants,* nor *the aged* escaped the fury of these monsters! When other prey was wanting they entered the houses to form the nightly chain by means of the domestics, and the first who came in their way. The inhabitants of the towns were prevented from eating fish lest in so doing they should feed on their own blood, and when at this very time sickness preyed upon the French troops exposed to vengeance and resentment of those who, to escape punishment, were obliged to conceal themselves in the woods, whence they carried on hostilities, at this very time the French ramparts were to be seen manned with Haytians, who defended them with ther arms and their courage till it came to their own turn to die!!

Such, general, were the amusements and recreations of *Leclerc, Rochambeau,* and the planters who excited them, and who, in the dread of being suspended, procured by an address *Rochambeau's* appointment as captain general. Their wishes were heard; alas! possibly they were those of France. This was the signal for the desertion of the Haytians to the woods to become almost general, and also for an increase of the cruelties of the French. I for one, withdrew to save myself from death. What were our hopes? Could we think it possible for us to repulse the French? Yet what was our alternative? Could we hesitate as to the conduct to be pursued? I dare to believe we were justified. God and our perseverance did the rest.

On the evacuation by the French army we returned to the towns, where we found every thing destroyed, and that every thing was to be recreated. Who will speak to us of our crimes—of our vengeance? Let him peruse the volume of our calamities, and thence form his opinion of our conduct. I have, I think, read somewhere in the melancholy annals of the world that, in those countries in which slavery prevailed, when the slaves succeeded in bursting their bonds, they forged them into arms against their oppressors: this was our conduct. The war between France and England was renewed. Isolated from all other nations and obliged to legislate for ourselves, our first act was to proclaim our independence, a measure which, under all the circumstances of our case, was but natural. We framed a constitution for ourselves with fixed and positive laws, and after the lapse of eleven years we undertook to guide ourselves. All the offices of state are filled with regenerated Haytians; we have raised an army; our flag waves and is respected over the ocean. We have been obliged to rise to the loftiness of our destinies. We have respected the laws of nations; in a word we can with truth say that we have had a share among the powers united against revolutionary France, in more or less directly aiding by our commerce, our supplies of provisions in the Antilles, and by our attitude, their operations, and we claim to ourselves a participation in the glory of co-operating to produce the results which followed. Let the indulgence of this vanity be allowed us.

I will ask your Excellency if we can possibly retrograde, if we can resign the advantages we have procured for ourselves, of liberty in the fullest extent of the word, of the most perfect equality of rights, and the guarantee which the arms in our hands afford us.

" The Haytians have been so often, and so cruelly deceived,
" that an almost insurmountable spirit of mistrust has arisen
" amongst them."

This is an unanswerable axiom, and, I will add, that this mistrust has been kept alive by the publications, the plans for attacking the country, and the proscriptions which have continually deluged France, and of which multitudes have reached us. The P. Alb. Délatre &c. &c. &c. all colonists, unbridled in their impotent rage, have calculated the method of subduing us: not content with wishing to recover their own possessions they have even disposed of ours and made them figure in a chapter of colonial receipts. Can any connection subsist between us and such men? Can confidence ever be renewed? Where have they been? To whose fortunes have they adhered? Not assuredly to those of Louis xviii. in England, but rather to those of the idol at whose feet they burned incense. The incense has escaped their hands, but the censer yet remains, and has been to us a Pandora's box. Do they, more fortunate than the emigrants, expect to recover their properties when the tried and faithful followers of their sovereign have been forced to resign theirs?

Your Excellency does me the honour to observe, that the times are totally changed. What a difference! What a contrast between the government of Louis xviii. and that which preceded it! I am far from entertaining a different opinion and ascribing to his most Christian Majesty sentiments so opposite to those he has uniformly expressed: we know him by his misfortunes: he knows us by ours. We never have offended him, and the same men who persecuted him, were equally our oppressors. What was the origin of the revolution? Against whom? The national cockade was imported from France, and the earliest disturbances broke out among the white French, against the government and its sovereign, whose authority was despised. What was our conduct then? Let them recollect Colonel Mauduit and his death, and they will see how we acted. To us the restoration of his most Christian Majesty was no surprise. It was the wish of the allied powers, and it was under the walls of the capital that this work was achieved in presence of their armies. The king's first act on his return to France was to promise an oblivion of the past, to consider the French in no other light than as loyal subjects, and to sacrifice to the repose of the world and the tranquillity of his kingdom the most distressing recollections, setting no value on these sacrifices. Shall we alone then be excluded from these benefits?

I do not dispute that men may reasonably lay aside mutual hostility, and enter into treaties of peace and amity for their reciprocal advantage. They are by their bodily organization framed to communicate with each other, and from their parleys reconciliations sometimes arise. By the law of nature they may at all times enter into such treaties, because they are on a footing of equality. That is the position in which we consider ourselves as standing with relation to France; but it does not appear to us that on her part we are regarded in the same point of view. It is of little importance in respect of commercial profits and their effects on the general interests of France, whether this country is in her hands or ours, for they will be the same in either case, and it is matter of demonstration that the country can be useful in our hands alone.

At what conclusion do we arrive from considering the subject in another point of view? War would necessarily occasion the loss of every thing, especially when carried on as it was in this island, where it was absolutely a war of extermination, and could no longer be a desirable system of policy to pursue. Your Excellency must be well assured that personal ambition has no influence over my opinions: we will consider nothing but our existence, our security, and our guarantee against every possible event.

I have the honour to acquaint you, that in order to be able to reply with precision to the principal proposition contained in your Excellency's official note, I have summoned a meeting of the chief authorities of the republic at Port-au-Prince for the 21st instant, when I shall submit it to their consideration; I have issued general orders on this subject, and shall have the honour to acquaint you with the result.

I address your Excellency with the greatest candour, and a perfect knowledge of the spirit of the people. Your stay amongst us will enable you to judge of their character, which unfortunately has never yet been sufficiently understood.

The President of Hayti seizes this opportunity to assure his Excellency General Lavaysse of his highest consideration.

(Signed) PETION.
Port-au-Prince, 12th Nov. 1814: 11th year of Independence.

No. 5.

Port-au-Prince, 19th November, 1814.
Mr. President,

The last letter your Excellency did me the honour of addressing to me upon the 12th was not delivered to me before the afternoon of the 14th, I had a fever the next day, and on the following I took physic, which weakened me so as to render me incapable of writing at any length.

In the letter in which I have now the honour to address to you, I cannot refrain from expressing my surprise at your Excellency's continuing, both in your oral and written communications, to blame the French for crimes committed in this island by the tools of a faction and a tyrant who had so long been the instruments of the Almighty's vengeance in oppressing our country.

With equal justice, Mr. President, might the inhabitants of Bourdeaux, of Nantes, of Lyons, of Marseilles, or of Toulon, be accused of the murders, the drownings, and enormities of every description, perpetrated in those cities by the same rapacious, sanguinary and unprincipled faction.

Providence, designing doubtless to punish, but not to overthrow France, has permitted her to acquire reputation by the glory of her arms and the grandeur and wisdom of her establishments, and she is at present governed by the wise and benevolent chief of that ancient family of kings, saints, and chevaliers, who have so long rendered her great and successful: in a word, by a Bourbon, a name at which every French heart beats with delight: a Bourbon, who prides himself upon being born a Frenchman.

May the inhabitants of this island, Mr. President, experience the same sentiments as their European brethren. The manner in which your Excellency concludes your last letter, leads me to indulge in this delightful hope.

Yet there is one thing which disturbs this pleasing idea, I allude to the facility, nay even eagerness with which some persons receive and propagate the most absurd reports and falsehoods which are equally injurious to the interests and the honour of our country.

And who are the fabricators and retailers of this tattle? What their object? They are wretches, the scum and outcasts of England and America, pitiful commission merchants, masters of droghers, men whom no respectable merchant in Jamaica, in England, or in France, would admit to his table. Yet here they start into consequence, and become very oracles.

You, Mr. President, who are so very enlightened and discerning, should not allow yourself to be influenced by their impudent absurdities, through which it is easy to discover their motives, and that it is their interest and their object to perpetuate discord, and prevent the reconciliation of the colony to the mother country.

After having been your blood-suckers, they next wish to act the part of the hyenas and jackalls who attend upon the lions, tygers, and other noble animals, in order to feast on the refuse of their prey. Such is the design of these worthless wretches who breathe only amidst civil wars and conflagrations, either that they may have an excuse for appropriating to their own use the funds of their employers, or gorge themselves with our spoils and rejoice over our misfortunes.

But we are all French, Mr. President. May then the august name of Bourbon be the signal of our rallying: may the wisdom and firmness with which you have so long governed this country amid the revolutionary tempests yet be her compass and her anchor. May France and her excellent monarch owe the possession of this country, not to compulsion, but to the genuine French feelings and the loyalty of its inhabitants. Your Excellency is worthy of accomplishing this great work. May you be entitled to the gratitude of your sovereign and your countrymen of both hemispheres.

Such is the ardent and sincere desire of him who has the honour to be with the highest respect, Mr. President, your Excellency's most humble and obedient servant,

(Signed) DAUXION LAVAYSSE.

P. S. I take the liberty of requesting your Excellency will communicate this letter to the magistrates and officers who are about you.

Liberty.   No. 6.   *Equality.*

REPUBLIC OF HAYTI.

Alexander Pétion, President of Hayti, to his Excellency General Dauxion Lavaysse.

I have the honour to acknowledge the receipt of the letter your Excellency addressed to me on the 19th inst. and I sincerely regret to find your indisposition continues, and shall learn with pleasure its termination.

I conceived it my duty to explain to your Excellency the nature and extent of the calamities with which our unhappy country has been afflicted ever since the commencement of the French revolution: and to shew who were the principal authors of them. This explanation was the more necessary, because after the patience of the Haytians had been exhausted by the rudest trials, the fate of their country was decided, and their emancipation as a people dictated by the atrocious conduct of those who, from the situation in which they were placed, might by a different mode of proceeding, have bound us indissolubly to France. It would be unjust to ascribe to his most Christian Majesty transactions in which he had no share, since at the time of their occurrence he was himself an exile from his dominions, and the victim of the very men who persecuted us so cruelly. His restoration to his throne, together with all those events which paved the way for it: the enlightened spirit of philosophy which appeared to have altered the politics of the world; and our conduct during this memorable struggle, seemed to justify our indulging a hope that we should have received the reward due to our sacrifices, by a spontaneous recognition of our rights. I will not repeat all that I have had the honour to say to your Excellency on this subject, since I am desirous of learning the wishes of the nation, which it was my duty, as chief magistrate, to consult. The time for this now approaches: since the principal members of the republic, to whom I shall submit all your Excellency's communications, are assembling in this town, and I shall lose no time in acquainting you with their determination. In this, as in every other act of my life, I shall prove to my fellow citizens that my principles and conduct are uniformly guided by public opinion, and that it is for them to decide in an affair which so materially concerns their dearest interests.

Your Excellency will be unjust to the Haytians if you believe them capable of being influenced by vague and unauthorised reports. They deserve more justice, and are fully capable of discriminating between credible and incredible intelligence. Persons are to be found in every country whose occupation it is to fabricate news. It is, if I may be allowed the expression, the trade of all the news writers in the world; and they always meet with persons who will circulate their falsehoods. To the known character of the foreign merchants resident in Hayti, to their honourable conduct under every circumstance, and in all their commercial transactions with us, I must give the meed of praise which is their due: they fearlessly employ numerous captains in their trade with us, and have made, as often as it was in their power, large advances both to individual Haytians, and to the government; all of which they have lost during the public commotions, and none have a deeper interest in the maintenance of order and tranquillity. They have always been under the special protection of government, they have never ceased to respect it, and have invariably confined themselves within the bounds of their own concerns, without seeking to exert any influence, or take any share in public affairs. Men such as your Excellency describes, if indeed they are to be found among us, undoubtedly merit the most profound contempt.

I beg your Excellency to accept my assurance of the high respect with which I have the honour to salute you.

(Signed) PETION.

Port-au-Prince 20th Nov. 1814: 11th year of Independence.

Liberty   No. 7.   *Equality.*

REPUBLIC OF HAYTI.

Alexander Pétion, President of Hayti, to his Excellency General Dauxion Lavaysse.

The generals and magistrates of the republic of Hayti, assembled to take into consideration the several dispatches of your Excellency which were laid before them, and invited to decide upon the proposition they contained, of forming a provisional government for Hayti in the name of his Majesty Louis xviii. were of opinion, that the several events of the revolution which have produced the present state of affairs in this country, were the result of the greatest sacrifices and consecrated by the purest blood of their fellow citizens who fell in defence of those rights of which it was attempted to deprive them, and which they acquired by their courage and perseverance, as well as by the divine protection: that their first movement on emancipating themselves was to proclaim their independence: that during the whole course of the coalition of the allied powers against revolutionary France, they did not cease to shew principles conformable to those which directed their operations, and that hence they conceive they have incontestible claims upon the justice of the sovereigns, and more especially upon that of his most Christian Majesty; claims the better founded since they have been unable to discover any blame which can be imputed to them, convinced that they had no other line of conduct to pursue, than that which they adopted, and which is justified by all the circumstances which provoked it. They cannot compromise their security and their very existence by any change in the state, the bare contemplation of it would draw down upon them a sudden and general overthrow, and infallibly destroy a country already too long torn by revolutionary fury, and which might hope to be allowed, like the rest of the world to repose beneath the shelter of peace. It is worthy of the greatness and enlightened philosophy of his most Christian Majesty to recognise the emancipation of a people whose misfortunes commenced with his own, and who, abandoned to the rage of his enemies, knew how after having defeated them to make a noble use of their victory, by taking as models those nations who succeeded in restoring him to his throne. It is gratifying to them to believe that his Majesty is guided in his proceedings with respect to Hayti much less by his own personal feelings than by a sense of what he owes to that portion of his people which loudly exclaims against the return of Hayti to France and the ancient regime. It will also be a source of lasting glory to his Majesty in granting to the Haytians a recognition of the independence of their rights, to reconcile it with what he owes to a part of his subjects in making others share in the benefits of a commerce whose abundant channels would promote the welfare of both countries. It is with such sentiments that I, as organ of the people over whom I have the honour to preside, will propose to your Excellency, acting in the name of his Majesty Louis xviii. and to give him a proof of the disposition which animates us, to establish the basis of an indemnity which we most solemnly engage to pay with every just security which can be required of us, and which shall be applied as he judges most expedient: this is worthy of him. Most sincerely do I wish that these propositions may prove agreeable to your Excellency; and in case they should not coincide exactly with the nature of your powers, I flatter myself that you will communicate them to the ministers of your sovereign, and that your residence in Hayti, by which you will have had an opportunity of becoming better acquainted with our national character, and what we really are, will induce you to do it in a favourable manner. I beg your Excellency to see nothing in this determination but the wishes of a people to whom their rights and liberties are dearer than their life, acting only from a deep feeling of what is due to their own preservation, without asperity or prejudice against France. In requesting your Excellency to support these propositions by your interest with the government, I give you a striking proof of the high respect with which you have inspired us, and to which I am happy to bear testimony.

I have the honour to be, general,
your Excellency's most humble servant,
(Signed) PETION.

Port-au-Prince, 27th Nov. 1814: 11th year of Independence.

No. 8.

Port-au-Prince, 29th November, 1814.

Mr. President,

I have the honour to acknowledge the receipt of your letter of the 27th, in which your Excellency acquaints me with the result of the deliberations of the assembly of the notables of your government. I shall lose no time in communicating it to his Excellency the Minister of Marine and the Colonies.

The closing of this assembly, together with your letter, having put an end to my mission, I ought not to lose a moment in returning to my country. In consequence, I yesterday, commissioned a merchant to charter a vessel to take me to Jamaica. He will have the honour of addressing your Excellency to-day or to-morrow respecting my passports.

I have the honour to thank you for the personal compliments contained in the conclusion of your last letter. If the fruitless issue of my mission has rendered me undeserving of them, those who have witnessed my zeal, I may even say my moral anguish, during a long and overpowering illness, will at least do me the justice of allowing that I have omitted nothing which could contribute to a more favourable result, and that I have neither been discouraged nor put out of patience by the daily and perverse machinators who are equally your enemies and ours, and with whom I venture to predict that you will yourself, Mr. President, be one day as much displeased as I am.

I have the honour to be with the highest consideration, your Excellency's most obedient and humble servant,

(Signed) DAUXION LAVAYSSE.

Liberty.   No. 9.   *Equality.*

REPUBLIC OF HAYTI.

The President of Hayti to the People and the Army.

Never did the annals of the republic present a more interesting epoch than that you have now witnessed, or one in which the national character has displayed itself more nobly. Haytians, we have fought during a period of twenty-four years for our rights and for our liberty; the attainment of our independence has been the glorious fruit of our labours; without it there was no security, no guarantee for our regeneration.—Known already by our military reputation, and our honourable character, the eyes of the world are upon us, and await the result of our conduct; it will be an example for posterity.—I will not recall any of the glorious traits which have distinguished those who have immortalised themselves in the cause of freedom. History has recorded them, and they will glow to the end of time in her commemorative page.

I address a people warmed with the purest flame of patriotism, a people free in fact as well as in right, and one that will never cease to shew to the world at large that it is worthy to be so. Nobleness and generosity are the natural characteristics of the patriot: I have always observed you to possess these noble qualities, and of this I have just received a fresh proof, for which I have the honour of expressing to you my liveliest gratitude. France has made peace. She reclaims her sovereignty over St. Domingo. She has lost for ever her claims upon Hayti, and it is to the French themselves that she is indebted for this loss. She wished nevertheless to retrieve it, and preferred employing for this purpose conciliation rather than force, which will always be impotent. An agent, General Dauxion Lavaysse, has presented himself. You have received and welcomed him; he has enjoyed the sacred rights of hospitality, and has lived with confidence in the midst of you. He has declared the purport of his mission: at a distance of two thousand leagues from his country, he has warmly urged the pretensions of his government without suffering any personal considerations to influence him. Your chiefs and magistrates have been convoked and consulted; they have listened calmly to the propositions of France. A government, conscious of its own strength, and founded on the solid basis of justice and reason, can listen to every thing, and is capable of duly discriminating. These propositions were incompatible with your principles and your institutions, and were unanimously rejected, as all propositions, which have a tendency to make you retrograde in the career you have run, will be.

Without fearing war, you were desirous of proving your wish of averting from your families and children the horrors she brings in her train, by the offer of pecuniary sacrifices to silence your persecutors, whose cries assail the French throne for the restoration of those possessions which they would tremble to approach, were they but convinced that on the instant of their appearance they would be converted into heaps of ashes. Your chiefs, the depositories of your intentions expressed in general terms, especially since the continental peace, have made this generous proposition in your name: a proposition which will give at once an idea of your wisdom, and make your enemies afraid of exciting your resentment.

Haytians! you have acted as you ought. The right of conquest has placed the country in your hands, it is your irrevocable property, and you are masters of it with full power to employ your property in such manner as you think proper.

Nations, by a mutual compact, from which they never swerve, respect the rights of nations. However culpable the intentions of an envoy may be, his character is always sacred. The French general, Dauxion Lavaysse, is gone, having ended his mission. You have not to reproach yourselves with any failure in what you owe to yourselves. You have not violated that fundamental principle which establishes the communications necessary for the maintenance of the political relations between governments. You have rendered yourselves estimable in your own eyes, and worthy of being considered so in the eyes of the world at large.

Victory is the uniform attendant upon a just cause; it is yours to say you are assured of it, should any presume to trouble you. In this case you will see me always at your head, resolute in either leading you to victory or falling with you.—Whatever be the lot Heaven has in store for us, we should be prepared for it. It is the duty of those chiefs whose paternal authority directs you, in the districts committed to their care, to provide secure retreats for the inhabitants in the interior of the mountains, and to employ for this purpose the artificers who are under their command. It is likewise their duty to multiply plantations of provisions of every description. It is the duty of the magistrates and justices of the peace to promote union, concord, industry and confidence, among their fellow citizens. The republic expects every man will do his duty, and I shall be the first to set the example.

I have directed the documents relative to the communications made by the French Government to be printed; they will be laid before you along with this address. You will there see what has been proposed, and what reply you ought to make.

Given at Port-au-Prince this third day of December, 1814: in the eleventh year of Independence.

Petion,

By the President.
B. Ingenac,
Commander of a squadron, and secretary.

Port-au-Prince:—Printed at the Government press. 1814.

C

FURTHER DOCUMENTS RELATIVE TO THE MISSION OF LAVAYSSE, MEDINA, AND DRAVERMANN, PUBLISHED BY ORDER OF KING HENRY.

No. 1.

Instructions for MM. Dauxion Lavaysse, de Médina and Dravermann.

IT being the paternal intention of his majesty to re-establish order and peace throughout his dominions by the mildest means, he has resolved upon not employing force to compel the insurgents of St. Domingo to return to their duty until every measure which his clemency can dictate has been found ineffectual. It is impressed with such considerations that his majesty has turned his attention to St. Domingo. Consequently, though he has directed a large force to hold itself in readiness to act if necessary, he has authorised the minister of marine and the colonies to send agents to St. Domingo to procure correct information respecting the disposition of those who at present possess any degree of authority there, the present situation of affairs, and the condition of individuals of every class. His majesty is disposed to make concessions to all who will promptly return to their duty, and contribute to the re-establishment of the tranquillity and prosperity of the colony. The report which the minister of marine shall make to his majesty after receiving that of the undermentioned agents will regulate the nature and extent of his concessions.

MM. Dauxion Lavaysse, de Médina, and Dravermann appointed by the king to execute this mission, will repair immediately in one of the English packet boats, which sail regularly twice a month from Falmouth, either to Portorico or Jamaica. From whichever of these islands they land at, they will proceed to St. Domingo, where they will at first only appear as persons who come to make commercial arrangements, either on their own account, or that of some mercantile house. Two of them will enter into correspondence as soon as possible, but yet with the greatest circumspection, with Pétion and his colleague Borgella: the third will do the same with respect to Christóphe. They must not open themselves more fully to these chieftains, until they have carefully sounded their dispositions, and made themselves acquainted with their internal resources, the degree of their preponderance in the island, and the spirit of their subjects; nor will they disclose their credentials, until they judge it expedient. It is impossible to lay down precise rules in this respect, much therefore must be left to their prudence and discretion.

When they have begun to negociate frankly with these chiefs they will discuss a plan of political organization which may suit their wishes, and to which the king can give his consent. They will receive from these chiefs an assurance of adhering to these plans, and that, protected by the royal power, they will bring all their subjects to submit. The agents on their side, without signing any formal treaty, a thing derogatory to the royal dignity, will assure the chiefs that his majesty is disposed to grant whatever shall be agreed upon by them, and that he will make this known, immediately on their return to France, by a declaration emanating from his grace. They will impress upon the minds of the chiefs that whatever the king has once promised, will be most irrevocably and religiously observed.

If the chiefs are, as is said, enlightened and intelligent, especially Pétion and Borgella, they will see that it is not enough for them to gain advantages for themselves and their successors, but they should also render them durable, and they will perceive that for this purpose they should not be excessive in *amount* as respects themselves, or in *extent* as respects the mass of the population. They will see that if the great mass of the blacks be not sent back and retained in slavery, or at least in a state of subjection resembling that which subsisted before the troubles, there can neither be tranquillity nor prosperity for the colony, nor safety for themselves. They will also see that for this numerous class, which constitutes in fact the population of the colony, to continue in submission to an exact though mild regime, it is requisite that the interval between them and the supreme head, should be filled by intermediate ranks, and that the example of a gradual superiority and obedience would render their inferiority less striking. From these considerations it is reasonable to conclude that Pétion and Borgella, satisfied with obtaining entire favour for themselves, and a small number of their necessary instruments, will consent to the rest of their cast being placed, notwithstanding their acquisition of nearly a perfect equality of rights, somewhat below the white cast: for, on the one hand, the perfect assimilation granted to them will be more marked and flattering, and, on the other, their cast will be better able to keep the blacks, both free and slaves, at their proper distance, from the circumstance of a shade of difference existing between themselves and the whites.

They must insist strongly upon this point, since it ought to be the first step in the progress of the negociation. It is of the first importance to preserve for the whites some superiority over the coloured class of the first rank, admitting nevertheless Pétion, Borgella, and some others, from this time forward absolutely and without reserve into the class of whites, and granting hereafter *lettres des blancs* cautiously from time to time to such individuals as may appear entitled to that indulgence, either by the fairness of their complexion, their fortune, their education, or their public services.

Should Pétion voluntarily consent to place the men of colour, including the mulattoes, a degree below the whites, it will facilitate the restriction of the privileges ot the cast next in succession (composed of shades intermediate between the mulatto and the negro) together with that of the free negroes; should these three intermediate classes be formed between the whites and the slaves.

Above all it is particularly recommended to MM. Dauxion Lavaysse, Médina, and Dravermann to adhere as closely as possible to the ancient order of colonial affairs, and never to deviate from it, except where it is morally impossible to do otherwise; and they should in their conferences on these subjects with the chiefs, uniformly adhere to this principle, that the King of France makes concessions wholly from his own free will, and that, far from admitting unreasonable demands, he not only will not grant any thing, but will make the full weight of his power to be felt, should his favours be rejected. In fact who can doubt, that if the King of France wished to bring all his forces against a handful of his rebellious subjects, hardly amounting to the hundredth part of the population of his dominions, destitute besides of the great military resources of Europe, and cut off from all foreign aid, who doubts, we say, his ability to reduce, and even to exterminate them, if he should be obliged to do so.

MM. Dauxion Lavaysse, de Médina, and Dravermann, should constantly remember in the course of their negociation, to urge this consideration to the chiefs, and always to exhibit the king's benevolence in conjunction with his power. There is no doubt that by employing these means adroitly, they may, without making too large concessions, render the employment of force unnecessary. It will also contribute to their success to shew Pétion and the rest how precarious their present situation must be if abandoned to themselves; that in a little time the mulattoes, far less numerous than the blacks, will be crushed by them; that the colony will be the prey of factions whose leaders will be successively overturned by more fortunate competitors; that on the conclusion of a durable peace between France and all the maritime powers, no foreign flag will be suffered to enter the ports of St. Domingo, and that the king will have only to send six frigates to cut off all external communication with the present inhabitants of the island, in which case they would cultivate the rich productions of their soil to no purpose, being no longer able to exchange them for the necessaries they require, and that they will soon be reduced to live like savages destitute of all the advantages of European civilization. Such considerations must necessarily strike Pétion and Borgella, and they will perceive that if the king abstains for the present from all compulsory measures, it is because he wishes to promote the welfare of his subjects of all classes, and does not suppose that his benevolent views will encounter any obstacles. Convinced that the present inhabitants of St. Domingo, weary of the troubles which have distracted them for twenty-five years, will hasten to embrace the certain advantages held out to them by his majesty's paternal government, the king suspends every rigorous measure, and does not send the most inconsiderable force to the shores of St. Domingo, for the present even abstaining from interdicting the trade carried on with them by foreign ships. But, on the return of the agents, to whom these instructions are given, and after their report, his majesty will send sufficient forces for their protection, or, if necessary, forces which no power within the island can possibly withstand.

Having once come to an understanding with Pétion and Borgella respecting those matters which concern themselves and the first class of coloured people, the agents will arrange with them the minimum of concessions to be made to the second class, consisting of persons of a shade deeper than the free mulattoes, without being absolutely black, and the third composed of free negroes.

For this once, should Pétion and Borgella judge it expedient, all mulattoes, whether formerly free by right, or recently free in fact, whether legitimate or the reverse, may be indiscriminately admitted into the first class. But from henceforward none who are illegitimate shall participate in the advantages of this class or cast. They will be limited to the simple enjoyment of the privileges which belonged to the free men of colour before 1789. Nevertheless, by intermarriage with the first class their children will acquire its privileges.

The same principle should be applied to the second and third classes.

APPENDIX.—C. NO. 1. [xxxvii

The marriage of an individual of a superior class with one of the next in order of gradation, may raise the offspring whether of the first or second generation, to the higher of the two: but it might possibly be better to arrange that the children of a marriage between an individual of the first and one of the third, should belong to the intermediate class.

The children of mothers, who are slaves or reputed as such, by concubinage with whites, mulattoes, or others, will invariably follow the condition of their mothers, and belong to their masters. The determination on this subject should be unalterable; nevertheless children of this description may be manumitted on payment of the sum of   to the proprietor by the father who acknowledges them. The amount to be paid will be fixed by a future regulation: children thus manumitted shall only enjoy the privileges which belonged to free men of colour prior to 1789. By intermarriage with one of the higher classes, their offspring will be raised to this last.

With respect to the most numerous class, that of the blacks attached to the cultivation and manufacture of sugar, indigo, &c. it is necessary that it should return to or continue in the situation in which it stood before 1789, with the exception of making such regulations respecting discipline as may secure its being sufficient for the maintenance of good order and a reasonable proportion of labour, without being too severe.— Means should be devised, in concert with Pétion to make the greatest possible number of blacks return to the plantations, and to subordination, so as to lessen the number of free blacks. Those whom it may be inadviseable to admit into this last class, and who might carry into the other a dangerous spirit of insurrection, should be transported to the Isle of Ratau,* or elsewhere. This should enter into Pétion's views, if he wishes to secure the fortune and interests of his cast; and nothing can be better than to have every thing prepared for accomplishing this plan, as soon as the moment for its execution shall arrive.

We have said that one of the three agents should repair to Christóphe: after sounding him, he will consult with his colleagues as to the expediency of following up a negociation with him, and determining upon what basis it should be conducted and whether in concert with Pétion and Borgella, or without their knowledge, as they may see fit: every thing in this respect must be left to their discretion.

As far as a judgment can be formed at this distance, the most important thing is to come to a good understanding with Pétion: after which, it will be easy to reduce Christophe with-

* See the explanation of this term given by Medina in his examination—C. No. 2. page 43.

out much effusion of blood. But as it is his majesty's intention to prevent bloodshed as far as possible, and to hasten the general pacification of the colony, the agents will omit no practicable means of disarming the followers of both Christóphe and Pétion.

The agents will embrace every safe opportunity of acquainting his majesty's ministers with their arrival, the commencement and progress of their negociation, and all the information they have been able to collect respecting the state of affairs in the colony. They will use a cipher for all communications which, if intercepted, might prove injurious. The moment an arrangement has been concluded they will return with all possible expedition to give an account of their mission. Should they judge it expedient that one or even two of them should await on the spot the arrival of the armament destined for the colony, they will do so, but at all events it will be right that one should return to communicate in person the particulars of the mission more in detail.

In these instructions is sketched the outline of a plan of political organization for St. Domingo, merely to give the agents some idea of what his majesty can consent to grant: the final arrangement must be the result of the information his majesty's ministers shall obtain from them. They must therefore use their utmost endeavours to confine the concessions within reasonable limits; the less these deviate from those formerly established, the better.

To sum up the whole they will promise nothing beyond what is stated below, after having done every thing to keep within it.

First—To Pétion, Borgella, and a few others, *the nearer their complexion approaches to white*, a perfect assimilation to the whites, and a participation in all their advantages of fortune and honour.

Secondly—To the rest of their cast *at present existing*, the enjoyment of the political rights of the whites with a few exceptions making them slightly inferior.

Thirdly—To all who are further removed from white than the free mulatto, a lower share of political rights.

Fourthly—To the free blacks *a still lower share* of these advantages.

Fifthly—To attach to the soil, and restore to their former masters *not only all the blacks at present employed upon the plantations, but likewise to send back to the plantations as many as possible of those who have emancipated themselves from this condition.*

Sixthly—To purge the island of *all those blacks, whom it* may be inexpedient to admit among the free, and dangerous to place among those attached to the plantations.

Seventhly—To check in the most effectual manner the increase of emancipation.

When these bases have been settled with the chiefs, the agents will add to them the following conditions.

First—It is perfectly understood that for the restoration of order in St. Domingo the laws of property, and all the principles which render it secure, must be established and respected in such a manner that every proprietor furnished with a legal title, whether by inheritance, purchase, or otherwise, may be put in possession of his lands and buildings in the state in which they shall be found, without regard to any arbitrary dispositions made by those who, previous to this period, had exercised any public authority.

Secondly—The admission of all the coloured class, to political rights, the assimilation which may take place of the principal proprietors of the first class to the whites, always reserving to the king and his representatives, the choice of those who may appear best calculated to fill employments of either a higher or lower rank, in the civil or military departments; in such a manner, however, that none of them shall be recognized as having an *acquired* but only an *accidental* right to these employments like the whites. As to those at present invested with the powers of the colonial government, it is understood that their entire submission to his majesty and the success of their influence with the cast in subjection to them, will secure to them the king's thanks, but without any stipulation that may bind him to any particular form of government. The aforesaid chiefs referring themselves wholly to his majesty's will and benevolence.

When all these points shall have been discussed and agreed upon with the chiefs, they will be reduced to a *process verbal* which, after their written submission, will be their effectual guarantee that nothing will be hereafter required of them which is not consonant to the present instructions signed by me the secretary of state, his majesty's minister.

MM. Dauxion Lavaysse, de Médina, and Dravermann, are strongly advised to read these instructions repeatedly over during their voyage, so as to comprehend their meaning fully, in order that in the progress of their negociation they may not deviate from it. (Signed) MALOUET.

Certified to be conformable to the original deposited in the archives of the state. DE LIMONADE,
Secretary of State for foreign affairs

APPENDIX.—C. NO. 2.

No. 2.

KINGDOM OF HAYTI.

SPECIAL MILITARY COMMISSION.

Process verbal of the examination of Agoustino Franco, sirnamed de Médina, a French spy.

This the 17th day of November, 1814, in the 11th year of Independence and fourth of his majesty's reign.

The *Special Military Commission* named by his majesty by virtue of his dispatch of the 11th of November, of the present year, composed of seven members, to wit,

His Grace the Duke de la MARMELADE, governor of the capital, President.

His Excellency the Comte d'ENNERY, lieutenant-general in the king's armies.

His Excellency the Comte de RICHPLAINE.

The Chevalier JEAN JOSEPH, field marshal.

The Baron de CADET ANTOINE, secretary general to the department of high admiral, secretary to the commission.

The Baron de LEO, colonel, &c. and JOSEPH LEONEL, lieutenant-colonel.

The commission having assembled at the hotel of his Grace the Duke de la MARMELADE, governor of the capital, for the purpose of instituting a criminal process against AGOUSTINO FRANCO sirnamed DE MEDINA, one of the three spies sent by the French cabinet, and arrested on the 11th of November in the present year, upon whom the definitive sentence will be pronounced after the affair has been thoroughly investigated.

AGOUSTINO FRANCO, sirnamed de MEDINA, having been brought into the hall of the meeting was sworn by the president to tell the truth, the whole truth, and nothing but the truth, and the said Médina having taken the aforesaid oath was examined by the president of the commission, as follows.

Quest. What is your christian name, your sirname, your age, and your profession?

Ans. I am called Agoustino Franco de Médina, about forty-seven years of age, a native of Santo Domingo, an inhabitant and proprietor at La Vega, formerly charged with the smuggling police at Bannie, afterwards appointed mayor by the late Governor Toussaint Louverture, and, under the French General Ferrand, adjutant-general commanding the department of Cibao, at present a colonel in the service of his Majesty Louis xviii. and an emissary of the Minister Malouet.

Q. How were you selected for the mission with which you are charged, to Hayti?

A. By a letter of invitation which I received about the middle of June, 1814, from one of the Minister Malouet's secretaries, desiring me to wait upon him. Before the appointment of this commission for the colonies it had been in contemplation to send the Comte d'Osmond, the Marquis de Fontenelle, Mazere, M. Degoute and the negro Louis Labelinaie, with some mulattoes, to sound the land: but M. Malouet ordered it otherwise.

Q. Did you wait on the Minister Malouet, according to his invitation, and at what hour?

A. I did wait on the minister of marine and the colonies at his hotel the next day at noon as I recollect, according to invitation.

Q. By whom were you introduced to the minister?

A. By one of the persons employed in his office.

Q. Who did you find with the minister?

A. One M. de Begon, an old officer of the French marine, Dauxion Lavaysse, and Dubuc now intendant at Martinique, the others were unknown to me. I also recollect that M. du Petit-Thouars was of the number.

Q. What conversation had you with the Minister Malouet in the presence of these persons, relative to your mission?

A. The minister spoke in these terms. *"It is in the king's name that I address you. His majesty desires to procure intelligence respecting the state of his colonies, especially St. Domingo. In consequence, M. Dauxion Lavaysse will go to open a negociation with Pétion at Port-au-Prince, in the name of his majesty, upon the basis of the last treaty concluded with Bonaparte. Dravermann will go to the South, having a correspondence with Borgella. You Mèdina,"* addressing himself to me, *" you will do what you can with Christóphe, I know he is hostile to France: but you will understand better what is to be done when you are on the spot."*

Q. Do you know the nature of the treaty concluded between Gen. Pétion and Bonaparte, and when it was ratified?

A. Since Gen. Ferrand was at St. Domingo, I have learned that Gen. Pétion corresponded with Ferrand and Bonaparte: but the treaty in question was concluded about the end of 1813.

Q. Are you acquainted with the provisions of this treaty?

A. I understood from the Minister Malouet, at the conference of which I have spoken, that France was to furnish Gen. Pétion with a certain quantity of troops and warlike stores.

Q. Do you know who negociated this treaty of Pétion's with Bonaparte?

A. M. Dravermann told me it was a man named Tapiau, a quarteron of the South, who was commissioned to carry on the negociation through the medium of the house of Perregaux, father-in-law to Marshal Macdonald, at Bourdeaux, to whom Pétion's vessel was consigned.

Q. Had Dauxion Lavaysse any instructions different from yours?

A. Yes. He had others particularly relating to Gen. Pétion, especially respecting the basis of the treaty he was to negociate with him.

Q. Do you know the nature of this treaty?

A. Yes; the object of this treaty was to prepare a landing for the French army, in case King Christóphe should refuse to submit to France: then Pétion was to unite his troops to the French, for the purpose of forming our advanced guards, detecting ambuscades and clearing the march for the troops. Dauxion Lavaysse was moreover charged to use every exertion to have his Majesty Louis xviii. proclaimed at Port-au-Prince.

Q. Do you believe it would be possible for Gen. Pétion to make his troops co-operate with the French in fighting against King Henry?

A. As for myself I know not: but the Minister Malouet assured me and told all present that Gen. Pétion would not consent to submit to the command of a negro: that the civil war would last for ever, and that Pétion was devoted to France.

Q. The council requires you to state in what manner you think Gen. Pétion could prevail on his troops to fight in the cause of the whites?

A. The minister said Gen. Pétion was to arrange these matters; moreover you see in my instructions the truth of what I say.

Q. What is the meaning of the expression, "Isle of Ratau,' in your instructions?

A. It is an invention of the Minister Malouet, not to wound the philanthropic feelings of his majesty, and signifies a method of freeing himself from men dangerous to the colony.

Q. Did the French design then to renew in Hayti the drownings and other horrors formerly committed?

A. I believe it to be the intention of the French cabinet to rid itself of all persons whom it deemed dangerous, since order could not otherwise be re-established.

Q. What do you mean? Are we *disorderly*?

A. The minister said that the negroes must be made to return to the plantations, and the planters should be put in possession of their properties as in Martinique and Guadeloupe.

Q. You declared publicly when you were arrested, that if the population would not submit to France it should be exterminated to the very infants?

APPENDIX.—C. NO. 2. [xliii

A. I believe it: and the Minister Malouet told us so in the conferences we had with him before our departure.

Q. Have you been often with the minister?

A. Yes: three times: it was the third time that Dauxion Lavaysse, Dravermann, and myself all met together there.

Q. What orders did you receive from the minister?

A. The minister said, pointing to Dauxion Lavaysse. "behold your chief: I recommend unanimity to you: your instructions shall be given to you: take your measures well, and act with prudence so as to ensure success to your mission."

Q. What further conference had you with the minister: was this the whole of what he said to you?

A. M. Dravermann wished to speak to the minister, but was interrupted by M. Dauxion Lavaysse to explain that M. Dravermann begged that letters of moment which he expected from Pétion and Borgella in the West and South, might be forwarded to him from Bourdeaux.

Q. Did they then rely much upon Generals Pétion and Borgella, in France?

A. Yes, great dependence was placed on Pétion and Borgella throughout France as I have already said.

Q. Through what channel had Dravermann written to Generals Pétion and Borgella?

A. I think it was through the United States of America, or rather by the same vessel of Pétion's which had arrived at Bourdeaux.

Q. Where did you go on quitting the Minister Malouet?

A. Each went his own way, and we met again at dinner at an hotel by an invitation from M. Dauxion Lavaysse.

The foregoing examination having been read to M. Agoustino Franco de Médina he declared it contained the truth, and that he had nothing to add to or take from it, and that he confirmed it. It was then signed by us,

Franco de Médina, de la Bande du Nord, Duc de la Marmelade, d'Ennery, de Richeplaine, de Jean Joseph, Baron de Leo, and the Cadet Antoine, secretary.

This 24th day of November, the Special Military Commission assembled in the hall of its sittings, when Agoustino Franco de Médina was brought in and examined by the president as follows:

Q. Were they making any hostile preparations against Hayti, in France?

A. Not at the time of our departure, they wait the result of our mission: one or two of our number were to return to give an account of it in order to enable government to determine its plan of operations, and a third was to remain in Jamaica.

Q. How did the Haytians of both colours, who are in France, act?

A. They were assembled at Bellisle and many other depôts: there are many of them in Paris; those at the depôts are soldiers who await the sailing of the French army.

Q. What do you suppose to be the force of the army destined against Hayti?

A. I know not: but I recollect that in the conference we had with the minister, M. du Petit-Thouars said, *"if the mi-"nister gives me frigates, I will go and speak with the chiefs to "know whether they are willing to submit to France, if they "should not I will cruize off the island to interrupt the com-"merce with the French part only."* Here the minister interrupted him by saying, *"You are not come here to talk in this "manner. This is not his majesty's intention: he is determined "to do all that may depend upon himself for the chiefs, as well "as for such subaltern officers as they may point out. The "most momentary shew of hostility would derange the whole of "our operations. When the time comes we will take into con-"sideration what measures should be adopted to reduce or "exterminate the revolted negroes."*

Q. What corps of the army do you think would be preferred for the expedition against Hayti?

A. That rests with the minister. But I heard it said that France would take advantage of this expedition to disencumber herself of as many bad subjects as possible.

Q. Who do you think likely to have the command of this expedition?

A. I know not; but the Prince of Angoulême has promised many commercial advantages to Bourdeaux. M. Dravermann told me *he wished for the restoration of the colonies and slave trade.*

Q. When did you leave Paris?

A. On the 28th or 29th of June, Dauxion Lavaysse, Dravermann and myself left Paris for Boulogne, whence in four or five hours after we embarked for Dover.

Q. How did you leave England?

A. From Dover we proceeded to London and thence to Falmouth, the Comte de la Châtre, the French ambassador, procured us a passage in one of the government packets at the disposal of M. Dauxion Lavaysse.

Q. At which of the islands did you first touch?

A. At Barbados, afterwards at St. Lucia, next at Martinique, whence we proceeded to Curaçao and finally to Jamaica.

APPENDIX.—C. NO. 2. [xlv

Q. Did you see General Hodgson at Curaçao?
A. No. It was M. Dauxion Lavaysse who landed: as M. Dauxion chose to be always decorated, contrary to the minister's intentions, we were at variance in consequence of the remonstrances I made on the subject. I presume this.

Q. And had you your decorations?
A. I had two crosses, one of his Majesty Louis xviii. and the other of the Emperor Napoleon; and my uniforms were in my trunk, part at la Vega, and part at St. Domingo.

Q. With whom had you left them?
A. At la Vega with the commandant, at St. Domingo with my sister Donna Anna.

Q. When did you reach Jamaica?
A. On the 25th or 26th of August.

Q. Where did you land?
A. At an inn.

Q. Did you all three land at the same inn?
A. M. Dauxion Lavaysse went ashore in a different canoe from ours, and lodged elsewhere. M. Dravermann and I were together at the same inn towards evening. Next morning M. Dravermann had a paralytic seizure, being a man of nearly seventy years old.

Q. About what age is Dauxion Lavaysse?
A. About forty.

Q. To what authorities at Jamaica did you apply, as bearers of dispatches from his Majesty Louis xviii?
A. M. Dauxion Lavaysse went to the capital to present himself to the governor, to shew the letters of recommendation he brought with him from London, and to talk to him.

Q. Who gave these letters of recommendation?
A. I do not know whether it was the French minister or ambassador. The Duke of Manchester was at that time governor of Jamaica. Dauxion Lavaysse saw the principal men: but Dravermann and I being ill did not: however, when we were recovered I saw them all except the Duke of Manchester.

Q. What steps did Dauxion Lavaysse take at Jamaica for the execution of his mission?
A. He told me he had written to Gen. Pétion. Lafond Ladebat is his secretary at present: he is almost blind: we brought no secretary with us. He waited Pétion's reply before he went to Port-au-Prince.

Q. Did not Dauxion Lavaysse write to Pétion alone?
A. M. Dauxion told me it was his intention to write to King Christôphe, and that he had a safe opportunity for doing so.

Q. By what opportunity did he write to Pétion?

A. I know not whether by a frigate, a brig, a king's vessel, or by one of the droghers which pass and repass.

Q. Which of you left Jamaica first?

A. I did. M. Dravermann was to proceed to the South: and M. Dauxion Lavaysse was to wait at Jamaica for Pétion's answer.

Q. Did you know of the meeting of the ex-colonists at an entertainment which took place at Jamaica?

A. Yes: this entertainment was given on the evening of our arrival, by all the French, in celebration of the general peace.

Q. Do you know any thing of the petitions of the ex-colonists to his Majesty Louis xviii. signed by fifteen hundred names?

A. Yes; I did know of these petitions. I saw many colonists at Jamaica, among others the Chevaliers Lafite and Dessource: there were not above a hundred colonists in all at Jamaica.

Q. By what opportunity did you reach the Spanish part?

A. By a small schooner. I landed at Monté-Christ, whence I introduced myself into this part.

The foregoing examination having been read to M. Agoustino Franco de Médina, he declared that it contained the truth; and that he had nothing to add to or take from it, and that he confirmed it: it was then signed by us,

Franco de Médina, de la Bande du Nord, Duc de la Marmelade, d'Ennery, de Richplaine, de Jean Joseph, Baron de Leo, Joseph Leonel, and Cadet Antoine, secretary.

No. 3.

From the Columbian, a New York paper, of the 19th Nov. 1814.

Negociation of General Lavaysse with Hayti.

This negociation has been grossly misrepresented.

General Lavaysse is made to appear the enemy to freedom by means of forged letters or expressions. The truth is that General Lavaysse obeyed the orders of his government faithfully, and served his country with fidelity. Whilst discharging his duty he acquired the esteem of the President of Hayti with whom he has always maintained a friendly intercourse.— At the period of General Lavaysse's visit to Hayti, the system of government which Louis xviii. had promised to pursue in France was completely and treacherously altered, it was at this moment that Pétion, who was always attentive to foreign transactions, said to this general that the men of the revolution, the Bonapartists were a proscribed race, they were, politically speaking, the mulattoes of France, and it was hard to know where this proscription would end.

We have seen the original of the letter of which the following is an extract.

We have also an authentic copy in French of which we conceive it will be sufficient to publish a faithful translation. We know not which this letter is more honorable to him who wrote or him to whom it was addressed: both being men of superior genius, and friends of liberty, and both having distinguished themselves in the annals of time, in the several sciences, in historic research, or in the profession of arms.

Port-au-Prince, 21st June, 1816.

Your letters dated from Paris, have reached me by M. Colombel. I see by what you send me all that you have had the kindness to write and speak in favour of our country and institutions.

I see, with new pleasure, by the contents of your last dispatch, general, that you retain your favourable sentiments respecting us and continue to advocate our cause with all governments, a cause which is that of reason, of justice, and humanity.

In whatever country or situation circumstances may place you it will always be glorious, honorable and even consolatory to you to recall to mind your having employed your pen and talents to overturn an order of affairs as absurd and revolting in its principles, as it is odious and atrocious in its consequences.

By devoting yourself to the defence of these great principles of public morality, of that sacred cause which guarantees to man the dignity of his being, you have entitled yourself to the gratitude of this portion of the human species which has been so long oppressed by a mercantile and monstrous combination: you have ranged yourself in the honourable ranks of those virtuous philanthropists who have always advocated the sacred cause of humanity before the tribunal of reason.

The memory of these true apostles of liberty, and benefactors of the world, praiseworthy on many accounts, will live from generation to generation. We rejoice in recalling to mind that these are the men who by unceasing perseverance and a profound erudition produced, by all the force of reason, the triumph of truth over those errors and prejudices which would annihilate her, and in acting thus you have given a death blow to that barbarous and stupid egotism of this set of men, sunk down in ignorance; vile and contemptible leeches who have no wish beyond that of fattening themselves on the blood of their fellow creatures.

It is gratifying to me, general, to have an opportunity of expressing the feelings with which the liberal principles you possess have inspired me.

PETION.

D

CORRESPONDENCE OF CATINEAU LAROCHE.

No. 1.

Copy of a letter from M. Catineau Laroche, an ex-colonist of St. Domingo, dated Paris, 16th February, 1815, to his Excellency General Pétion, President, at Port-au-Prince.

My dear friend,

They talk much, as I have already acquainted you, of sending troops to Gonave, the Cayemettes, Isle á Vaches, and la Tortue, who will be left there in order to become seasoned to the climate. Among other things they speak of sending a thousand men from hence to la Tortue. One part of the troops who have been just sent to the windward islands will either join them, or remain in the other islands to be seasoned. Meanwhile emissaries have been sent to sow disturbances in the North, and they proposed that you should take the command of the European troops in order to carry on hostilities against the King of Hayti.

I am much afraid my express may arrive too late: nevertheless, as the troops are not yet embarked, and money is not more plentiful here than the means of transporting them, I hope it will reach you in time: these circumstances may occur more than once, and you must judge of how much consequence it is that you should furnish me with the means of corresponding with you. You ought to have vessels and agents in England constantly at my disposal.

At this moment especially, your interests may suffer materially from a want of the means of correspondence.

It is it seems the agents you have received who have occasioned the idea of seizing on the smaller islands, and establishing a blockade.

I beg you to accept the assurance of my respectful consideration, and my constant friendship.

(Signed) CATINEAU LAROCHE.
Rue du Fauxbourg Saint-Honore, No. 84.

P. S. I open my letter to acquaint you with a mixed plan which is going to be adopted.

It is in contemplation to name you governor of the whole colony, and they talk of sending commissioners with the warrant of your appointment.

It remains to be known whether the government would not require to have the interior administration in its own hands. In this case, notwithstanding your nomination, slavery will be re-established, in a few years at least, unless laws are made to the contrary, or that of the 2d of Feb. 1794 be confirmed.

This project is attended with the greatest danger: it will produce a war between you and King Henry, and the disposable forces of France will be insufficient to enable you to maintain the contest long. If you have war, the colony will be overturned.

No. 2.

Copy of a letter from M. Catineau Laroche, dated Paris, 17th February, 1815, to his Excellency General Pétion, President, at Port-au-Prince.

My dear friend,

They talk much at present of your favourable disposition with respect to France, and it is reported that you have offered to grant her commercial advantages, as favourable as she enjoyed in 1789, and that you wish to retain the internal administration and a kind of independence. They add that you are going to send commissioners to treat on these bases.

You act wisely in retaining the internal administration; for if France had seized on it, her navy would have sent back the old planters to produce troubles, and you would soon fall a prey to the factious.

All persons of sense are of opinion that it is essential for France to obtain from St. Domingo such articles of commerce as she requires in exchange for the products of her own soil and her manufactures. None but the colonists think that government should trouble itself about the restoration of property; and indeed it matters little whether the Antilles be cultivated by free men or slaves, by blacks or whites. The only subject of consequence is to have the lands cultivated and their produce employed in French commerce.

It follows from this opinion, which prevails generally among enlightened men, that if you persist in demanding to have the internal administration left to you, on admitting consuls for the interests of the French commerce, and on offering to restore the commercial intercourse with France to the same footing as before 1789, this demand and these offers will eventually be acceded to.

My proceedings will ultimately I believe have the effect of preventing the military expedition altogether; the scheme appears to be adjourned to May.

As to the restoration of property you will doubtless reconcile justice to circumstances; and if the properties of some worthy people who have proved their attachment to you, have been disposed of, you may make them compensation out of a public fund. For the rest doubt not my zeal to serve you.

Accept my best wishes, and the homage of my respect, with the assurance of my unceasing friendship.

(Signed) CATINEAU LAROCHE.
Rue du Fauxbourg St. Honoré, No. 84.

P. S. I have spoken of the necessity of having one or more commissioners, it will be expedient to give them powers and instructions to conclude an arrangement with France. Had I possessed authority from you to negotiate I would have obtained for you six months ago from the king a declaration confirming your rights and liberty, and preserving your authority.

At all events, I send the form of a power and instructions which you may give me in common with other commissioners.

No. 3.

Inclosures in the foregoing letter.

(A) *Form of a Power for a Commissioner.*

COLONY OF SAINT DOMINGO.

We the undersigned military and civil chiefs of the colony of St. Domingo, actuated by a desire of concluding an amicable arrangement between this colony and France, and wishing as far as possible to contribute to the re-establishment of commercial intercourse, to efface the calamities of war, to cause property to be respected, to secure public order and an oblivion of the past, to assist the unfortunate French proprietors in this colony, and to guarantee the rights of all the inhabitants, appoint M. ———— ————, our commissioner general to his majesty the King of France and Navarre, for the purpose of negociating the terms of an accommodation between the colony of St. Domingo and the French government, according to the bases laid down in the instructions which we transmit to him under the date of this day.

Promising to ratify the aforesaid terms so far as they do not essentially differ from the above mentioned instructions.

We therefore pray his most christian majesty and his government to receive M.———— ————, our commissioner furnished with powers to negociate for this accomodation, and to acknowledge him as far as is necessary in the aforesaid capacity.

Done at ————, this ———— ——.

(B) *Instructions for M.* ———— ————, *commissioner general appointed by the military and civil Chiefs of St. Domingo to negociate a treaty of alliance with his Most Christian Majesty.*

The negociator will acquaint his majesty the King of France and Navarre that the chiefs of the colony are anxious that the negociation should not be conducted by the minister of marine, a man notoriously under the influence of the faction which has produced, and prolonged for upwards of twenty-five years, the calamities of St. Domingo. The negociation should be carried on, either with the minister of the king's household, or the minister of the interior officially charged with the great interests of trade and manufactures, or the minister for foreign affairs.

The negociator will propose in the name of the chiefs of the colony,

1st. To admit French traders into the harbours of St. Domingo upon the same terms as in 1789, and to impose no other duties upon goods imported and exported by these vessels, than those which existed at that period; that is to say, to grant to France the exclusive trade of the colonies, without prejudice to the modifications allowed in favour of foreign commerce by a decree of council of the 30th of August 1784.

2d. To restore to European proprietors their respective possessions in St. Domingo, subject however to the undermentioned modifications, to wit:

That all property let out on lease by the colonial government prior to the conclusion of this concordat, shall continue to be cultivated by the leaseholder till his lease expires, and the proprietor shall only demand the rent.

That on the expiration of the leases, and previous to taking possession, the proprietors shall indemnify the farmers for the improvements made, and buildings which shall have been erected, by paying their value for them, unless the contrary has been expressed in the contract.

That the properties disposed of by government from the year 1794 inclusive, whether by way of indemnity, reward, gift, or otherwise, shall continue in the hands of their present possessors: the chiefs of the colony being under an obligation to indemnify the original owners either by grants of domains belonging to the state, or, in default of a sufficiency of these, out of special funds raised by a general and extraordinary contribution, or in any other manner which may be deemed expedient, and according to a valuation of the said estates made in the usual manner.

3d. To grant a free ingress into the colony to all the French except the ancient planters, who are not to be admitted without previous permission from the government of St. Domingo; but this permission will not be necessary for their wives or children under age.

4th. To give shelter within the ports of St. Domingo to all French ships of war or privateers, whenever France is engaged in a maritime war; and to place at her disposal three thousand regular troops for her West Indian expeditions, which troops are to be paid and maintained by the colony during their period of service.

5th. On every new reign to pay homage and swear allegiance anew to the king by three deputies from the colony, and pay him the sum of three millions of livres as a subsidy upon the happy event.

6th. To admit into the colony a consul general and two French consuls to superintend and protect the commerce of France.

In return for these concessions the negociator will demand,

7th. That his most christian majesty renounce for himself and his successors all right of interference in the internal affairs of the colony.

9th. That he will protect the flag, property, and inhabitants of the colony with his navy.

10th. That he admit an agent from the colony to reside at the seat of government with the title of consul general and one

APPENDIX.—D. NO. 4.

consul at each of the ports of *Marseilles, Bourdeaux, Nantes, Bayonne, Havre, St. Malo,* and *Dunkirk.*

This *projet* of a treaty in which we have been forced to consult private interests, as far as the present situation of the colony will permit, and whose provisions are all politically beneficial to France, since they in fact give her all the advantages without any of the expences of the colony, will probably be assented to by his most christian majesty: provided the discussion of it is left to statesmen. We wish it may be so; since we love France, and have long panted for a time when we might be allowed to live in peace with her. M. ———— will insist on the adoption of these propositions, and while exerting himself to secure the essential provisions, he will consent in detail to such modifications as appear upon discussion to be just and reasonable.

Done at ————, this ———— ——

No. 4.

Copy of a letter from M. Catineau Laroche to General Pétion, dated New Orleans, 25th January, 1816.

Mr. President,

My last letter written to you from New Providence, and transmitted by the master of a vessel from Charlestown, which took General Lee to Port-au-Prince, acquainted you with the disaster which befell me on the Bahama banks, and the heavy loss I sustained in consequence. I informed you it was my intention to remain a month at New Providence, but a ship from Sumatra having come in, and been declared fit to proceed on her voyage, and not expecting for a long time to find a better opportunity for going to New Orleans, whither I was obliged to proceed in order to save the wreck of my little fortune, I was compelled to embark in this vessel.

I reached this place in four days, leaving the ship, which made slow progress, in the river. Such were my losses that my family and myself arrived almost in a state of nudity, the greatest part of our personal property having been thrown overboard with my goods.

There was no opportunity either for Jamaica or St. Domingo from hence. This disappointment added to the necessity of attending to my own little interests will force me, to my great regret, to continue here some time. Should I nevertheless fail to receive any communication from you, or see any person sent by you to whom I can explain matters relating to your government and that of King Henry, in the course of next month, I will at all hazards proceed to St. Domingo in the best manner I can.

You will see the occasional arrival of vessels which are either French or dispatched from France, whence they will come either directly or after touching at Cuba. Most of these expeditions are made on account of the government by the minister of marine in the interests of the planters, with a view of learning what passes in St. Domingo, and producing misunderstandings. Prudence seems to suggest that these passengers should not all be equally well received, and you cannot safely repose the same confidence in all.

Strong prejudices have always prevailed in France against St. Domingo. The old planters continually cry out for war, and talk perpetually of exterminating the male population of all colours. The court, which is generally desirous that matters should be replaced upon their old footing, and shudders at the very name of liberty, listens with much complacence to the projects of the old colonists. Age has not indeed added vigour to the arms of these exterminators, but they are sanguine in their hopes that government will place troops at their disposal to complete the task they commenced in 1803. On the other hand the foreign powers who at present in fact govern France, will not be sorry to see her rid herself of the remnant of Bonaparte's old troops, by sending them to St. Domingo, as a hearse to convey them to the tomb, and King Wellington, say they, would be rejoiced to see King Louis adopt this resolution. The British government doubtless would not suffer France to complete the conquest of St. Domingo, were such an event possible; but a war in which Frenchmen should cut each others throats would, I say, be quite to her taste, since it would have the farther effect of completing the devastation of a country whose productions enter into competition with her own in the great markets of Europe.

They build their hopes of success upon a misunderstanding between you and King Henry, and in whatever harmony you live with him, the French newspapers periodically announce that your troops are slaughtering each other, and indulge in all the dreams of the planters on the subject. M. Charmilly, formerly a resident in the Plaine du Nord, and afterwards in the South near Plymouth, and who joined the English army in 1796 or 1797, is one of the most clamorous and violent for war. He arrived in Paris from London last year with English funds which he offered to government for the first expence of the expedition, and demanded the appointment of administrator in chief of St. Domingo. His gold took effect, and from what he shewed, those who were about the king, voted for war.

Had a misunderstanding subsisted between you and King Henry, a French expedition would have joined one of you to exterminate the other, and the victorious party would be exterminated in its turn. Men of all colours and parties might lay out their account for being sacrificed, should the colonists ever again enjoy power.

Nevertheless the opportunity is favourable for securing your common independence by means of the government of the King. I have furnished you with the means of accomplishing this by the intervention of persons of sense and influence: but you should in some degree aid my undertaking as far as possible without committing yourself. The developement of these means requires an interview, since they must be reasonably modified according to the existing state of the country with which I am not sufficiently acquainted, and particular circumstances of which I am ignorant. The most important thing is, that you should remain your own masters: this is the end. As to the means we will come to an understanding respecting them either by a personal conference, or through the medium of a confidential person whom you will send to me. Should I not have an answer in February, I will present myself at Port-au-Prince in the course of March, unless a second shipwreck should cast me upon some desert or inhospitable shore, or no opportunity should offer except for the Cape.

I beg to be kindly remembered to my friends, if there are any of them about you, and I beg you to accept the homage of profound respect with which I am your Excellency's most humble and most obedient servant,

CATINEAU LAROCHE.

House of MM. Vincent, Nolte and Cie.

P. S. Should I meet no opportunity except for the North, I will take advantage of it and afterwards proceed to you. The common interests, and those which concern all the inhabitants without exception, are at stake.

No. 5.

Copy of a letter from Catineau Laroche addressed to M. Gentil, dated New Orleans, 28th January, 1816.

Doubtless, my dear sir, you must have reached St. Domingo. I flatter myself you have written to me since your arrival.

But it is a fact that with the exception of two letters you addressed to me from London, before you went to Portsmouth, I have received no tidings of you. I know not even whether the letters with which I charged you are not left at Dover with the trunk which the Custom-house officers seized.

In the state of uncertainty in which I am on this subject, I have determined on proceeding to St. Domingo, where I should have now been but for the disasters I experienced at sea.

I am at a loss how to secure your receipt of this letter to which I request you to reply fully if, as I trust, you have arrived.

I wish you every happiness, and am wholly yours,

C. LAROCHE.

House of MM. Vincent, Nolte and Cie.

E

[Documents printed at the government press at Port-au-Prince.]

DOCUMENTS RELATING TO THE CORRESPONDENCE BETWEEN THE COMMISSIONERS OF HIS MOST CHRISTIAN MAJESTY AND THE PRESIDENT OF HAYTI.

No. 1.

To General Pétion.

At sea, on board H. M. frigate Flora, 2d Oct. 1816.

General,

The flag, which you have defended so long and so courageously, has been displayed with enthusiasm for upwards of two years over all the countries formerly subjected to France. St. Domingo alone hesitates to hoist it, a circumstance which grieves his majesty's heart most severely. Occupied with remedying the calamities which his subjects have experienced from the neglect of their duty towards him, this excellent prince wishes to re-unite all the members of his family in the bonds of friendship, and his children in St. Domingo are not less dear to him than those who belong to Europe.

The criminal attempts of the usurper, and the evils they have occasioned, have retarded the execution of his majesty's design. Now, however, that his return has given peace and security to Europe, and order is re-established within his dominions, his majesty has directed us to repair to St. Domingo for the purpose of consulting with those in authority there on the measures to be employed to give this country a security which it cannot enjoy in its present precarious situation; to legalize in his name all the necessary establishments; to reward the care and services of those who have restored and maintained order in the colony; to consolidate by his royal will all such institutions and changes in the state of persons and of things in this island, which the course of events may have rendered necessary, and which are neither incompatible with the dignity of his crown, or the acknowledged interests of the colony and the mother country.

The calamities which have desolated St Domingo, her public and private misfortunes, are all known to the king, nothing which enhances the glory of the French name has escaped him, while every thing which tends to tarnish its splendour is blotted from his memory. More happily situated than the provinces of France, St. Domingo, also laid waste by the man who so grossly abused his power, separated herself from France, as long as the latter was separated from her king. His majesty is not ignorant that if one portion of the inhabitants of this island have constantly resisted the usurpation, they have displayed equal courage when they thought themselves threatened with a foreign yoke: these are the only recollections he is desirous of preserving.

Should malevolence seek to raise any doubts, or awaken any fears respecting the object of our mission, repose in us, general, the same confidence we repose in you and the authorities the king has ordered us to recognize. It is for you, and for them to point out to us whatever may be an object of desire or uneasiness to the people, whatever may contribute to their peace and their prosperity, and you will soon, like the French, enjoy the blessing of having found in the king the best of fathers.

Full of confidence in your loyalty and character, general, we feel no apprehension as to the reception which his majesty's commissioners will experience. We send your colonel the Chevalier de Jouette, and the Chevalier Dominge, chef d'escadron, who are the bearers of this letter, together with M. le Dué, one of your countrymen, who has expressed a wish to accompany them, in a light vessel commanded by Captain Bégon, and will follow ourselves immediately after in one of his majesty's frigates.

Your old general the Viscomte de Fontanges, he under

whose command you and your countrymen so honourably defended the royal cause when perjured subjects dared to attack it, is the head of this pacific mission. He has regarded neither his age nor his infirmities, nor has he hesitated to cross the seas once more, for the purpose of conveying to men whom he has long loved and defended, the benevolent intentions of the king.

We beg you, general, to accept the assurance of our high respect.

The Viscount de FONTANGES,
Lieutenant-general, commander of the order of St. Louis,
and an officer of the legion of honour.
ESMANGART,
Counsellor of state, knight of the royal legion of honour.

Liberty.   No. 2.   *Equality.*

REPUBLIC OF HAYTI.

Alexander Pétion, President of Hayti, to MM. the Commissioners of his Most Christian Majesty to the Republic of Hayti.

Port-au-Prince, 6th October, 1816 : 13th year of the Independence of Hayti.

Gentlemen,

We have in truth defended the French flag with the greatest courage and most unbounded devotion : while doing so we were far from anticipating the conduct of those who alienated us from it, a conduct unparalleled in history. Since that period the institutions, moral character, progress of learning, experience, and circumstances, have made the citizens of this republic a new people. Already had they entered upon their career and begun to merit respect by the good faith they observed towards strangers, as well as by the renown of their arms, when peace was restored to Europe by the simultaneous efforts of the sovereigns, and it was settled that his most christian majesty should remount the throne of his ancestors.

We might have expected that this great epoch of the world would have been that likewise in which we should have appeared in our turn before the tribunal of public opinion, and upon examining our own hearts, and judging favorably of men under the happy influence of an enlightened morality, justice, philosophy, and religion, we felt no apprehension respecting the result. Our conduct towards his most christian majesty has been irreproachable. His known character before the revolution, his mild principles, his unprecedented misfortunes, with those of all his family, a contest as protracted as it has been cruel and sanguinary, the uncertainty of his fate which has only been decided by long delayed and extraordinary events, our tacit adherence to the league which supported him, all led us to expect that we should form a particular exception in the view of a wise policy: we also regarded as favourable to us the efforts and immortal success of a distinguished government, which has established as a moral axiom that the traffic in men was not only horrid in itself, but contrary to the spirit of christianity, and has obtained proof of the possibility of sugar and coffee colonies prospering without having recourse to this barbarous and disgraceful measure. Whatever our blindness was then, we have since pierced the veil, and the simplest logic has explained to us that if there was no slave trade there would be no slaves. This plan is not yet realized, because virtue is unable to counteract hatred and want of reflection, but events are in a state of preparation under the guidance of wise and benevolent men who devote themselves to the task and will accomplish it.

What have we then to fear? The wickedness of our enemies and oppressors, and those obstinate and incorrigible men who are the real authors of their own calamities: the difference of our epidermis, which in the eye of colonial prejudice assimilates us to the brutes; the reservation of a continuance of the slave trade for five years, made by his most christian majesty; the clamours of the *ci-devant* proprietors in this country, their writings, the inflammatory publications which issue from the French press under the very eyes of the king, shew us how rapidly our favourable expectations have vanished, and that our sole attention must be henceforward devoted to preparations for war even whilst we desire peace, and to furnishing our magazines with arms and ammunition, as if we were threatened with immediate invasion. It might even be allowed us to presume that our prognostications were well founded, and that an armament was actually fitting out at the important crisis of Bonaparte's re-appearance in France.

During this interval, General Dauxion Lavaysse arrived at Jamaica and assumed the character of a royal commissioner. A work published under his influence appeared a brand of discord hurled amongst us to create disunion, to set the family at variance with its heads and the heads with the family; a qualified slavery was there depicted in the most specious colours, and the people were called back to it in the mildest manner; while the lot of the leaders was to be that of mischievous savages, DEATH OF BANISHMENT TO THE ISLE OF RATAU, after having aided in seducing and reloading with chains their brethren, their friends, the companions of their arms and their glory. Notwithstanding all this, General Dauxion Lavaysse dared to present himself at Port-au-Prince, where he was received with kindness: the acts of his mission were made public, his instructions were unmasked and avowed by himself. In what point of view could his mission be regarded? As an *espionnage!* In this case what risk did he not run? Nevertheless these instructions were signed and sanctioned by a minister in the confidence of the king, and thus bore the stamp of authenticity. What a subject of reflection for us! All these documents were, we are well assured, long under his most christian majesty's consideration, and no doubt often carefully examined by him. The public prints of all Europe have resounded with them; and they have been repeatedly republished with remarks, much to our credit; and in which our wisdom and moderation have been approved of. General Lavaysse has returned to France, after having received every testimony of the most sacred hospitality.

The commissioners whom it has pleased his majesty to send to this republic will find, as soon as they land, how sacred the laws of nations are held by this government; and that the whole world, without exception of colour or of nation, enjoys here under the protection of the laws, the most perfect equality.

Appointed by the nation the guardian, not the supreme disposer of its destinies, I will receive in its name all proposals which concern its welfare and its rights, conforming myself to the exercise of those powers with which I am invested.

I beg you to receive, gentlemen, the assurance of my high consideration.

PETION.

No. 3.

On board his majesty's frigate Flora, 6th October, 1816.
General,

We think proper to transmit to you a copy of the king's ordinance by which we are named commissioners extraordinary to St. Domingo.

The utmost we could say or write would assuredly be less satisfactory than his majesty's own words. This ordinance ought to calm every uneasiness and fill all hearts with hope. It will acquaint you likewise, general, with the extent of our powers, and the paternal intentions of the king; in a word, it will demonstrate to you that the welfare of the colony at present wholly depends upon those who possess power and authority, and we doubt not that under this new consideration it will be more indebted to you than to all the rest.

Receive, general, the assurance of our high respect,
The Viscount de FONTANGES,
ESMANGART,
Commissioners of the king.

No. 4.

ORDINANCE OF THE KING.

Louis, by the grace of God, King of France and Navarre, to all present and to come, greeting!

Since our return to France, our whole care, after having concluded peace, has been directed to repair the evils which have resulted from the usurpation.

Our colonies, even the most remote, have been ever in our recollection. We must ascertain the state in which they are, the extent of their misfortunes, and the nature of their wants.

The colony of St. Domingo has particularly fixed our attention. We have conceived it would be useful to send commissioners to calm the uneasiness which the inhabitants of that island may feel respecting their situation, to put an end to their uncertainty, to determine their future condition, to legalize the changes which events have rendered necessary, those especially which tend to improve the future lot of our subjects.

Our commissioners will confer with the existing authorities on every thing connected with the legislation of the colony, the internal administration and public order; as also the civil and military functionaries, respecting the state of persons and the restoration of commercial intercourse with the mother country. They will point out to us such of our subjects as are deserving of our favour, and entitled to be rewarded for their attachment and fidelity to our person.

For this cause, and upon the representation of our secretary of state for the department of marine and the colonies,

We have named, and do name as commissioners, MM. the Viscount de FONTANGES, lieutenant-general in our armies; ESMANGART, a member of our council of state; DU-PETIT-THOUARS, captain in the navy; and the Sieur LAUJON, secretary general to the commission.

APPENDIX.—E. NO. 5.

The Sieurs JOUETTE, colonel of infantry, and COTELIER LABOUTERIE, our attorney-general in the tribunal of the first instance at Gien, are appointed supernumerary commissioners.

The necessary instructions will be given to the commissioners by our secretary of state for the marine and the colonies, in order that they may conform themselves to them.

Given at Paris, at the Chateau des Tuilleries, this twenty-fourth day of July, in the year of grace 1816, and of our reign the twenty-second.

(Signed)   LOUIS.

By the king.
(Signed)   The Viscount DUBOUCHAGE.

A true copy.
And a little lower (Signed) The Viscount DUBOUCHAGE,
Secretary of state for the marine and colonial departments.

A true copy.   The Viscount de FONTANGES,
Lieutenant-general, commander of the order of St. Louis, officer of the royal order of the legion of honour.

ESMANGART,
Counsellor of state, knight of the royal order of the legion of honour,
Commissioners of the king.

A. de LAUJON,
Secretary general to the commission.

No. 5.

Port-au-Prince, 8th October, 1816.

General,

After what you did me the honour to communicate the day before yesterday, I beg you will have the goodness to name the time at which you can receive us. M. Esmangart and myself are anxious, general, to have a private conference either with you singly, or with such members of the government as you may think fit to have present.

As for the rest we will consent to whatever may seem advisable to you respecting it.

I beg you, general, to receive the assurance of my high consideration.

The Viscount de FONTANGES.

Liberty.   No. 6.   *Equality.*

REPUBLIC OF HAYTI.

Alexander Pétion, President of Hayti, to Monsieur de Fontanges, Commissioner of his Most Christian Majesty.

Sir,

In reply to your letter, which I have just received, I have the honour to acquaint you, that I shall be ready to receive you and M. Esmangart, at seven o'clock this evening, and that the principal authorities of the republic will be present at our conference.

I beg you, sir, to receive the assurance of my high respect.

PETION.

No. 7.

On board H. M. frigate Flora, 23d October, 1816.

General,

Detained nearly ten days by calms between St. Marc and the Môle, our absence in the North has been extended beyond our expectation.

Our first care, general, is to send you a copy of the letter we addressed to General Christóphe, under cover to the commandant of Gonaïves, of which we sent him a duplicate by one of his majesty's brigs, commanded by the Chevalier Bégon, the pilot of the Cape not having answered the frigate's signal.

The object of this letter was, as you will see, general, to acquaint General Christóphe with our arrival in the colony, and his majesty's intentions.

On our return to the roads of Port-au-Prince, we hasten, general, to renew with you the communications which are the object of our mission.

We will reply, general, in the briefest manner to your letter of the 6th instant, in answer to ours announcing our arrival.

We will not indulge in any recriminations, in consequence of the reproaches you make to France, it being our wish that the evils which are past should be mutually forgotten, and this, most assuredly, is the first desire of the king.

St. Domingo is indisputably the spot on which the shock of the revolution was most forcibly felt; it is indisputably the country in which the greatest barbarities, crimes, and cruelties have been committed. The king regrets these evils, as well as those which overwhelmed France in his absence, and it is this recollection which determined him to send commissioners to the island to see, in concert with the existing authorities, what may be the means of saving this unhappy colony. If the king has forgiven all his personal injuries, every individual ought to bury his grievances in oblivion. This is due to the public peace, and to prevent reproaches from producing recriminations which tend to render reconciliation impossible.— Therefore, general, let us not dwell longer on these disasters than is necessary for concerting measures for remedying them, and above all for seeking whatever may conduce to preserve the colony in future.

Tell us all that your situation, your experience, your regard for virtue, and your knowledge of the temper of the people suggests to you on these subjects, and we shall soon come to an understanding respecting the means.

With regard to your remarks on the mission of M. Dauxion Lavaysse, we can only repeat what we said to you on the day we had the honour to see you and the principal functionaries. M. Dauxion Lavaysse never had any power from the king. His majesty had no knowledge of his mission, except from its results and common report: he has caused it to be officially disavowed.* He has found fault with the mission and still more with the conduct pursued. We cannot therefore speak after the king, his disavowal is sufficient.

His majesty, equally unacquainted with your wishes, your wants, and the changes occasioned by the revolution, has given us the most ample powers to reply to your demands, and do all that is possible to prevent this colony from becoming again the theatre of civil war.

It is not the desire of repossessing himself of a country laid waste and torn by civil commotions, which has dictated the paternal overtures he now makes. It is rather the fondness of a parent, who, after having been deserted by his children, stretches out a saving arm to snatch them from the brink of the precipice, to which a most dreadful revolution has impelled them. He furnishes at this moment an example of moderation and benevolence, which will be recorded by history, not only to Europe, but to the whole world,

France, exhausted by her own victories, after having made an unfortunate and imprudent trial of every variety of government, has found happiness and hope under princes who for upwards of eight centuries raised her to the first rank and acquired an untarnished glory. Our only ambition now is to maintain our legitimate government, and remain agriculturists

* Appendix, F. No. 3.

and manufacturers. Without anxiety for the future, each individual now applies himself in peace to industrious pursuits. The object of our mission is to offer you similar advantages. Placed over a volcano, you dare not undertake or repair anything; your houses are in ruins, your fields waste, and your plains deserted. Perpetually in dread of the misfortunes which may assail you to-morrow; your only care is to defend yourselves, and your torches are ready for your own destruction.

Those whom you mistrust, come with the olive branch in their hands to offer you security and repose. The king who sends us does not wish even to chuse the means of preserving them to you, fearing lest he should again deceive himself; it is he who consults you as to what may give them to you. Speak, and you will soon see how far the king's benevolence, moderation, justice and love for his people can lead him.

Receive, general, the assurance of our high consideration.

The Viscount de FONTANGES,
ESMANGART,
The commissioners of the king.

P. S.—You have surely, general, received the copy of the royal ordinance which has named us commissioners for St. Domingo. We transmitted it to you in our letter of the 7th inst. We think we ought to remind you that having sailed the next day for the North, you have not acknowledged its receipt.

No. 8.

Copy of a letter from MM. the King's Commissioners to General Christôphe.

At sea, on board H. M. frigate Flora, off Gonaïves,
12th October, 1816.

General,

After twenty-five years of trouble, of civil dissensions, wars and battles, France has been restored to herself, and found repose by throwing herself into the arms of her king. From this moment she repairs the evils, which those seasons of disorder brought upon her and which the goodness of the king causes her every day to forget.

His majesty, in resuming the exercise of her rights, has in his wisdom felt fully convinced that it would not be for the interest of his people to restore all that the revolution had destroyed : he has on the contrary been desirous that all the passions should be checked; he has demanded fresh sacrifices from his most faithful servants, of which he himself set the first example; he has consolidated by his royal will those changes which he thought conformable to the national inclination. All, now divested of anxiety for their children respecting the future, have seen doubt exchanged for certainty, and have hastened with zeal to serve so good a prince, in their several ranks and stations.

The king is desirous of extending to St. Domingo, the blessings he has bestowed on France. It is with this intention that he has ordered us to come hither for the purpose of consulting with the civil and military authorities respecting all those measures which may be able to fix the lot of the colony.

His majesty has desired that we should repair to Port-au-Prince as a central and intermediate place from whence we can communicate with both the North and the South, so as to make known to all, his royal and paternal intentions.

Invested with the command of the North, it is more especially in your power, general, to enlighten the people with regard to the truth, and the fatherly disposition of the king; to remove all those doubts which malevolence, private ambition, or avarice may endeavour to excite respecting the object of our mission; to declare to the citizens of all classes that it is his majesty's desire that none should suffer by his return; that all those changes, which they are taught to apprehend, meet his approbation only in proportion as they conduce to the general welfare. That he has no wish to send forces to a country in which there already exist an army, generals, public functionaries, and subjects who will be faithful to him : and that his majesty's only design in sending commissioners furnished with powers, is to consolidate and legalize all that can exist without derogating from what is due to the dignity of his crown, to justice, and to the interests of his subjects.

We will await, general, all the communications you may make to us, and we doubt not for an instant, that you will seize with avidity the opportunity of proving to your countrymen that in such important circumstances you are desirous of promoting their welfare.

We feel it right to subjoin to this letter the ordinance of the king who has sent us to St. Domingo. It will acquaint you better than all we could write, how benevolent and paternal his majesty's intentions are.

(Signed)   The Viscount de FONTANGES,
Lieutenant-general, commander of the order of St. Louis, officer of the royal order of the legion of honour.

(Signed)   ESMANGART,
Counsellor of state, knight of the royal order of the legion of honour, Commissioners of the king.

A true copy.   The Viscount de FONTANGES,
ESMANGART,
Commissioners of the king.

Liberty.   No. 9.   *Equality.*

REPUBLIC OF HAYTI.

Alexander Pétion, President of Hayti, to MM. the Commissioners of his Most Christian Majesty.

Port-au-Prince, 25th October, 1816:
13th year of Independence.

General,

I have the honour to acknowledge the receipt of your letter of the 23d instant, dated on board the frigate Flora, together with the copy of that addressed to General Christophe at sea on the 12th, as also the ordinance of his most christian majesty, naming you his commissioners, inclosed in your letter of the 7th, to which your absence prevented my reply.

After the horrible crimes perpetrated by the French, crimes which shame the page of history, the independence of Hayti has been solemnly sworn, over the yet smoking remains of our unfortunate compatriots, by the intrepid warriors who achieved its conquest. This sacred oath, pronounced for the first time by an enraged people, has never ceased to echo from every heart; it is annually renewed with fresh enthusiasm; it is the palladium of public liberty; to retract it, or to entertain a thought hostile to it would be a disgrace and infamy of which no Haytian is capable; to alter it would be to bring down upon ourselves merited calamities; our laws imperatively forbid it; and, as first magistrate of the republic, it is my most sacred duty to cause it to be respected. I have sworn this in the face of heaven and of men, and *I have never sworn in vain.* To make us swerve from this holy resolution is beyond the utmost stretch of human power. We possess, and deem ourselves worthy of preserving our independence: to wrest it from us we must first be exterminated. Well! should this even be possible, we would determine to endure it, rather than retract.

We may be allowed to think that our character, little known, especially in France, where they are accustomed to judge of us by the colonial feeling, would have perhaps created an idea of our being upon our guard, from a mistrust of the guarantees which might be offered to calm our apprehensions for the future, and that the most probable means of leading us to the end proposed, would be the adoption of those forms which were most likely to be pleasing to us; that they would have seen how much the mission of General Dauxion Lavaysse had irritated our minds, and that it did not escape us that it had the semblance of that authenticity which usually attends the acts of government; since his instructions, which are in our possession, and were acknowledged by him, have the signature of the minister of marine. You do me the honor to repeat to me that this mission has been disavowed by his majesty. I assent to this, and, in consequence, to the nullity of all the proceedings arising out of it. I will therefore speak of it no more. His majesty, since his restoration to the throne of France, has had every official transaction of our government before his eyes, none of the periods of our revolution can be unknown to him, and he must be convinced that we cling to our independence as to our existence; and although we separated him from the misfortunes which have so long afflicted us, we could believe that he would have unreservedly acknowledged our independence, as he has confirmed other arrangements which must have been still more painful to his feeelings, had he not been prevented by the opposition which he encountered in the public mind. For when pressed in 1814 by the allied powers to renounce the shameful traffic in slaves, he nevertheless demanded its continuance for five years; and yet in 1815 he himself acknowledged that it had been his desire to renounce it on his return to France, but that he had at that period been obliged to yield to circumstances. Should he not at the present day then refuse with still better reason to grant that which is demanded by interests perfectly isolated, and which would cost such oceans of blood? Such is the opinion we would form to ourselves of the sentiments of his most christian majesty, and deeply should we be grieved to find ourselves obliged to change it.

The whole face of the world is altered, that is to say renewed by a revolution of five and twenty years: every individeal has created for himself habits and employments to satisfy his wants; prescription seems to have overthrown those ancient pretensions which no longer exist except in recollection, while the majority of those interested in them are no more.

The return of order and peace has recalled men to labour and industry; the most urgent wants of governments have deep wounds to heal; the results of war are every where the same; deserted plains, ravaged fields, every thing languishes until the return of confidence, which cannot take place all at once: this is a principle of general application, and does not, while calling them into play, destroy the internal resources which every country possesses within itself. It is a fact, that ours could only exist by ourselves; it is necessary then with peace to seek resources, to stimulate labour, to encourage manufactures; but where are these to be found if not in industry and commerce? The Frenchman can have no interest in the restoration of the ancient order of things: he is in want of support, he requires encouragement, and to make useful profits for himself and his government, he only asks to be relieved from the impediments which prevent his giving full scope to his speculations.

Manufactures also require the same advantages and the necessary openings for their maintenance and improvement.— None can be ignorant that this country, though it produces little, consumes largely; because it is the disposition of the Haytians, who all enjoy the fruits of their own labour, to procure for themselves every possible comfort.

In order to reply with frankness to the communications you have done me the honour to make respecting the very ample powers of your mission, which you announce as perfectly pacific and disinterested, and not originating in any wish to re-annex this country, ravaged and wasted by intestine wars, to France, that I have felt it necessary to enter into some details free from all recrimination, and every thing at variance with what is just and reasonable, yet highly important for the purpose of explanation.

If his most christian majesty's intentions agree on this point, and your powers correspond with this spirit of justice and moderation, then, forgetting every selfish motive and influenced solely by the love of truth and the desire of doing good, you will regard us *as a free and independent government,* whose consolidated institutions depend upon the will and love of the nation.

You will not hesitate to admit this as an essential basis between us, and thus entering into the spirit of our laws, you will enable me to correspond with you on all matters which may be reciprocally advantageous to both countries, without swerving from my duty.

Every thing leads me to believe that, when you left France you were fully satisfied that we could not admit any other principles: by recognizing them, you will bear away with you the most glorious fruit of your mission, and acquire the highest claim to our esteem and regard.

I have the honour, gentlemen, to salute you with the highest respect.

PETION.

No. 10.

General, Port-au-Prince, October 25th, 1816.

We came here with the most perfect confidence in the town and territory you command, assured that every thing connected with the rights of nations would be respected. We have no cause to regret this confidence, and it is this circumstance which induces us to acquaint you with what passes between the Carthagenians and Mexicans who are here, and our sailors. The former enlist our men, and lead them to be guilty of insubordination. Complaints have been made to us on this subject, and we are assured that on communicating them to you they will be redressed. We claim your authority to have a search made for our men by the police, and that they may be given up to us. It would be an affront to your government to insist upon a demand of this nature which belongs as much to a well regulated police as to the laws of nations.

Receive, general, a renewed assurance of our high consideration.

The Viscount de FONTANGES,
ESMANGART,
Commissioners of the king.

Liberty. No. 11. *Equality.*

REPUBLIC OF HAYTI.

Alexander Pétion, President of Hayti, to MM. the Commissioners of his Most Christian Majesty.

Port-au-Prince, 26th October, 1816:
13th year of Independence.

Gentlemen,

I have received your letter of the 25th inst. in which you complain of the conduct of the Carthagenians and Mexicans here, and the sailors of your squadron. It is not in vain that you claim the interference of government to put an end to this disorder. I shall give particular orders to the general commanding the arrondisement not only to prevent your sailors being enlisted under any flags, but also to back by force the search after the deserters.

Be assured, gentlemen, that you will, under every circumstance, find whatever protection you can desire with respect to the police of your squadron.

Receive, gentlemen, the assurance of my high respect.

PETION.

No. 12.

General, Port-au-Prince, October 30th, 1816.

We received on the 27th the letter you did us the honour to address to us on the 26th of this month.

France, like St. Domingo, has experienced reactions. The parties which succeeded each other, each in its turn vanquishers and vanquished, have exercised, as is usual in civil wars, vengeance and reprisals, equally blameable on both sides: but since his majesty's return no one has thought of blaming the king for the misconduct of the opposite faction, or making it a pretext for refusing to acknowledge the royal authority and rights. Each on the contrary, taught by experience, was convinced that truth alone and legitimacy could put an end to the violent dissensions and ambition which for twenty-five years rendered France so unfortunate. All measures adopted in favour of one party against the other, the laws and regulations, all have become as though they had never been, each party being satisfied that cautionary measures alone were necessary against its opponent faction. But on the sovereign and legitimate authority resuming the exercise of its rights, these precautionary measures the protection of the several parties, became useless. Their laws became virtually repealed, and nothing has remained, but what the king in his wisdom thought it right to preserve. All besides has ceased to be obligatory even upon those who had sworn to it; since the effect ought to cease with the cause.— To maintain those laws and regulations would have been to perpetuate civil dissensions; to commit hostilities after peace.

His majesty felt, nevertheless, fully convinced that twenty-five years of revolution had changed the manners, habits, and even the thoughts of the people. He legalized every thing which could be allowed; he has bestowed on us laws suited to our new character, and thus given repose to all families.

Nor has the king's anxiety for St. Domingo been less, as

our former letters, general, have sufficiently informed you: he however cannot do any thing but what appears to him just and beneficial for his subjects. He ought to consult their wants only, and not their passions, this it is which will guide him, as it has in France, in the measures to be adopted for this country.

To despise the king's bounties and the value of his royal sanction, without which, however, all you acquired by the revolution in rights, in honors, in fortune, in wealth and dignities, will remain in a state of perpetual uncertainty; you oppose to us an act which of itself would demonstrate to the king the impossibility of abandoning you to yourselves, since by so doing he would leave you on the brink of that horrible precipice to which your own imprudence has brought you. On a cool and dispassionate perusal of the first pages of this act which forms the ground-work of your institutions, it is immediately manifest that it carries with it the germ of your own destruction. To prove this it will be sufficient to quote the three following articles which declare that,

Article xxxviii.— "*No white man of any nation, can set his foot on this territory in the capacity of a master or proprietor.*"

Article xxxix.—"*Those whites are recognized as Haytians who form part of the army, those who discharge any civil functions, and those who were admitted into the republic at the publication of the constitution of the 27th of December, 1806; and no other can in future, after the publication of the present revision, pretend to the same rights, neither be employed, nor enjoy the privileges of citizens, nor acquire property within the republic.*"

Article xliv.—"*Every African, Indian, or their descendants, born in the colonies or in foreign countries, who may come to reside in the republic, will be recognized as Haytians, but shall not enjoy the rights of a citizen till after twelve months residence.*"

By these articles you re-establish in a more absolute manner than any ordinance had done, that distinction of colour which philanthropy has been labouring for upwards of half a century to destroy. You commit an act of hostility against Europe, you come to a rupture with her, and justify her in confiscating, by way of reprisal, the property of all who bear the name of Haytians amongst you, and depriving them of the right of inheritance and the other political advantages they enjoy in their fullest extent and without distinction.

By a caprice unexampled in the history of revolutions, after having fought for twenty-five years in support of an opposite principle, your very first act, your fundamental law, has established the very distinction which you strove to overthrow at the price of your blood.

Were Europe to judge from your laws, she would be far from supposing the urbanity of your government to be such as we have experienced it, and of which we conceive it our duty to make our report.

In fact you exclude every civilized nation in order to adopt exclusively, as the only ones fit to associate with you, on one hand the Barbary powers, whom Europe is at this moment endeavouring to reduce, and on the other, nations amongst whom the very name of civilization has not yet penetrated. Should the philanthropists, no more exempt than others from the proscription you have declared against their complexion, should they nevertheless protest against the reprisals adopted against you in Europe, they are answered by your own constitution: the principle has been laid down by yourselves; what right then have you to complain?

Such, nevertheless, general, is the system you ask the king to sanction. He could not do so without derogating from what he owes to himself, to his subjects and to other powers; could he even sanction it with advantage to yourselves?

We repeat to you, general, that it is the king's wish to do for this country all the good which is compatible with the dignity of his crown, and the interests of his subjects. His only desire is to secure the happiness of the present inhabitants of St. Domingo in the most permanent manner.

You have asked us to point out the means by which this is to be accomplished. We make the same request of you in our turn. Judge for yourselves, general, after the observations we have made to you, whether the end which the king proposes is attainable in the way you point out.

You are not ignorant, that as subjects have duties to fulfil towards their kings, these likewise have duties to fulfil towards their subjects. Kings cannot abandon them even in their errors or their misfortunes. The greater the danger into which they have brought themselves, the more incumbent is it on their monarchs to hasten to their assistance. His majesty, more than any other king, gives to the world a proof of that parental anxiety which ought to attach all hearts to him in this country as well as in France.

When we were honoured with his confidence, we were convinced that we should only bring you nearer to the precipice, and abuse the power entrusted to us were we unreservedly to grant what you demand, in a moment especially when your passions are at their height.

We do not reply by recriminations to the fresh reproaches

you cast upon France. France has doubtless committed great errors; above all she has been eminently guilty towards her king.

Like all other nations in commotion, she has been the theatre of the greatest excesses, but her errors and her faults, even her crimes will, in the records of history, be lost in a forest of laurels.

God has at length broken the rod he sent to scourge us. He has restored to us our king, our legitimate princes; let us then think only of fulfilling our duties and repairing our losses.

Should we be so fortunate as to convince you, general, and the authorities who surround you, we shall have no reason to regret having introduced into this discussion that moderation which always prevails in the king's heart, when the object is to recall to his arms children whom false and pernicious theories have alienated from him.

Receive, general, the assurance of our high consideration.

The Viscount de FONTANGES,
ESMANGART,
The Commissioners of the king.

Liberty.   No. 13.   *Equality.*

REPUBLIC OF HAYTI.

Alexander Pétion, President of Hayti, to MM. the Commissioners of his Most Christian Majesty.

Port-au-Prince, 2d November, 1816:
Gentlemen,   13th year of Independence.

I have received the letter you did me the honour to address to me on the 30th of last month.

It belonged to the nineteenth century to produce extraordinary events; it was also reserved for it to remove the bandage which prevented the most unfortunate and oppressed portion of mankind from discovering in the great charter of nature their imprescriptible rights and the object of the Divinity in their creation. It is owing to the intolerant spirit of the parties that France has caused to succeed each other in this lovely country, that the sacred arch of the independence of Hayti has been reared amidst oppression and injustice. In swearing to maintain it we were as far from thinking that it would affect the authority of the king of France, as from anticipating that he would one day triumph over the French, and set up claims against us which our arms had overthrown: idle claims which policy revokes, which reason disapproves, and which are far less necessary to the dignity of the crown than a multitude of other privileges which circumstances have led him to abandon, no doubt from powerful considerations. We may add that in reclaiming our unacknowledged rights we are influenced solely by a regard for our own security; happy to have shaken off the most hideous yoke, we have desired nothing more than that, in the midst of universal peace, we should be able to enjoy what we already possess. And, since the resources of our country would become unproductive unless cultivated by our hands, which we could not employ under any other influence than that of the family feeling which unites us, we might appear culpable indeed in the eyes of a sordid policy, while at the same time we should stand acquitted before the tribunal of justice and equity which legalizes our rights.

We have never feared inquiry, and far from losing by it we could not be otherwise than gainers; especially if the inquiry be conducted calmly and dispassionately. This is perhaps the the reason of our being so accessible in so delicate a cause; because we are strong in ourselves, and have drawn up our social compact, which is the declaration of the national will, with due consideration.

In calling my attention to the 38th, 39th and 44th articles of our constitution, you seem to me to fling down the gauntlet, and to wander from the subject under consideration, for the purpose of converting a *particular* into a *general* case affecting all the powers of Europe: this appeal to such clear sighted governments will be very slow, since they have not regarded in the same point of view what you denominate a mark of hostility towards them. These articles are contained in the act of independence; in those which followed, in the constitution of the 27th of December, 1806, they have received a fuller explanation, by the 39th article of the revision, which is merely a paraphrase of the 27th article of the constitution. They have never ceased to be in force, and have no other object than our security, which the French government alone can dispute with us, as you do at present; while the other powers have no interest in them, since they have a constant intercourse with us, as you can satisfy yourselves by ascertaining the presence of an accredited agent from the United States of America to the republic; by the *order in council of the 14th December, 1808 by the King of England, which has never been revoked; and by the foreign ships in our ports into which they are admitted as ours are into theirs. You may see multitudes of Europeans in this town trading with us unimpeded by the proscription of colour.

* See a copy of this at the end of the Appendix.

Is there a reciprocity of advantages in the commercial intercourse between foreigners and the island of Hayti? The question I think is resolved. Is there any incompatibility with regard to property and the rights of citizens? The answer would not be difficult.

We rely on the justice of our cause, and purity of our intentions. We do not conceive that Europe arms herself against us because we wish to enjoy freedom under the only form which can secure its existence, or that the philanthropists, who are the objects of our admiration, would blame a conduct which they themselves would no doubt have recommended. If from all this, motives can be derived to effect our extermination, we must prepare ourselves for it: and, placing all our dependence upon HIM who is the Lord of the lords of the universe, receive from HIM new strength to defend ourselves: this is our part—we have none else to chuse.

The allusion you make to the Barbary powers is answered by the conduct we pursued towards England and America during the war between them. Never did a government give proofs of a stricter neutrality or a stronger regard for the rights of nations, so that there was not the smallest complaint on their part.

It is an acknowledged and indisputable principle that every government has a right to regulate itself by its own laws. Louis xiv. by his revocation of the edict of Nantes, excluded the French from the very bosom of France. No power interfered, and all benefited more or less by the advantages resulting from this emigration.

In Japan, China, and among other polished nations, they have, as a precautionary measure, forbidden the entrance of strangers into the interior, and yet we see commerce carried on and flourishing with a people whose political existence gives no disturbance to the peace of other nations. It would be easy to cite examples of the same nature, did we wish to relate them.

Whatever judgment be passed upon our efforts during the revolution, history cannot disguise that we have been sacrificed and deceived, and likewise that our arms have been crowned with laurels.

If your powers are not sufficient to allow of your negociating on the basis I have had the honor to propose, or you do not deem it expedient to use them; I must acquaint you that, under these circumstances, I do not conceive my duty will allow of my continuing longer to correspond with you on the subject of your mission.

Whatever be the result, I shall not have to reproach myself with having neglected the smallest opportunity of securing peace and prosperity to my fellow citizens, as I shall always shew myself worthy of their confidence by causing, to the last moment of my existence, their rights and privileges to be respected, without swerving from the principles which I have uniformly professed.

Receive, gentlemen, the assurance of my high respect.

PETION.

No. 14.

General,   Port-au-Prince, 10th November, 1816.

Your health being re-established, we proceed to transmit to you the reply your indisposition delayed.

In your letter of the 2d instant, as in all which preceded it, you continue to speak to us of the violence and injustice you have experienced. According to the pacific character of our mission, we have abstained from replying by recriminations to the charges you bring against certain violent Frenchmen. We will persevere in this system of moderation to the last.

You nevertheless admit that, during the usurpation, when the king was incapable of exercising his rights, you found yourselves compelled to chuse some form of government. That independence, being that form which of all others appeared to offer the greatest security, had been selected by the nation: but that nothing had been done to the prejudice of the king.

All this, general, perfectly coincides with what we had the honour to remark in our last letter. Hitherto you have committed no act of hostility against the king. Your measures have been directed against the enemies of his crown. They are weapons you have forged to resist them, and which you could not legally employ except against them. But when the king resumes the exercise of his rights; when all his subjects hasten to range themselves beneath the banners of the laws, will you alone refuse to avail yourselves of that which has been achieved against those who are equally his and your enemies in order to oppose him? Such an attempt could arise only from a wish to excite a fresh struggle against legal power, which will be injured and invaded without provocation; it would be nothing less than open rebellion. The rights of the king as sovereign, are indisputable. The contract between him and his subjects is indissoluble; in a word, his rights, which are imprescriptible, cannot be in any degree affected or impaired by his having experienced a temporary suspension of their exercise. Thus, until the king shall have decided otherwise, the state of war will become permanent, and every thing will remain uncertain, till a peace of which none can anticipate the period. All this is so self-evident, that we shall not dwell longer upon it.

If in our last letter we have spoken to you of certain articles of your constitution, it was solely with a view of pointing out what you proposed to the king to recognize in sanctioning your independence, and to demonstrate to you that the fundamental law of your institutions carries with it the seeds of your own destruction. Be assured it was far from our intention to make, as you call it, an appeal to foreign governments.— France, by separating from her king, experienced the greatest calamities, but her honour as a nation was far from being lost, and the king is sufficiently able of himself to maintain her rights according to his good will and pleasure without claiming assistance from any power.

Nor has it, general, been any more our intention to avoid or elude a question, the discussion, of which has no terrors for us. Had we nevertheless (we think we ought to assure you general) followed our first inclination we should have limited ourselves after the receipt of your letter to taking leave and embarking to communicate to the king, the obstinacy with which we found you pertinaciously maintaining, and this without shewing its necessity or advantages, an independence which is in fact nothing but a disposition to resist the authority of his Majesty.

But the king, who ordered us to conduct this discussion with all that persevering moderation which is so congenial to his own heart, would have blamed us had we quitted this country abruptly, without an endeavour to prove the injustice of such obstinacy, and the danger to which a government such as you are desirous of adopting would necessarily expose the country. If our remarks can bring you to reason, we shall have cause to congratulate ourselves upon not having been hasty. We shall even have rendered a signal service to you yourself, and have fulfilled both the orders and intentions of the king.

We proceed then, previous to concluding our mission, to offer those remarks which our duty and the interests of the colony dictate, on the subject of this independence, in the same manner as we have already done on certain articles of your constitution.

To be independent, you should be certain of being able at all times and in all places to cause your independence to be respected.

You should also have within yourselves a sufficient force to repel the attempts as well as the ambition of those who might take umbrage at your prosperity.

APPENDIX.—E. NO. 14.   [lxxix

You ought to be able of yourselves to protect your subjects both at home and abroad, and to avenge injuries. If the state which wishes to declare itself independent does not possess within herself these powers; if she is obliged to call in the aid of a foreign power, she ceases to be independent and her political existence is every instant in danger.

See what the present state of this colony is, feebler than the smallest province in France! Relying on your courage and climate you are disposed to insult all the powers of Europe, if it be necessary, to support a pretension which cannot be maintained at the present day upon any rational principle. You do not even possess within yourselves any resources for war: you must procure every thing from abroad, and if, in consequence of any war with a leading power, your foreign communications should be cut off, the climate which destroys its forces will in a little time also spoil your arms and every other implement of war. The want of these, which you may experience at the end of a certain time, has already rendered you dependent upon strangers. Nor are you less dependent through the new wants and habits you have acquired, the privation of which would be painful and even become a source of suffering to most of you. Hence it is manifest that the day in which the king declared you independent, would leave you dependent upon the whole world.

As to your internal means of defence, it is admitted by all that, when threatened by an imposing force, you have no others than to lay your town and crops in ashes, to carry fire and destruction every where throughout your plains, and retire with your wives and children to the mountains, and there defend yourselves to the last.

This might be the result of a noble resolution, but it is also a striking proof of great weakness. A nation which has no other means of opposing invasion but by its own destruction, cannot exist without the support of a powerful protector. Situated as you are at present, the mere shew of attack by any power whatsoever would reduce you to the most frightful extremity; since, on the first demonstration of hostility, armed with the torches stored in your arsenals, you would become the most useful auxiliaries of your enemies.

On a review of all your resources, it is evident that your external means of maintaining your independence are still weaker than your internal. For you cannot, with your scanty marine, either inforce respect to your flag or punish any insult offered to the subjects of the republic.

Your present independence is consequently an absolute chimera, a pretension which cannot be maintained, which will be ruinous to yourself, and still more so to those on whose behalf you stipulate; and should the king, weary of opposition, grant your mad request, he would in a little time be fully avenged.

In thus frankly explaining to you, general, the true political situation of your country, our only object is to open your eyes to what you owe to your dearest interests. There is no glory in needlessly maintaining a struggle in which there is a certainty of your being sooner or later subdued and your people destroyed. Such temerity is culpable, and equally repugnant to humanity and to reason.

For the rest, desirous, general, to approach as close as possible to that independence which you say can alone determine the happiness of the people, we shall now state the concessions we are permitted to make in the king's name: viz.

Article 1. It shall be declared in the king's name that SLAVERY is abolished in St. Domingo, and NEVER SHALL BE RE-ESTABLISHED.

Article 2. That civil and political rights shall be granted to all the citizens, as in France, on the same condition.

Article 3. The army shall be maintained on its present footing. The general and other officers shall be confirmed by the king in their respective ranks, and all shall enjoy the same pay, allowances, honours and distinctions, as those of the royal armies in France.

Article 4. The king will never send European troops to St. Domingo. The defence of the colony shall be always entrusted to the courage and fidelity of the indigene troops, who never shall be employed out of the colony.

Article 5. The president of the republic, with the senators, shall retain his prerogatives, and the senate its privileges. It, as well as the administrative and judicial authorities, shall remain provisionally as they exist at present; subject however to such modifications as they themselves shall propose and decree in concert with his majesty's commissioners: and in case of a change hereafter, they shall only be affected in the manner fixed in the revision of the constitutional act.

Article 6. The old planters will not be suffered to come and reside within the colony, unless they submit to the established laws and regulations, those especially relating to persons and civil rights.

Article 7. A general rule shall be established, respecting property, by the existing authorities in concert with his majesty's commissioners, in order to settle all doubts, and prevent such disputes as may delay the re-establishment of the colony.

Article 8. The existing president shall be appointed governor general of the colony; and the present commander in chief shall be appointed lieutenant-general of the government. They shall each retain his present powers, subject however to such modifications as the situation of affairs may demand, but this shall not be done without their consent. In future, they shall be appointed by the king upon the presentation of three candidates chosen by the senate.

Article 9. The ports shall continue open to all nations on the same terms as at present. The senate shall have a power of modifying these terms according to circumstances, and on the demand of the governor general representing the king.

Article 10. The king shall exert his interest with his holiness to obtain for this colony a bishop, and all those spiritual succours which yield a nation the greatest consolation.

Article 11. All these concessions shall extend to the north as well as to the south and west of this colony.

Article 12. The constitutional act shall be revised by the senate in concert with the king's commissioners in the course of the year, so as to make all its arrangements coincide with the order it is desired to establish. The king shall be requested to have the goodness to accept it after the revision, and to guarantee its observance by himself and his successors.

From these concessions it will be evident to the whole world that the king wishes to give you, instead of an imaginary, a real independence, and one the more durable and certain from its injuring no one, interfering with no interests, being maintained by yourselves at home, and finding a powerful protection abroad. In a word, is there a nation more independent than that which has the choice of its own magistrates, generals, and functionaries; legislates for itself; raises its own army, which has a certainty of never being employed on foreign service, and has, for the maintenance of its prerogatives, the support of a powerful prince who governs a nation of twenty-four millions of heroes. To despise the advantages of such concessions is to reject the substance and grasp the shadow.

In what other manner could the king recognize the independence of a country in which two hostile governments, directly opposite each other, are accurately balanced, one of which (the battles being daily) must fall before the efforts of the other. The king, in recognizing your independence now, would in fact recognize your republic; and if, notwithstanding your courage and resolution, you should, by the ordinary chances of war, be vanquished, the republic would be immediately suspended by the semblance of a monarchy horribly absolute; and the king, had he yielded to your wishes, would have signed the death warrant of his subjects.

APPENDIX.—E. NO. 15.

We trust, general, that the spirit which has dictated these observations will be duly appreciated. They are the result of a sincere desire to see this colony peaceable and happy, and thus fulfil the dearest wish of the king. We will continue our pacific mission to the foot of the throne: we will supplicate the king, however just his anger, to allow the inhabitants of this colony time to weigh these new considerations well, and to consider cooly, what more may be offered to them, what further demands you can make, or what the king can grant. His majesty, who hopes to meet here, as elsewhere, grateful children and faithful subjects, will be deeply grieved to find himself obliged to command as a king, where he had ever wished to speak as a parent.

For ourselves, general, our stay here becoming both useless and inconvenient, we shall depart upon receiving your acknowledgment of this letter. We thank you for the hospitable reception you have given us, and shall make a favorable report of it. We depart with sincere regret at having failed to do the utmost for the welfare of this colony and the peace of the inhabitants; and should the future be less prosperous than it ought to be, should fresh calamities desolate your country, you have only your own refusal and obstinacy to blame, and not the benevolence and justice of the king.

Receive, general, the assurance of our high consideration,

The Viscount de FONTANGES,
ESMANGART,
Commissioners of the king.

Liberty.   No. 15.   *Equality.*

REPUBLIC OF HAYTI.

Alexander Pétion, President of Hayti, to Messieurs the Commisioners of his Most Christian Majesty.

Port-au-Prince, 10th November, 1816:
Gentlemen,   13th year of Independence.

I have received the letter of this date which you did me the honour to address to me. I have observed the developement of the same principles and the same ideas as those announced in your former communications, and which all tend to a recognition of the sovereignty of the king of France over this island. This, I think, I have answered in my former letters; and if the terms of the oath I have taken to the nation according to our laws, were not graven deep enough in my heart, I should only have to read them over to be convinced that I have done my duty, and that it is the fixed determination of the nation, which I communicated when I acquainted you, that no change in the state could be allowed.

You seem yourselves in this discussion to agree and justify the choice of the government we adopted for our security in the first epoch in which we consecrated it. From the change of circumstances in France you infer that they should also be changed here. It would be reasonable to suppose that if the motive was legitimate in its principle it would be more natural at the present day to recognize than reject it.—By this solemn act of the King of France's will, all the consequences of the misfortunes you anticipate would be obviated: the precautions you employ in the mixed form of government you propose, would become needless; nothing could alter the prosperity of the republic in relations honourably formed with the French government, and all mistrust would cease.

In declaring their independence, the people of Hayti did so to the world at large, and not to France in particular. Nothing could be done to make them swerve from this unalterable resolution; they know by the experience of past misfortunes, and by wounds yet unhealed, that its only guarantee is to be found in itself and without partition.

They have weighed all the force and extent of this measure since they preferred devoting themselves to death to retracing their steps, without designing to put themselves in a state of hostility against any person whatsoever.

It is in the name of the nation of which I am the head and interpreter that I address you, I never will compromise its sovereignty, and my duty is to conform myself to the bases of the social compact it has established. The people of Hayti wish to be free and independent; I participate in their wish; hence the cause of my refusal, of my obstinacy.

To alter our institutions belongs to the decree of the nation, not to that of its head.

I am gratified by your assurance, on announcing your departure, that you have experienced, during your residence in the republic, all the attention and hospitality which was due to you.

Receive, gentlemen, the assurance of my high consideration.

PETION.

APPENDIX.—E. NO. 16.

Liberty.   No. 16.   *Equality.*

REPUBLIC OF HAYTI.

PROCLAMATION.

Alexander Pétion, President of Hayti, to the People & the Army.

    The French flag has appeared on our coasts, and the king of France has sent commissioners to Hayti.
    Under what circumstances have they presented themselves? At the moment we were about to consecrate the edifice of our laws. It was in the midst of the enthusiasm of a nation the most jealous of its rights, that they dared to propose to compromise them; and for what advantages? Are there any then preferable to those we enjoy? Is there a Haytian so lukewarm in his feelings as to consent to retrace his steps? Our duties are marked out for us, we trace them from nature; she has made us equal to other men; we will maintain them against all who may dare to form the wicked design of subjugating us. They will find on this land nothing but ashes mingled with blood, a destroying sword, and an avenging climate.
    On this, as on all former occasions, you have shewn the same circumspection, the same respect for the laws of nations. You have calculated your strength, and, in leaving to your magistrates the care of explaining your dearest interests, you have calmly waited till they should acquaint you with what they had done for you. Your confidence never shall be abused.— Their authority is derived from your will, and your will is to be free and independent. You will be so, or exhibit to the world the dreadful example of burying ourselves beneath the ruins of our country rather than return to a state of slavery, however modified.
    When all Europe has combined, at the voice of philanthropy, to annihilate the last trace of that most shameful traffic, the traffic in men; and when the most polished nations prepare and meditate a general plan of emancipation for those who yet groan beneath oppression; we see with regret that governments, which pique themselves on being the most religious, cherish principles which both justice and humanity condemn.
    Haytians! your security is in your arms! reserve them for those who attempt to trouble you, and avail yourselves by your labour of the advantages which a most fertile soil affords you.
    I have ordered the printing of my correspondence with the commissioners of the King of France: it shall be submitted to your inspection.

I have done my duty, and my duty is yours.

Given at the national palace of Port-au-Prince this 12th day of November, 1816: in the thirteenth year of the independence of Hayti.   PETION.

By the president.   B. INGENAC.

Port-au-Prince: printed at the government press, 1816.

F

No. 1.

KINGDOM OF HAYTI.

DECLARATION OF THE KING.

Full of confidence in the justice of our cause, and the legitimacy of our rights; taking God and the universe as judges of the unjust and tyrannical pretensions of the French; and having no secrets to keep from our subjects, our interests being the same, and indissolubly connected; we have made it an imperative law to ourselves to discuss in the most public and solemn manner all matters which concern the liberty and independence of the Haytian people.

Moved by such considerations, we have published the overtures and propositions made to us directly or indirectly on the part of the French cabinet.

We have deemed it our duty to deviate from the ordinary policy of governments, and by our frank and honorable conduct we have declared our sentiments, and made known to the world our unshaken resolution either to live free and independent or to die.

It was with this view that we published our manifesto of the 18th of September, 1814, wherein we laid before the sovereigns and nations of the world the justice of our cause, and the claims of the Haytians to liberty and independence.

Europe had, at that period, been rescued from the oppression of France. After twenty-five years of war, of bloodshed and of battles, the nations of the earth began to taste the sweets of repose. Louis XVIII. was restored to the throne of France by the allied powers. It might have been presumed that under a prince, said to be enlightened and a foe to prejudice, a change would have been made in the perfidious and destructive system pursued with respect to Hayti. It might have been presumed that France, content, like other nations, with forming a commercial intercourse with us, would have renounced her desire of subjugating a people whom she had already unsuccessfully employed every effort to re-enslave. It might have been presumed that I is majesty Louis xviii. moved by feelings of justice and humanity, would have recognized our independence, and have repaired and effaced, by this act of justice, the incalculable evils we experienced from the French under the government of Bonaparte. In a word, it might have been presumed that by our unceasing efforts to combat and defeat the armies of the oppressor of Europe we should on the general restoration of peace, have been deemed worthy of enjoying some advantages, after having endured all the miseries of a barbarous and destructive war. These our just hopes were grounded on the moral principle of justice and equity which guide the enlightened sovereigns and nations of Europe.

The treaty of Paris was concluded without the slightest mention of Hayti France reserved, and the powers of Europe left to her the right of conquering St. Domingo, and, in despite of the noble, magnanimous and generous endeavours of the BRITISH nation and government to compel France to renounce the SLAVE TRADE, she retained, by the treaty of Paris, a right of continuing this odious traffic for five years, with the sole view of preserving the means of replacing the population of Hayti, in case of its destruction in the meditated war of extermination.

In defiance of the act of independence of the 1st of January, 1804, wherein the Haytians, driven to desperation by the injustice, the cruelty and unheard of crimes of the French, declared in the face of the universe, that they renounced France for ever, and would die rather than submit to her cruel, tyrannic and unjust dominion:

In defiance of our above mentioned, manifesto wherein we have explained the just motives which led us to proclaim our independence, and our determination to bury ourselves beneath the ruins of our country rather than submit to any invasion of our political rights:

In defiance of the laws of nations, of reason, and of morality, contrary to all the principles of humanity, of justice, and of equity, the French cabinet conceived and resolved upon the odious project of making the Haytians return to all the horrors of slavery from which they had emancipated themselves after twenty-five years of battles, sacrifices, and struggles;

APPENDIX.—F. NO. 1. [lxxxvii

The history of the crimes committed against mankind by the most cruel tyrants furnishes no similar example. But, what the world would hardly believe, did not the most incontestible documents establish its truth, to the shame of France and the enlightened age in which we live, the cabinet of Louis xviii. has not scrupled to employ the same treacherous measures with that of Bonaparte in order to entangle us in its snares, and reduce us to bondage. It was with such base intentions that the French cabinet sent out three agents, or we may more truly say three emissaries, charged with taking the preparatory steps for the execution of its criminal designs, as a patient perusal of the official papers relating to them must convince every unprejudiced person.

The whole world is acquainted with the termination of this mission of *espionnage* and perfidy, in the disgrace of the government and minister who sent it.

In the letter* addressed to us by Dauxion Lavaysse, chief of the mission, one may read, amidst the most deceitful promises the grossest insults, along with a threat of *exterminating the Haytians, and replacing them by other unfortunate wretches torn from the bosom of Africa;* and the more effectually to intimidate us, we are threatened with the *co-operation of the maratime powers of Europe, should we refuse to return beneath the yoke of France and* SLAVERY.

Faithful to our principle of always taking our people as judges in their own affairs, we have submitted the propositions of the French to a general council of the nation solemnly convoked for the purpose.

The grand, noble and magnanimous resolution, adopted by the Haytians, of suffering themselves to be exterminated to the last man rather than renounce their liberty and independence, is known both in Europe and America.

In this state of affairs the fresh proofs of zeal, of love, and of fidelity, which we have experienced from our fellow citizens unanimously, have imposed new obligations upon us, and rendered it more than ever our duty to devote the whole of our life to render them all free, happy and independent.

In his letter to General Pétion, amidst the flatteries which this emissary has bestowed upon him, may be found a threat held out to the Haytians of a part of the West and South, of being *treated as mischievous savages, and hunted out as Maroon negroes* ! ! !†

History will judge how he who dared to pen so hateful a menace could, after writing it, presume to shew his face at

* See Appendix F. No. 2, p. xcvi.   † See Appendix B. No. 1, p. xv.

Port-au-Prince, and how the chief to whom it was addressed could welcome with the kindest cordiality the man who presumed to make it.

Whilst one of these emissaries (to our shame be it spoken) was bartering away with a traitor at Port-au-Prince, the civil and political rights of the Haytians, the second returned to France with the earliest intelligence; and the third, named Médina, introduced himself into the North of the kingdom in order to accomplish the purpose of his mission. The secret instructions of M. Malouet, then minister of marine and the colonies, which he bore, clearly demonstrate to the entire world what *were* and what *are* the true designs of the French cabinet with respect to the Haytians. To be able fully to comprehend the abominable, crafty, and treacherous policy of this cabinet it is necessary to peruse these instructions with care.*

In these may be discovered the grand and favourite plan of the French cabinet, ever influenced and governed by the ex-colonists, namely to divide us and arm one part of the population against the other. They are ignorant then that, whatever the private differences among the Haytians, at the call of their country every feeling of animosity will be suppressed, and that they will always be firm and united when required to oppose the French. They are ignorant then that any promises which may be made to them by a factious man become vain in execution being contrary to the interests and the will of the nation. They are ignorant too that the cause of the Haytians of both colours is one and inseparable, that their interests are common and indissolubly united; that all are embarked in the vessel of independence, and must save her from shipwreck, or perish with her. It is to no purpose then that the French labour to sow dissention. The Haytians will be unanimous *on this point at least*, TO FIGHT TO EXTERMINATION RATHER THAN SUBMIT AGAIN TO THE YOKE OF FRANCE AND SLAVERY.

We are too well acquainted with the wily policy, and criminal designs of France respecting us ever to fall into her snares, We can easily figure to ourselves the abyss of calamity into which we should be plunged, were we blind or weak enough to be deluded by her fallacious promises, or intimidated by her odious threats. Were we so imprudent or unfortunate as to confide in the cabinet of Louis xviii. we should, as under Bonaparte, be the victims of our misplaced trust. To form a correct idea of this truth, it is necessary to read the letters of these emissaries, and compare them with their secret instructions and the examination of Médina,† who was one of them.

---

* See Appendix B. No. 1, p. xxxii.   † See Appendix C. No. 2, p. xl.

The French cabinet never has disavowed this mission of *espionnage* and perfidy. His majesty Louis xviii. has only expressed his high displeasure at the clumsy manner in which the agents attempted to execute it. It is not the less true, and it is indeed admitted by M. Beugnot, successor to M. Malouet in the ministry of marine and the colonies, that *they were commissioned " to collect and transmit information respecting " the state of the colony:"** and the most hasty perusal of their instructions will serve to convince us that the French agents acted strictly in conformity with them, both in their correspondence and their conduct towards the Haytian chiefs, even to the threat of EXTERMINATION if they refused to return to a state of slavery, and of the co-operation of the European powers to effect it.

So true is it that the French cabinet relished this abominable project; that the ex-colonists wrote and freely published thousands of pamphlets in which they unblushingly disclosed plans of destruction which make nature shudder, and are repugnant to the religion, the morality and the learning of the age wherein we live. These pamphlet-mongers propose to EXTERMINATE our generation *without distinction of* SEX *or* AGE!!—infants under the age of six years being alone excepted, to be retained in bondage, because these little innocents could not at so early an age have received the first impressions of FREEDOM.

After the pamphlets of the ex-colonists; the letters and instructions of the French agents; after all the authentic documents before our eyes, is it not most satisfactorily demonstrated that the French cabinet of Louis xviii. has adopted, like that of Bonaparte, projects of destruction, of guilt, and of blood.

Whilst this mission of *espionnage* was executing its designs in Hayti, France prepared an expedition in all her ports to add weight to her threats.

None can doubt at the present day that DEATH OR SLAVERY is the only alternative which France would offer to us.

None can doubt, that she has excluded the Haytians from the circle of social relations; that she has violated, with respect to us, all laws, human and divine; and that it is her intention to destroy us like wild beasts, as the aboriginal population was exterminated in an age of ignorance and barbarity.

The return of Bonaparte to France prevented the departure of this expedition, and averted, for a season, the projects of France.

---

* See an extract from the Moniteur of the 19th of January, 1815, inserted in Appendix F. No. 3.

Political views, led Bonaparte to abolish the slave trade.— He sounded our disposition towards France by his agents, but his proposals were rejected with contempt.

During the interval which preceded the second restoration of Louis xviii., the French government, embarrassed with its own affairs, was unable to molest us.

But scarcely was Louis xviii. reseated on the throne of his ancestors by the allied powers, before the ex-colonists recommenced their intrigues: they employed hireling under-agents to make us indirect overtures which have been printed and published. The French cabinet, being as yet unable to act openly, left us in peace till this moment, when it has renewed its useless efforts.

Could it be believed that, after what had passed during seven and twenty years between the Haytians and the French, as well as recently, together with our perfect acquaintance with their true intentions, the French cabinet would dare to persist in overtures containing disgraceful propositions?— And again, by whom are they made? By commissioners who are all ex-colonists; all men sunk and disgraced in the estimation of the Haytians. How infamous? It is with these *ci-devant masters* that Louis xviii. wishes their *ci-devant slaves* to negociate the manner of their return to bondage!

How did these ex-colonists shew themselves on our coasts in the execution of their mission? Like pirates, before the ports of a civilized nation coming to pillage! What steps did they take to open a communication with us? They took advantage of an American ship, which they diverted from her course, to transmit their letters; which were instantly returned, because their superscription was insulting to the Haytians.— At length they had recourse to a stratagem to transmit them under a borrowed cover. Had it not been for the obligation we have imposed upon ourselves of publishing whatever comes from the French we should have consigned these documents to the contempt and oblivion they merit.

In their letter of the 12th of October* they announce that they were proceeding to Port-au-Prince as a central and intermediate place for communicating with both the North and the South: whilst we are well informed that they called at Port-au-Prince on the evening of the fifth. † The traitors! hardly had they appeared, and yet they endeavoured to intrigue—and had recourse to fraud to disunite us!

And what do they propose to us in these communications?

* See Appendix E. No. 3, page lxv.
† See a corroboration of this in Appendix E. Nos. 5, 6, and 7

To renounce our independence! to renew our commercial intercourse with the mother country, in short to become again a French colony. In other words, to rob us of our rights, our institutions, our laws, and all the advantages we have purchased by our courage, our perseverance, and by twenty-five years of sacrifices, of battles and of bloodshed.

They *no longer* propose to us DEATH OR SLAVERY! it would cost them too much; the execution is impossible; but they endeavour to attain the same end by palliatives.

It is after reading our act of independence, our manifesto, and the act of the general council of the nation; it is after our detection of all their projects, that they have dared to offer us proposals as insulting to us, as they are disgraceful to those who have the impudence to make them. In fact they must imagine that we are deprived of understanding, or rather must not they themselves have totally lost their senses, to dream that such proposals could be favourably received by us.

To renounce our independence! or, what to us is synonymous, to renounce our glory and our lives; to consent to become slaves again, or perish by an ignominious death; to renew our commercial intercourse with the mother country! this proposition is as false and unfounded, as the former is hateful, insulting and unjust. It is now fourteen years since we renounced this *soi-disant* mother country. To give her our commerce! would not this be an admission of her supremacy? and even after she has recognised our independence we cannot grant her an exclusive commerce; since doing so would not only be a violation of our laws, but injurious to our national interests; and France having forfeited all her claims of sovereignty, we never will admit conditions which can again give her the right of exercising any supremacy whatsoever within the kingdom of Hayti.

France not only has done, but yet wishes us too much harm to be entitled to hope for partiality in her commercial intercourse with us. Do we not know the French? Have we not had sufficiently dear bought experience to convince us of their designs and our own real interests? Are we ignorant that all their publications sufficiently shew that it is not their wish to treat sincerely with us, but that they are bent upon the revival of slavery. *No slavery, or no colony*—this is their system; and if they make other proposals, and pretend to qualify them, it is only from inability to reduce us to bondage by main force; hence they wish to cheat and lull us asleep under the faith of treaties *framed in the intention of violating them on the first favourable opportunity.* It was *by venturing* *to negociate with them*, that Toussaint Louverture, with a multitude of others of our fellow-citizens, became their victims. Bear for ever engraven on your memories, ye Haytians! the goodly and flattering promises—nay OATHS, of " OUR BRETHREN, BEFORE GOD AND THE REPUBLIC."* You have experienced their sincerity. Remember likewise the *promises* of Louis xviii., and the instructions of his minister to his agents. You have the same proof of *their* sincerity. Bear these instructions continually in your mind, and recollect that *had it not been for the events which took place in France* we should before this have experienced from the French under Louis xviii. the same unjust cruelties and horrors as under Bonaparte. You are witnesses that *the same overtures and the same oaths* have been employed to deceive us, the *effects only are wanting*, and this has wholly arisen from the force of circumstances. Should we then trust them again? Should we wait to see a repetition of those horrors of which we have already been the victims, before we adopt such strong, prudent and decisive measures, as the safety and welfare of the Haytians demand.

As far as *we* are concerned there is *no change*. The government of Louis xviii. differs not from that of Bonaparte; its crafty policy is unaltered, its estimate of crime and bloodshed continues the same. If they fail in sowing dissention, and arming one part of the population against the other, they endeavour to detach the cause of the people from that of their government; as though the cause of the one was not that likewise of the other: as though the ruin of the one would not bring with it that of the other also. As far as respects us, the French will always be French, that is to say, our most cruel tyrants and most implacable enemies. What treaty can subsist betwen *ci-devant* masters and their *ci-devant* slaves? What could be its conditions? Where its guarantees? That which is to us a source of happiness and prosperity, causes misfortune and sorrow to them. *They* cannot wish for *our* freedom and independence, which are the sources of *our* happiness. Nor can *we* treat with *them*, without first obtaining the guarantee of a great maritime power, and such conditions as they shall be unable to violate: for, for if they treat with us without such guarantees, it will be with a predetermination to cheat us We must therefore insist on these guarantees, without which you can neither have a durable peace nor the slightest security.

* See the Proclamation of the First Consul, inserted in Note, page 27.

HAYTIANS! should you renounce your independence to-day, you will be required to renounce your liberty to-morrow: and should you renounce both at the same moment—should you consent to live as slaves to the French, you would have perpetually to die an ignominious death!—for no sooner will their power be re-established, than the GIBBETS, the FUNERAL PILES, and the SCAFFOLDS will be prepared for you. On the least symptom, the least whisper, the least sigh which the loss of your liberty may extort from you, you will be abandoned by your executioners to the severest punishments

Thus then you have not even the choice of living as slaves beneath the disgraceful yoke of these tyrants. You have no alternative worthy of you, worthy of men who have achieved the conquest of their rights, except the magnanimous resolution we have adopted, of either vanquishing these odious tyrants by the points of our bayonets, in order that we may live free and independent, or perishing manfully in the field of battle. Should they even recognise our independence we must require such conditions in the treaty as may deprive them of the power of troubling and eventually subduing us: and, independent of these conditions, we must have besides such precautionary regulations of police, as may insure our most remote posterity from ever again falling beneath the yoke of France and slavery.

For, without these securities, no sooner will they have concluded a treaty with us than they will seek means to execute their projects of slavery and destruction. First they will commence, under commercial pretexts, by insinuating themselves amongst us: they will soon after find excuses for meddling in our politics, intriguing and gaining partisans amongst us so as to rekindle a civil war; and when they find that our debased population has lost its moral force, and has become incapable of resistance, they will recommence hostilities and wage a war of treachery in which they will turn our own weapons against us.

Should we not, in such a case, be obliged to maintain an active and vigilant watch over those factious men who will flock amongst us merely for the purpose of creating disturbance? Will not the acts of severity we shall be compelled to employ against them be an incessant source of complaint and disagreement with France? Will she not likewise be able to throw in, with a view to invasion, (by means of her ships of war and merchantmen, which will have free entrance into our ports,) a mass of population which she can reinforce from time to time at will; landing upon our shores, by means of her navy, an army, to take us by surprise, as was the case after the peace of Amiens.

Then, in the state of perpetual war and alarm in which our want of foresight in neglecting to require guarantees will have placed us, we shall be unable to better our lot without violation of the treaty. In this case, compelled to keep our armies on the war establishment, and perpetually harrassed by the French, we shall have to endure all the cost and peril of our situation without enjoying any of the advantages of peace: we shall be unable to apply either to agriculture, commerce, the sciences, or the arts, since these can only be cultivated with success in a state of secure and lasting peace. Is it not infinitely better to be in a state of *open and declared* war, than to have only the phantom of peace? Is it not better *to fight to the last man*, than consent to a peace which would be more ruinous and burthensome than the most destructive war?

Such is the candid exposition of the real situation in which Hayti stands with respect to France. It is shewn that we cannot negociate with her without endangering our existence, both as a nation and as individuals, unless we first obtain those securities which we have a right to demand.

We have not only to labour to secure the lives, the liberty, and the independence of the existing generation, but we should also labour to secure the possession of these inestimable blessings to our latest posterity; and it is only by the most unceasing efforts, the most unremitting vigilance, and the most active foresight, that we can accomplish this.

The sovereign of France has declared, that in negociating with us, nothing should be done which could detract from *what he owes to the dignity of his crown, to justice, and the interests of his people!* And we—we also declare that we shall not be found wanting in what we owe to the interests of our people and the dignity of our crown.

The high interests of the Haytian people, together with our duties, oblige us to make known to the world the powerful motives which have led to the adoption of this determination, in order to put a final period to all the aggressions and insults of which the French government is perpetually guilty with regard to the Haytian people; as well as to destroy all those unjust and illusory pretensions to sovereignty which the cabinet of France may yet entertain respecting the free and independent kingdom of Hayti.

For these causes we have declared, and do solemnly declare, that we will not negociate with the French government on any other footing than that of power with power, and sovereign with sovereign. That no negociation will be entered upon by us with this government which has not for its preliminary basis the independence of the kingdom of Hayti, as well in affairs of government as commerce; and that no definitive treaty shall be concluded with this government without having previously obtained the good offices and mediation of a great maritime power which will guarantee the faith of the treaty from being ever broken by the French:

Whenever we negociate we will withold our consent from any treaty which does not comprehend the liberty and independence of the whole of the Haytians who inhabit the three provinces of the kingdom, known by the names of the North, the West, and the South, our territory; the cause of the Haytian people being one and indivisible:

No overture or communication from the French to the Haytian government, whether oral or written, shall be received, unless made in the form, and according to the usages established in the kingdom for diplomatic communications:

Neither the French flag nor individuals of that nation shall be admitted within any of the ports of the kingdom, until the independence of Hayti has been definitively recognised by the French government:

We declare anew, that *our invariable determination is, never to interfere directly or indirectly in matters foreign to our kingdom:*

That it shall be our unceasing endeavour to live in good understanding and harmony with the friendly powers and their colonies in our neighbourhood, TO MAINTAIN THE STRICTEST NEUTRALITY, *and prove to them by the prudence of our conduct, our laws and our labours, that we are worthy of* LIBERTY *and* INDEPENDENCE:

We declare and protest, in the face of the Omnipotent, of monarchs, and of nations, that we have been moved to make this declaration solely by the general interests of the Haytian people, and for the preservation of their rights and their existence:

We declare and protest, that, whatever be the menaces employed by the French to intimidate us, whatever their attempts to subjugate us, the nature of their attack, or the magnitude of the crimes and barbarity they count upon employing for the attainment of their end, nothing shall for an instant shake our determination. Should the whole universe conspire for our destruction, the last Haytian will resign his last breath rather than cease to live free and independent.

We leave the justice of our cause in the hands of that GOD who always punishes the unjust and aggressors. We will maintain the dignity of our crown, with the rights and interests of the Haytian people; and we rely with confidence on their bravery, their zeal, and their patriotism, to second all our efforts in defence of their rights, their liberties, and their independence.

> Given at our palace of Sans Souci, this 20th of November, 1816; in the 13th year of Independence, and sixth of our reign. HENRY.
> By the king. DE LIMONADE,
> Secretary of state, minister for foreign affairs.

No. 2.

Letter from General Dauxion Lavaysse, dated Kingston, the 1st of October, 1814, and addressed " To his Excellency General Christóphe, supreme Chief of the government of the North of Hayti," in the following terms:

General,

You have been informed of the important mission with which I have had the honour to be charged to your excellency; and it had been my intention on arriving here to address your excellency and General Pétion at the same moment: for I am not come, as you well know, to be the messenger of discord, but as the precursor of peace and reconciliation.

A few days after my arrival I paid the tribute to the climate along with my travelling companion M. Dravermann, and I could not meet here more than one confidential person to assist me in the capacity of secretary.

Meanwhile, I have conversed with some worthy persons who possess, they assure me, your confidence, and confirm what fame had already told me of you.

But previous to having the honor of corresponding directly with your excellency, I ought to have procured more certain information respecting you, and every thing which the success of my mission rendered it necessary for me to know; and I confess with pleasure to your excellency that all I now know serves greatly to enhance my hopes, and encourages me to address you with the frankness of a soldier and the interest which cannot be refused to those who have followed a military career.

The virtuous king who is at length restored to France—this king equally deserving of admiration for the firmness and benevolence of his character, the extent of his knowledge, and the contempt he professes for every illiberal prejudice, Louis xviii., has lamented more than any one, the atrocious measures adopted against General Toussaint, at the peace of 1802.—This loyal and enlightened chief had, with nearly the whole of the inhabitants of Hayti, taken arms in favour of the royal cause. He had maintained himself with energy for many years, and had restored order and agriculture in the most astonishing degree. But, when the whole of Europe had bowed beneath the yoke of Bonaparte, he felt himself compelled to submit to this acknowledged usurper. None of the acts of general Toussaint had declared independence, nevertheless, Bonaparte, either for the purpose of sacrificing a part of those immense troops which embarrassed him at the peace,* or of appropriating to himself imaginary treasures, sent an army to St. Domingo when he ought only to have sent rewards.

The effect of this barbarous expedition was a second destruction of the colony and the loss of General Toussaint.

The king would have considered this loss as irreparable, had not your excellency succeeded to the power of this celebrated man: and, convinced that you are perfectly acquainted with your true interests, and with all that has taken place in Europe; certain that the welfare of your country, of yourself, of your family and your friends will serve as the rule of your conduct, he doubts not that you will act with him as Toussaint would have done had he lived.

I come then, general, by the orders of my august sovereign, to bear to you words of satisfaction and of peace. And while from the height of a throne the most splendid in Europe, he commands an army of five hundred thousand men, he sends me alone to negociate with you on the subject of your true interests.

We live no more in the time of Bonaparte; all the sovereigns of Europe leagued themselves together to overthrow that usurper; they continue united to secure the tranquillity of all parts of the world. At this moment you see England punishing, at a distance of fifteen hundred leagues from her shores, the United States of America, who dared to lend their aid to that enemy of order, and the repose of the world: already has the capital of this new empire been laid in ashes; already has her chief been put to flight; nor will England cease to crush the United States beneath the fearful weight of her vengeance, till they profess the same principles as the sovereigns of Europe: thus so long as there is a spot in the universe in which order is not restored, the allied powers will not lay down their arms, but remain united to perfect their great work.

If you doubt this truth, general let your excellency consult by your agents the disposition of England, hitherto hostile to

---

* Nearly the whole of these troops had served under Moreau, to whom they continued strongly attached; but the generals were mostly partisans of Bonaparte.

France, but now her most faithful ally, and they will attest what I say.

General, if Bonaparte with a large portion of the forces of France, has been subdued by the troops of the allies: who can now resist France, united with all Europe—France allied to England? And who doubts that Bonaparte would have completed the infernal work of destruction he began in 1802, had not England in 1803 declared war against France, and thus cut off, by her immense fleets, the communication between France and St. Domingo?

Every thing has been foreseen in the treaty of peace between the sovereigns of Europe. Unacquainted with the wisdom and principles of your excellency, they imagined you might hesitate as to the conduct you should pursue; and it was agreed that, to replace the population of Hayti, which, in this case, would be totally annihilated by the forces sent against it, it would be necessary for France to continue the slave trade for yet many years, with the double view of replacing the hands wanting for agriculture, and forming soldiers in imitation of the English.

It is doubtless unnecessary to enter into details with a man of an understanding so superior as your excellency's, but it is right perhaps that these grand considerations should be offered to those honoured with your excellency's confidence.

Had the alliance of the European powers only for its object the restoration of order and the overthrow of the usurper who was perpetually troubling them, the august monarchs who compose it, would not on this account have shewn less esteem for those worthy pillars of the glory and independence of France; for those gallant warriors who, through twenty-five years of misfortune, never shrunk from the post of danger, and saved their country from all the horrors of civil distractions, and the humiliation of a dismemberment of France. The king, the wisest and most generous in the world, the virtuous Louis xviii., has felt more sensibly than any of his great allies, the claims of these heroes, as well to royal munificence as to public gratitude: they are now loaded with honours, enjoying immense estates, and blessing the events which have given to their splendid fortunes a stability unattainable under a usurper.

Follow their example, general, proclaim Louis xviii. in Hayti, as they have proclaimed him in France: and not only shall honors and rewards be presented to you, but those whom you may point out, shall receive marks of the satisfaction of our sovereign and the gratitude of our country; and the reign of prejudice which was overthrown along with the ancient regime, will oppose no obstacle to their rewards being made fully equal to the extent of their services to the king.

Doubtless, did Bonaparte address you from the elevation of the throne of France, the words which I bear you, I should be grieved to deliver his success in politics arose from his arts of deceit; his treachery equalled the power of his arms, nor was General Toussaint the only victim who learned this by sad and cruel experience. But the legitimate King of France, the august successor of so many illustrious sovereigns, the descendant of St. Louis and Henry iv. he indeed needs not the vile arts of an usurper, his royal word is as sacred, as his family is old and venerable; and like one of his magnanimous ancestors, Louis xviii. has said, that if good faith was banished from earth she ought to be still found in the bosom of kings. Thus, general, whatever he promises will be sure and unalterable; of this you cannot entertain a doubt.

But I am aware, that there are among your generals some who fear that the chiefs sent by the king, forgetting the instructions they have received, and yielding to the influence of the creoles and emigrants, may gradually re-establish the reign of prejudice. But believe me, general, the reign of prejudice is at an end for ever. It will no more revive in the French colonies, than in France, and who can suppose that any yet exists in that country? when by the side of the Montmorencies, the Robans and the Perigords, are seated the Soults, the Suchets, and the Dessoles; when men of so different an origin, but equally illustrious, the one by their exploits the other by their ancestry, sit in consequence as equals in the Chamber of Peers, and equally share the high offices of state? The king, desirous to avail himself of merit wherever it is to be found, will act, you need not doubt, like the monarchs of Spain and Portugal, who by lettres de blanc, raise an individual of any complexion to the condition of a white. His royal power, which has placed the Neys, Soults, the Suchets, and the Dessoles on a footing of equality with the Montmorencies and the Robans, by an act of munificence and equity, which all France has applauded, is equally capable of rendering a black or coloured man not only in the sight of the throne and the law, but also in social intercourse, equal to the whitest men of Picardy.

Compel us not, general, to make soldiers of the negroes we are now importing from Africa; compel us not to have recourse to all possible means of destruction. Do not expose yourself to behold the desertion of your battalions who will soon learn that French discipline, the most perfect in the world, employs not that excessive severity which you so often exercise. We are acquainted with all your means of defence; when I tell you I wish to speak to those who are under your command.

For I believe you to be too cool headed, too enlightened and too noble, not to be satisfied with becoming a nobleman and a general officer under the antient dynasty of the Bourbons, which Providence has seen fit, contrary to all human calculation, to continue upon the throne of our dear France; you would prefer becoming a distinguished servant of the great sovereign of the French, to the uncertain lot of a leader of revolted slaves. And if it be necessary to point out examples for your imitation, see Generals Murat and Bernadotte, for many years chiefs or kings, of nations whom they rendered illustrious by their arms, nobly descending from the thrones to which they had been raised by the French revolution. See them, I say, descending nobly and voluntarily from these thrones, to become great and illustrious nobles, and preferring legitimate and durable honours for themselves and their posterity, to the hateful and precarious title of usurpers.

For do not deceive yourself, general, the sovereigns of Europe, although they have made peace, have not yet returned their swords to their scabbards; and you doubtless are not ignorant of what all Europe knows although there has not yet been anything publicly diplomatic respecting it, that the principal article of the compact signed by all the European sovereigns upon their royal honour, is to unite their forces if necessary and to contribute all the assistance requisite to overthrow all the governments that have arisen out of the French revolution, whether in Europe or in the new world. Know that Great Britain is the party most concerned in this convention, to which in a few months sooner or later, every government must submit; and that all governments and chiefs who do not submit will be treated as traitors and brigands; while those who will voluntarily and with a good grace be sufficiently reasonable and sufficiently upright to adhere to this principle and contribute to make those they govern return to obedience to their legitimate sovereigns, shall obtain from those sovereigns an existence and establishments as honourable as durable.

The last consideration which I shall offer to your excellency is the integrity which distinguishes the present minister of marine. All the world knows that in the time of the constituent assembly, in which he was always one of the most strenuous defenders of the cause of the king, he insisted on the justice of ameliorating the lot of the blacks and the men of colour. To pronounce the name of Malouet is to awaken the recollection of the highest virtues, and the most inflexible integrity. Every promise made by such a man will be as sacred and as certain as if it were (pardon the expression) the Divinity himself who uttered it.

Accept, general, the sentiments of high respect wherewith I have the honour to be your excellency's most obedient humble servant, DAUXION LAVAYSSE.

P. S. Colonel Medina, an associate of my mission, will repair to your excellency, whose entire confidence he merits.

In proof of the candour with which I act, I subjoin a copy of my letter to General Petion. Hardly had I written it before I felt ill, which deprived me of the honour of addressing your excellency at the same time.

No. 3.

Official censure upon the mission of Lavaysse, Dravermann, and Médina, by the Minister of Marine and the Colonies.

The minister secretary of state for the marine and the colonies has placed before the king the letters inserted in the public papers, and which were addressed from Jamaica on the 6th of July, and first of October last, to the present chiefs of St. Domingo, by Colonel Dauxion Lavaysse. M. Dauxion whose mission was altogether pacific and had for its sole object to collect and transmit to government information respecting the present state of the colony, had no authotity for making communications so contrary to its object. The king has expressed his high displeasure and orders his disapprobation to be made public. The Count BEUGNOT,
Minister of State, having the department of the marine and the colonies.

Extract from the " *Moniteur de France,*" for the 19th January, 1815.

No. 4.

Address of the General Council of the Nation to the King, on the arrival of the French emissaries, Dauxion Lavaysse, Médina, and Dravermann, with his Majesty's reply.

Sire,

We shall seek in vain among the annals of nations for an instance of overtures of peace made under such frightful auspices, and accompanied with such disgraceful circumstances as those commenced by the French general, Dauxion Lavaysse, in the name, and as the agent of his Majesty Louis xviii.

Nations, sovereigns, and even private individuals possess

rights which are respected by the most barbarous people, and no person whatever is allowed to infringe them; but if the world at large be agreed to respect rights consecrated by custom, and by public consent, how much more deserving is he of contempt who, in the capacity of envoy from an enlightened monarch and people, has openly dared to violate them.

What? The most abominable tyrants, when desirous of oppressing their subjects, have had recourse to perfidy, and have masked their design beneath some specious pretext because they feared openly to violate the rights of the people, whilst the royal envoy of France has unblushingly set decency at defiance, and offered the most cruel insult possible to a free people, by proposing to them the dreadful alternative of SLAVERY or DEATH!!! To whom has this vile agent dared to address himself, for the purpose of making known the base designs of his government?—To your majesty—to the vanquisher of the French—to the defender of freedom and independence! To you SIRE, who have devoted your whole life to the maintenance of the eternal and indestructible rights of man! To your majesty, who has uniformly made the honour, and glory of the Haytian people the sole rule of your conduct! It is to you that he has dared to propose that you should descend from that throne whereon the love and gratitude of your fellow-citizens has placed you! O! height of infamy and presumption! He dared to believe you capable of such horrible perfidy!—To whom has he dared to talk of *master* and *slave?* To *us!*—To a *free* and *independent people!*—To warriors seamed with honourable scars received in the field of battle—who have destroyed to the last fibre, the antient tree of prejudice and of slavery! To those warriors who have in a thousand combats defeated those barbarous ex-colonists, whose remains, escaped from our just vengeance, dare again to speak of reviving that hateful system which we have eternally proscribed! No—never shall either MASTER or SLAVE exist again in Hayti!

Could your majesty have expected such an aggravated insult from a sovereign, whom fame has represented to us as wise, good, and virtuous—brought up in the school of adversity—the foe to illiberal prejudices, and distinguished for his justice and humanity!!! How false do we find fame, Sire, when we compare the results with her previous professions! The first overtures of peace—the first conciliatory words addressed to us in the name of the prince, of whom we had been led to form so favourable an opinion, were cruel and unfeeling insults: they proposed to men who had been for five and twenty years in the enjoyment of freedom—and who had arms in their hands, to lay them down for the purpose of resuming their chains, and bowing anew beneath the yoke of a fearful bondage! Whilst suggesting these horrors, they artfully veiled them beneath the specious mask of peace and reconciliation! They masked the poignard of the assassin beneath the honourable, and seductive exterior of *liberal* sentiments, and the friendly disposition of the French monarch with respect to us. But, on a sudden, this vile agent, changing his tone, and displaying the atrocious character of his mission in all its naked horrors, *menaces the extermination of our race and the substitution of another in its room!* What justice! What liberality! What humanity!

Does not this last proceeding of the French, Sire, clearly demonstrate that the cause of the Haytians is distinct from that of all other nations? Indeed to what other people or sovereign would they dare to offer *such* proposals?—proposals as base as they are insulting! They despise us, and believe us to be so stupid as to be destitute even of that instinct with which nature has endowed the very dullest of the brute creation for their own preservation. What madness! What assurance! to dare to propose to us to surrender anew to the French and submit to their hateful dominion! Is it on account of the *benefits* we have received from them, that we are to resume the chains of SLAVERY? Is it for a sovereign who is a total stranger to us, of whom we have no knowledge, who has done nothing for us, and whose name they employ to insult us, that we are to change masters? Is it in short, for the sake of being again given up to dogs to be devoured, that we should renounce the fruits of twenty-five years of bloodshed and of battles? What have we then in common with this nation? Have we not burst every tie which could unite us to them? Have we not changed our name, our habits, and our manners! We bear no resemblance whatever to the French! They are a people we abhor, and which has incessantly persecuted us. Wherefore then should we be doomed to groan again beneath their tyranny?

The barbarians! they have dared to despise us! they imagine us unworthy the blessings of liberty and independence! They fancy us incapable of those sublime sentiments, of those generous transports which constitute heroes, and give man the command of his destiny. Such is their idea, but they deceive themselves: little do they know the magnanimity, the courage, and the energy of the people they dare to insult. Our wish is to be free and independent, and we will be so in despite of our tyrants.

Ah! if ever our cause be separated from that of other

nations, if they conceive they have a right to menace, insult, and blot us out of the number of the living—if, in this enlightened age, injustice prevail over equity, even though our tyrants should ultimately triumph over us, still will the glory of the Haytians stand unrivalled in the annals of the world. Yes! we are resolved.—May our whole race be exterminated, rather than renounce our freedom and independence! This is our unalterable resolution. To this indeed we subscribe! But before France establishes her power here, may the plains of Hayti become one mighty desert, may our towns, our manufactories and our plantations be destroyed by the flames; and may each of us augment his strength, and redouble his energy and courage for the purpose of sacrificing to our just resentment millions of these tigers drenched in our blood. May Hayti exhibit nothing but a mass of smoking ruins, and may the affrighted spectator behold only vestiges of death, of desolation, and of vengeance. May posterity, beholding these ruins exclaim, *Here dwelt a free and noble race whose tyrants attempted to rob them of their freedom; but they preferred the noble alternative of extermination!* Posterity will applaud this magnanimous act. Where, indeed, is the man so ungenerous as to withold from us the tribute of his applause, admiration, and good wishes?

In wars between civilized states, while the armies fight, the people live in peace; but, in a war of extermination, like that with which they threaten us, when called upon to defend our homes, the tombs of our fathers, our liberty and our independence, nay—what do we say—our very existence, with that of our wives and children—the war is between man and man—the very women and infants partake in it: all are in arms: it becomes a duty to injure the enemy in every possible manner: every art of destruction is admissible, and we will revive the dreadful example of the exasperation of a people who have terrified the world!—Posterity will tremble with horror, but, far from blaming us, will impute our desperation solely to the perverseness of the age, to our tyrants, and to necessity.—But no, this will not be, it is impossible! Hayti is invincible! and the justice of her cause will triumph over every obstacle! No, this execrable enterprise never will take place. The honour and the glory of the sovereigns and people of Europe are at stake; and Great Britain, that liberatress of the world, will prevent such an abomination.

Sire!—The insult offered to the sovereign and people of Hayti, the outrage offered to the august person of your majesty, equally affects us individually and collectively, and, in our just indignation, the vengeance shall if possible, equal the offence.

The council, penetrated with a lively sense of your majesty's exertions for the glory and prosperity of Hayti, has the honor of presenting to your majesty, in the name of this brave and generous people, its determination to *live free and independent, or to die,* and to express its sentiments of devotion, of fidelity, and of gratitude to the august person of your majesty, and the royal family. Twenty-five years of experience, and of services rendered to the Haytians, are sure pledges, that the happiness and prosperity of your majesty are closely connected with the general welfare. Our first inclination then is to cry to arms, and our second to respect your majesty, to whom the nation has intrusted its destinies. We offer you, Sire! unanimously, our arms, our lives, and our property, for the service of your majesty, our country, our liberty, and our independence, and we renew at the foot of the throne the sacred oath of *obedience to the constitution of the realm, and fidelity to the king.*

The council received this address amid acclamations of *Vive le roi! Vive la liberte! Independence or death?* In an instant all the members hastened to the bureau to affix their signatures.

Signed, by their royal highnesses *Prince Noel* and *Prince John.* His serene highness the Prince of *St. Marc.* Their Graces the Dukes of *Anse, Fort Royal, Artibonite, l'Avance, Marmelade,* and *Dondon.* Their excellencies the Comtes de *Valliére, d'Ouanaminthé, de Laxavon, de Cahos, de Limonade, de Trou, de St. Louis, du Terrier Rouge, du Gros Morne, de Lèogane, de Richeplaine, de Terreneuve,* &c. &c. Field Marshals *de Barthèlemy Choisy, de Jean Joseph, de L. Fregis, de Deville, de Chevallier, de Raymond, de Joseph Jerome.* Barons *de Thabares, de Henry Proix, de Sicard, de Dossou, de Ferrier, de Bastien Fabien, de Cadet Antoine, de P. Poux, de Cap, de Bottex, de Leo, de Montpoint, de Dupuy, de Beliard, de Stanislas Latortue, de P. A. Charrier, de J. B. Petit, de Vastey, de Dessalines, de Lucas.* Chevaliers *de Lacroix, de Blaize, de C. Leconte, de C. Petigny, de Desormes, de Prèzeau, de Dupin,* Colonels *de David, de Prophile, de Laurent Desir,* &c. &c. &c. Officers of administration, *G. Desmangles, Djaquoy, Achille, Menard, Darmey, Auguste jeune, T. Guèrinet, N. Gaulard, Brevoltaire, Gallo Birame, Dufresne, C. Warloppe.* Counsellors *B. Lemoine, Hector, Guisot, Dubois,* &c. &c. &c. Lieutenans de Juges, *James Lallemand, Corasmain, E. Tollo,* &c. &c. &c.

HIS MAJESTY'S REPLY.

Haytians! Your generous resolution is worthy of you, your king will always be worthy of you.

Our indignation is at its height! Hayti should be, at this moment, one vast camp. Let us prepare to combat these tyrants who threaten us with chains, with slavery, and with death.

Haytians! The eyes of the whole world are fixed upon us: our conduct then should be such as to confound our detractors, and to justify the opinion formed of us by philanthropists. Let us rally: one wish alone animates us all, that of exterminating our tyrants. Upon the harmony of our union—the promptitude of our measures—and the perseverance of our efforts, will depend the success of our cause.

Let us transmit to posterity a grand display of valour. Let us fight gloriously. Let us rather be blotted out of the rank of nations, than resign our liberty and independence. King! We will know how to live and die such! You will always find us at your head, participating in your perils, your hardships, and your privations. Should we chance to die previous to the consolidation of your rights; remember our conduct, and should your tyrants endanger your freedom and independence, exhume our bones, they will conduct you anew to victory, and make you triumph over your implacable and everlasting enemies.

HENRY.

Done and passed in council, this twenty-first day of October 1814, in the eleventh year of the independence of Hayti.

(Signed) The Prince DU LIMBE, President,
Comte DE LA TASTE, Vice-President,
Comte D'ENNERY,
Baron DE DESSALINES, } Secretaries.

G

PROCLAMATION.

The King to the Haytians of the West and South.

Haytians! The civil dissentions which have afflicted our country have always deeply grieved our paternal heart; and we have never ceased to make every exertion to extinguish them without shedding Haytian blood; that precious blood which we ought to preserve for the defence of our country against the common enemy.

Whilst the only obstacle to our reunion yet lived, the Haytians have witnessed all the overtures we made to procure peace by means of conciliation. We have not hesitated to make the first advances, and it will always be pleasing and honourable to sacrifice every personal feeling to the general welfare and prosperity of our compatriots.

At present when there no longer exists any obstacle to peace, reunion, and the extinction of civil war, we call upon all good citizens, all good fathers of families, in a word, all Haytians who love their country, and value good order and tranquillity, to second us with all their might in labouring to accomplish the reunion of the Haytians, to terminate our dissentions without bloodshed, and produce a new order of things which shall be just and reasonable, honourable and advantageous for all.

Our first duty and our most ardent wish is to labour with all our ability for the welfare of the Haytians, and to bestow upon them all those advantages which ought to attend a just and paternal government, to introduce public instruction,* to promote religion, and to make the arts and sciences, agriculture and commerce flourish, but to the effectual accomplishment of this it is necessary to consolidate our internal peace.

We are informed that the evil-disposed, who desire to see a renewal of the horrors of civil war, have circulated a report that, under the pretence of visiting the kingdom we avail ourselves of the new circumstances which have arisen, to march an army to Port-au-Prince, while the real object of the circuit we are now making through the kingdom accompanied by our family is to examine personally into the situation of the people and their plantations, to promote law, order, and justice, to ameliorate and reform every thing susceptible of improvement.

To dissipate these false reports whose only object is to produce animosity, to excite mistrust, and prevent the reunion of the Haytians into one and the same family; we have felt it necessary to make known our real views and paternal intentions.

It is for the purpose of fully and entirely accomplishing this, that we have determined upon prolonging our stay at the town of St. Marc that we may be nearer to communicate with the Haytians of the West and South; and they should not consider the troops which occupy the lines of the cordon of the West otherwise than as friends and brothers who come not to contend with but to welcome and fraternize with them.

---

* See a proof in the Report of the Schools, Appendix I. No. 1. p. 115.

In consequence, not to leave it at all in the power of the enemies of the public welfare, of order and tranquillity, to spread fresh reports tending to throw a shade of doubt over our pacific and acknowledged intentions, and that no one may be able to plead ignorance, we declare and proclaim the following articles which shall be religiously observed towards all who acknowledge or declare themselves in favour of reunion, and the royal and legitimate authority.

1. Security of persons and property.
2. No one shall be called to account in any manner for his past conduct by reason of the civil dissensions.
3. A confirmation of rank and employment to all the civil and military officers.
4. We promise the most splendid rewards and honours to all who shall spontaneously acknowledge the legitimate authority, and shall display the greatest zeal in labouring to effect a prompt reunion of the Haytians.
5. The troops of the line shall be maintained, clothed and paid, they shall continue in their respective garrisons for the protection of their homes and their fellow citizens; and the chiefs in their several commands as at present.
6. We will renew our orders to the generals commanding the arrondisements of Arcahaye and Mirebalais not in any manner to disturb the Haytians who return to their homes, and those who place themselves under our protection, but to receive them with kindness, and treat them as brethren and fellow citizens.

Given at our royal palace of St. Marc, this ninth day of June 1818, in the fifteenth year of independence, and eighth of our reign. (Signed) HENRY.
By the King
The Comte DE LIMONADE,
Secretary of State, Minister for Foreign Affairs.

No. 2.

Letter addressed by the King to Messieurs the Generals and Magistrates of part of the West, and of the province of the South, assembled at Port-au-Prince.

St. Marc, 28th June, 1818: 15th Year of Independence.
Messieurs Generals and Magistrates!

The necessity of terminating our dissensions, and uniting the Haytians into one and the same family, has determined us to send to Port-au-Prince, to the generals and magistrates therein assembled, messieurs the Barons de Dessalines, major general, Baron de Bottex, colonel, and the lieutenant commissary Armand, aides de camp employed about our person.

Messieurs generals and magistrates, these three officers are commissioned on our part to make known to you our pacific intentions and to deliver to you our proclamation of the ninth of this month. You may rely fully on what they will tell you, and on the contents of the aforesaid proclamation, it being the frank expression of our heart.

You are witnesses, messieurs generals and magistrates, that we never provoked the civil war. It has always been repugnant to our feelings, not only as being contrary to the true interests of the Haytians, but as encouraging the enemies of Hayti in their barbarous and criminal hope of making us the instruments of our mutual destruction, and reducing the survivors to a complete state of slavery. Hence results the necessity of endeavouring to effect the reunion of the Haytians, and the extinction of our dissensions, in order to bring back peace, union and happiness amongst us.

On our side there can be no difficulty to impede or retard this union, so necessary and indispensible to the general welfare. If any obstacles to this peace and reunion should yet remain, notwithstanding our endeavours to attain an object so salutary, we request you to communicate them. We are ready to obviate them, satisfied that you cannot propose any that are not just and reasonable.

On your side messieurs generals and magistrates, we are convinced that you are no less desirous than ourselves of this reunion, being equally alive to its necessity. You will doubtless contribute all in your power to accomplish it, and the happy results we shall obtain, cannot fail to redound to the glory and advantage, of all who shall have contributed to it.

Persuaded, messieurs generals and magistrates, that the welfare, the interest, and the prosperity of the Haytians imperatively demand this union, we have never hesitated on every opportunity which presented itself, to offer those overtures which our desire to promote the public welfare dictated, for the purpose of obtaining a general pacification; and it is with an equally pure intention that we have frequently sent to Port-au-Prince, persons possessing the public confidence, as bearers of terms of peace and conciliation; and if our overtures have not been crowned with all the success we had hoped for, we had the satisfaction at least of believing that this was not owing to any fault of ours.

At the present day nothing can prevent our knowing how to introduce into our public affairs a new order of things which shall be just and reasonable, and in which every one shall enjoy peace and security.

Animated by these noble and generous sentiments, we call upon the generals, the magistrates, all respectable persons, all fathers of families, in a word all Haytians, to join with us in re-establishing peace, harmony, and union, which never should have been interrupted among the Haytians, who have so much reason to avoid divisions. We invite you to second us with all your power, so as to enable us to attain so desirable an end.

Messieurs generals and magistrates, the necessity of terminating every thing amicably for the welfare of our common country, leads us to request an affirmative reply to these important propositions; and moreover, to enable us the better to come to an understanding, it is indispensably necessary to open a conference at which wise and prudent men of both sides can explain themselves respecting the interests of the country and the means of terminating our public calamities.

(Signed) HENRY.

No. 3.

Reply of the Magistrates of the Republic.

Port-au-Prince, 1st July, 1818:
15th Year of Independence.

The Generals, Magistrates and Chiefs, of the Republic of Hayti, assembled at Port-au-Prince, to General Christóphe.

The generals and magistrates of the republic could not express any other than the deepest indignation at the perusal of the perfidious letter and fallacious proclamation of General Christóphe which his excellency the president read in the presence of his deputies.

To dare to propose to them to betray their oath, to declare themselves in a state of revolt against the chief whom they have selected whom they have recognised, and to whom they have sworn allegiance, in conformity with the law which is the declaration of the general will, is the height of insanity.

To address a part of a people when they have a chief who governs them, is a public insult, a ridiculous lure which can only provoke contempt against the person who used it.

On reading General Christóphe's letter and proclamation we could hardly contain ourselves. Nothing but the respect due to the character of a deputy could command our moderation.

What does General Christóphe mean, what can he propose to us? We are free, independent, and republicans, we will maintain our rights at the hazard of our lives against all who invade them, wherever they appear, and whoever they may be.

What does he pretend? That we should acknowledge him for our chief, which we are unwilling to do; and by what right should he prevail? Is it by all the innocent blood he has shed? He is responsible for it both to God and man.

We declare in one word that nothing can ever disunite us; that General Christophe will in vain endeavour to accomplish this, and we will die rather than submit to him.

Let him address himself to his generals; let him ask them what the opinion of the generals and magistrates is? Let him learn from them the degree of love and confidence which they manifest towards the president of Hayti. Let them acquaint him with the enthusiasm and happiness which was displayed in their presence. From these he will learn the feeling of the people and the army, and understand that he never can command us.

We have already explained ourselves. No communication. No correspondence. We do not wish to have any thing in common with General Christóphe or with his royalty.

H

Address of the King to the Haytians on the anniversary of the 29th of November, 1803.

Haytians! Behold the memorable anniversary of the expulsion of the French army from the territory of Hayti!

With what noble sentiments should not the recollection of the brilliant exploits which led to this glorious event, and thus crowned our arms with success, inspire and animate you!

Fort Labouque, the Tannery, Trois Pavillons, la Croix, Cardineau, Sainte Suzanne, Les Écrivisses, la Crête à Pierrot, the Defiles of Dondon, le grand Gilles, le Bonnet, the bridge of Pérard, Blanchard, Petit Goave, Acquin, Torbeck, Cagnet, Ma-

zères, *Haut-du-Cap, Vertieres,* and a thousand other places ennobled by victory, and at which, the far famed splendour of the French arms was sullied and eclipsed before the victorious phalanxes of a people, resolved either to perish, or achieve the conquest of their liberty and their independence. Imperishable monuments! eloquently do ye proclaim the skill, the valour, the patriotism and the perseverance of the Haytian soldiers.

After having freed ourselves from tyrants, who had too long polluted the soil of freedom, we established the independence of our country, and laboured to consolidate the interests of the public.

A testimony of national gratitude and respect was due to the memory, not only of those gallant heroes who fell, covered with glory, in defence of the sacred cause we maintained, but to that likewise of our less fortunate brethren who expired amidst the unheard of cruelties of our butchers.

With this view we have ordained a solemn service to take place on the anniversary of our deliverance; for, although the first tribute of our gratitude be due to the God of armies for the blessings of this day, the chief object of our joy, it cannot be amiss to blend with the aspirations of our thanks to the throne of the grace, a tribute of respect to the memory of our fellow citizens, and to offer up our vows to the Almighty in union with our prayers for the souls of our fellow-labourers in the field of glory, who have cemented with their blood the stately fabric of their country's independence.

To these let us likewise add the tribute of our praise for the virtues they displayed, the fortitude they evinced, and the example which they left. It was not till after we had the fullest experience of the perfidy of our oppressors, and beheld the majority of our troops disbanded and disarmed, and the mass of our population loaded by them with chains, and groaning beneath their tortures, that indignation fired our souls, and vengeance nerved our arms to a successful struggle not for our rights merely, but for our very existence.

Without pausing to estimate the force of our enemies, or weigh the probabilities of success, we plunged into the contest with a thoughtless improvidence, and with inadequate resources for maintaining it; hence we were often obliged to contend, man for man, with such weapons as chance threw in our way; yet, encircled by privations, after a thousand battles in which we disputed the ground inch by inch, often defeated but never dismayed, we maintained ourselves by courage and perseverance against the unexampled efforts of our enemies, surmounted every obstacle, and at length succeeded in expelling our oppressors, triumphing over the impotence of their rage, and rearing upon their downfall the lovely superstructure of our liberty and independence.

Gratitude this day fills our hearts, and inspires our accents; honour then! immortal honour be to the deathless memory of those generous asserters of our freedom who are no more, having fallen in defence of the most upright, the most just, the most holy of all causes! Honour be to those martyrs of patriotism, who, by combatting the dastardly abettors of slavery have approved their claims to freedom. If, in this noble struggle, their lot has been to fall, their eyes, in closing, have had the satisfaction of beholding the discomfiture of the oppressors of their country, those vampires who have sucked her blood and fattened upon her vitals; if it has been their lot to fall, glory, has shed her brightest beams upon the moment of their dissolution, and they have carried with them to the depths of the tomb, the consolatory hope of vengeance, and the fond anticipation of their country's emancipation. Whilst then these heroes slumber in the night of death, let us who have survived them in the common race, pour forth the song of praise to their memory, and offer upon the hallowed altar of their tombs, the mournful homage of an approving country and an admiring army.

But the tribute of our regret is not bounded to those heroes who signalised themselves in the field of battle, and sought repose on the gory bed of victory: our sorrow likewise extends to the melancholy shades of those who fell victims to French perfidy, to French ferocity: for they were our friends, our relatives, and our brethren. – If in the deep recesses of the tomb—if in the holy place of their abode with the Divinity, they can hear our hymns, or regard the prayers we offer up to the Almighty Disposer of events upon this memorable occasion, they cannot but feel satisfaction. The blood of these unhappy victims has fecundated liberty, while their bones have given birth to independence. They have bequeathed to us important duties to fulfill, first, to imitate their bright example, and next to visit their butchers with interminable execration and ceaseless vengeance.

Let us then, on this memorable day, rekindle the torch of that inextinguishable hatred which our hearts have vowed; let us graft it in the hearts of our babes; let them suck it in with their maternal milk; let them inhale it with the air they breathe; and let their conduct ever manifest its effects upon the sight of a Frenchman.

May the rising warriors of Hayti ever bear before their eyes the generous sacrifice made by those heroes whose loss we this day deplore, and may they from their noble example take a lesson HOW TO DIE FOR THEIR COUNTRY!

Haytians! Amidst the other virtues which it is our duty to practice, never let us forget that we carry arms in our hands solely for the protection of our fellow citizens, and the defence of our country and our rights. Arms alone can effectually guard our liberties, when the dictates of reason cease to be efficacious. Our tyrants still cling to the idle hope of re-enslaving us; yet, illusory and chimerical as this hope may be, and however regardless you may feel of its effects, bear incessantly in mind that it is only by *a strict observance of discipline, a due submission to the laws, and such harmony and unanimity amongst ourselves, as prevailed in those days in which we first asserted our freedom,* that we can find the strength requisite to the defeat and punishment of our oppressors should they again assail us.

It is only by the cultivation of those social virtues which characterize *good parents, good children, good husbands, good wives, and good Haytians,* that you attain the happiness you merit.

By the sage measure of the sale of the property of our former tyrants, the Haytians, will, in their turn, become proprietors of those estates which they have so long watered with their tears, with their sweat, with their blood. If they have hitherto defended their country for her own sake, what an additional inducement will they not have to cherish and protect her now that they have found her so kind, so tender and so considerate a mother; and how will they not, in the hour of her peril, rally around her standard as one family, one household, one people!

Learning has shed her wholesome beams upon the mass of our population; she will more particularly instruct them in their duties and their rights, and thus eminently contribute to the welfare of both the present and the rising generation.

We will punish those tyrants who have conspired against us—we will confound the calumniators of our race by proving ourselves inferior in no respect in moral or in physical powers to other inhabitants of the globe; and shewing that we are capable of acquiring and practicing the sciences and the arts, and attaining to an equal degree of improvement and civilization with Europeans.

HENRY.

I

State of Education and Commerce in Hayti.

No. 1.

State of Education.

The following report of the state of public instruction in Hayti appeared in the New Times for the 2d of October, 1821, and cannot fail to interest those who rejoice in witnessing the amelioration of their species; the translator has therefore felt little hesitation in subjoining it to this appendix.

Previous, however, to laying the statement before his readers it is proper to observe, that these schools are all royal endowments, and that the young scholars are educated *altogether gratuitously*. Of the eleven schoolmasters, there are but two, Mr. Gulliver and Mr. Simmons, who are not natives of the island, and of the remainder not one could understand a syllable of English four years ago.—This circumstance alone, which the translator is able to state from his own personal knowledge, while it reflects the highest credit upon the zeal and abilities of Mr. Gulliver, furnishes a most satisfactory answer to those who would represent the blacks as incapable of mental improvement.—Besides the schools noticed in this report, there is a school of medicine under the superintendance of an ableand indefatigable physician, which, when the translator left St. Domingo, held out the fairest promises of success, but of which he has not since received any accounts.

The commercial abstracts, which cannot fail to interest the mercantile world, were made on the spot by the translator, from the official documents, and may therefore be relied upon for their accuracy.

ROYAL ACADEMY.*

Professor.	Class 1. Latin.	Class 2. French & Eng. composition.	Class 3. French & Eng. composition.	Class 4. Grammar.	Class 5. Geography.	Total.
J. Daniels, MA.	11	17	25	19	16	61

* This Establishment is under the care of a Scotch gentleman of considerable literary attainments, and a graduate of one of the Scotch Universities.—*Transl.*

Fifteen pupils have left the Academy since the last Report, six of whom have passed into the schools of Sans Souci, Port de Paix, Fort Royal, St. Marc, and Limbe. The eleven pupils of the 1st, and sixteen of the 6th class, are comprised in the numbers of the other classes.

NATIONAL SCHOOLS.

Classed and taught after the British System.

When founded.	Where.	Masters.	Reading the Bible.	Arithmetic.	Total.
October 1816	Cape Henry	T. B. Gulliver	98	121	249*
May 1817...	Sans Souci	J. Emmanuel	28	30	36†
April 1817..	Port de Paix	T. Papillon	55	83	133‡
May 1817...	Gonaïves	W. Simmons	48	53	120§
Novem. 1817	St. Marc	T. Duchèsne	58	100	172
Decem. 1819	Fort Royal	J. Hilaire	—	—	100
	Limbé	H. Désoubry	—	—	60
	Borgne	— Antoine	—	—	60
January 1820	St. Louis	— Phanor	—	—	60
	Jean Rabel	Pierre Louis	—	—	60
	Plaisance	H. Fontaine	—	—	60
Total......			287	386	1110

* Thirty-three pupils have left this School since the last Report. Of these twenty have gone to the Academy, four have gone as Monitors to the Schools of Borgne, St. Louis, Jean Rabel, and Plaisance: the remaining nine to other employments.
† Left since the last report three.
‡ Left eighteen: ten of whom passed to the Academy.
§ Left ten.

Certified to be conformable to the Reports presented to the Chamber by the inspectors and superintendents,

DE LA TASTE,
President of the Royal Chamber.
DE DUPUY, President.
DE VASTEY, Secretary.

No 2.

GENERAL VIEW OF THE COMMERCE OF CAPE HENRY, HAYTI,

from 1st *January to* 19th *August,* 1817.

Tonnage.	English.	American.	Danish.	Bremen.	Prussian.	Dutch.	Swedish.	Spanish.	Grand Total.
Under 50..	1	2	7	—	—	—	—	—	10
Under 100..	1	16	3	—	—	—	—	1	21
Under 200..	5	19	—	1	1	2	—	—	28
Under 400..	3	6	—	1	1	—	1	—	12
Total Vessels	10	43	10	2	2	2	1	1	71
Total Tonnage	1619	4998	502	426	401	336	210	50	8542

PORT OF GONAIVES.

Tonnage.	English.	American.	Danish.	Bremen.	Prussian.	Dutch.	Swedish.	Spanish.	Grand Total.
Under 50..	3	1	2	—	—	1	2	1	10
Under 100..	8	3	4	—	—	—	—	1	16
Under 200..	1	1	—	—	1	1	—	—	4
Under 400..	3	—	1	—	1	1	—	—	6
Total Vessels	15	5	7	—	2	3	2	2	36
Total Tonnage	1678	349	589	—	400	471	89	60	3636

No. 3.

ORDER IN COUNCIL FOR A FREE TRADE WITH HAYTI.

At the Court at the Queen's Palace, the 14th of Dec. 1808,

Present,

The King's Most Excellent Majesty in Council.

His Majesty, by and with the advice of his privy council, is pleased to order and declare, and it is hereby ordered and declared, that those ports and places of the island of St. Domingo which are not in the actual possession of France, and from which the British flag is not excluded, shall be considered as not being in a state of hostility with his majesty, and that his majesty's subjects and others, are at liberty freely to trade thereat, in the same manner as they may trade at neutral ports and places.

Provided, nevertheless, that nothing herein contained, shall be construed to effect any question now depending in his majesty's tribunals, respecting the character of the said ports and places; but such questions shall be decided in the same manner as if this order and declaration had not issued.

And the Right Honourable the Lords Commissioners of his Majesty's Treasury, the Lords Commissioners of the Admiralty, the Judge of the High Court of Admiralty, and the Judges of his Majesty's Courts of Vice Admiralty, are to take notice of his Majesty's pleasure hereby signified, and govern themselves accordingly.

(Signed)   WM. FAWKENER.

/972.94V341E1969>C1/